The Two Faces of Justice

The Two Faces of Justice

Jiwei Ci

Harvard University Press

Cambridge, Massachusetts, and London, England | 2006

Printed in the United States of America

Library of Congress Cataloging-in-Publication Data
Ci, Jiwei, 1955–
The Two faces of Justice / Jiwei Ci.
p. cm.
Includes bibliographical references and index.
ISBN 0-674-02160-6
1. Justice (Philosophy) I. Title.

B105.J87C52 2006
172′.2—dc22 2005043545

For my parents
and in memory of my grandmother

Acknowledgments

Working on the first draft of this book was, for better or for worse, largely a solitary experience. A number of people subsequently gave me valuable help in improving the manuscript; I especially thank Annette Baier, Neil Cooper, Chris Fraser, Liang Zhiping, Wang Xiaoying, and Wu Fen. For intellectual conversations, in person or by writing, that have contributed in more or less direct ways to making this a better book, I am indebted to Daniel A. Bell, Nicholas Bunnin, Joseph Chan, Raymond Geuss, David Konstan, Christopher New, Dan Robins, Joan Scott, Michael Walzer, Wan Junren, Wang Yunping, Xu Ming, and Xu Yinong. My deepest thanks go to Raymond Geuss for the most wonderful support, help, and encouragement imaginable.

I am grateful for fellowships awarded by several institutions for projects that were, or turned out to be, related to work on this book: the National Humanities Center, Research Triangle Park, North Carolina; the Virginia Foundation for the Humanities and Public Policy; and the School of Social Science, Institute for Advanced Study, Princeton.

In two chapters of the book I draw on material that has appeared before, in *History of Philosophy Quarterly* 15 (1998) and *Political Theory* 33 (2005). I thank North American Philosophical Publications and Sage Publications, respectively, for permission to do so.

I owe special gratitude to two anonymous referees for Harvard University Press. One of them, Thomas Pogge, has shed his anonymity, and it is a pleasure to thank him for extremely enlightening and probing comments. The other referee, equally deserving of special mention, captured the drift of my argument with such an amazing combination of sympathetic understanding and critical detachment that I have gratefully taken the liberty of borrowing locutions from the referee's report to improve the formulation of a number of my ideas. I also thank the philosophy and law syndics of Harvard University Press for helpful suggestions.

Lindsay Waters has been a superb editor, guiding me through crucial stages of the process with his distinctive combination of scholarly discernment and wealth of editorial experience. Susan Abel and Thomas Wheatland, friendly and wonderfully professional, have been a pleasure to work with, as has Amanda Heller, whose care and judicious, light touches as copyeditor have made a real difference.

Contents

The Two Faces of Justice

Introduction

Consider the following, at first sight rather simple, phenomenon: When acts of injustice (by standards internal to the society in question) by some are not effectively stopped, more and more people otherwise not inclined to perpetrate acts of injustice tend to participate in an ever-expanding vicious cycle of injustice, while those who are unable or unprepared to take part are consumed with resentment, until many of them become indifferent through overexposure and others lose the ability to hold back.[1]

In this admittedly "abnormal" phenomenon, certain perfectly "normal" features of justice stand out with particular salience, such as a just person's reliance on effective legal sanctions *against others* as a motivational cushion for himself, his proneness to resentment, and hence the contagious nature of injustice. Here I mean "abnormal" in the sense of being peculiar, say, in degree or scale, to one or more societies at a particular time,[2] and "normal" in the sense of being true in general. Thus, what seems peculiar to one society in this regard is something that, given the general mechanisms at work, could happen to any society, and attending to the general as foregrounded in the seemingly peculiar affords an exceptionally lucid access to the general.

The features I have noted suggest that justice is a conditional virtue—and that it is only when the conditions involved are regularly *not* satisfied that the basic characteristics of justice as such a virtue come to the fore. A number of questions immediately arise. What is the nature of such condi-

1. Within this kind of distressing picture can also be found those who are moved to make courageous, even selfless efforts to restore justice. But such people are almost always few and far between, and their exceptional behavior reveals little directly about the ordinary moral psychology of justice.

2. Anyone can pick his or her own examples. I have in mind Chinese society at various times, not least in the post-Mao era, where the phenomenon is sometimes quite striking.

tions and what does it take to satisfy them? How can everyone be reasonably assured that others will do their part in a society-wide scheme of cooperation? Does the desire to be just depend entirely on that assurance, or does it also contribute to it, and in either case, how and to what extent? How are we to explain the fact that the desire to be just may nevertheless appear to be unconditional, if only under reasonably favorable conditions, and how are we to square this with the fact that justice is a conditional virtue? Ultimately, what do our answers to such questions as a whole tell us about the possibility and limits of justice, both as a virtue of individual human agents and as a property of social institutions?

What gives the phenomenon under discussion, and the questions prompted by it, some degree of distinctness is that it is quite possible for there to be no disputing, and no disputing of, the unjustness of the acts in question, even by those who perpetrate them. In other words, what we find, principally, is not disagreement over substantive conceptions of justice, although such disagreement may exist to some degree, but the failure of significant numbers of people to comply with what are generally regarded as more or less acceptable norms, or worse, the failure of the state to enforce such norms seriously and effectively, and as a result, the gradual unraveling of the whole social fabric of justice. This kind of injustice is clearly distinct from the injustice that results from the effective implementation of norms that are themselves regarded as seriously flawed. To be sure, these two phenomena of injustice are more analytically than empirically distinct, but there can be circumstances in which they are also empirically separate to a significant degree.

Given their analytical and possible empirical distinctness from each other, these two kinds of injustice point, it seems to me, to two distinct types of subject matter for the study of justice. The first (to oversimplify for the moment) has to do with the nature of the disposition to follow more or less just norms whatever these norms may happen to be, the second with what should count as just norms by some appropriately high standard.

I am also of the view that these two types of subject matter are of equal importance. In order to understand justice as a virtue of individuals and as a property of social institutions, it is as important to give an account of the generic disposition toward justice as it is to take note of the normative principles that make up its culturally and historically specific content. Whatever normative principles of justice may be adopted in a society, the manner in which they tend to be practiced—or not practiced, as could easily happen—has a lot to do with the nature of the disposition toward justice itself. To be sure, actual principles of justice give substance and direction to a just disposition: they are what a just person in a particular society is disposed to act on and judge by. But the disposition toward justice itself, by virtue of being the disposition toward justice and not some other ("higher" or "lower") disposition, has certain features—call them *structural*—that are necessarily present regardless of the normative principles that happen to form its content.[3] Moreover, these structural features, such as a just person's proneness to resentment and the dependence of her willingness to perform just actions on certain conditions, seem to constrain, though they do not determine, the *kinds* of normative principles that can be taken up as principles of justice (as opposed to, say, principles of benevolence). It is these features, and what they tell us about the possibility and the limits of justice, that form the main subject matter of this book.[4]

There is a great deal to be studied, or, as I prefer to say, explained, about this subject matter. But since the subject matter itself does not, *ex hypothesi,* involve significant disagreement over normative or substantive questions of justice, such questions are suspended or bracketed in the explanation. In this sense, what I aim to develop is a purely *explanatory* the-

3. I do not mean to suggest that any principles whatsoever can be made the content of a just disposition. I make the point, in Chapter 1, that the generic disposition toward justice, by virtue of its structural features, already contains *some* basic normative content. Over and above this basic normative content, however, though in keeping with it, the disposition toward justice is capable of assimilating different kinds of normative content under different social and cultural circumstances.

4. There is a sense in which much of this book belongs to the category of philosophical attempts to explain how something, in this case justice, is possible. To one degree or another, all such explanations leave room for saying that what is shown to be possible in one way may also be possible in some other way. If this inability to rule out all alternatives categorically is something of a drawback, it can be outweighed by the significant speculative (and, in the case of the present study, genealogical) insights this kind of inquiry is uniquely capable of yielding. It may take other, more or less empirical kinds of study to move from the possible to the actually true, but a good "how-possible" explanation can help point us in the right direction. In any case, I try (in ways to be explained in Chapter 1) to minimize the room for alternative explanations by (a) attending carefully to various dimensions of the necessarily intermediate character of justice, whose independence and integrity depend on its being distinct from unconditional virtues on the one hand and from (rational) egoism on the other, and by (b) starting from phenomena that are clearly part of the *empirical* psychology of justice (for example, a just person's proneness to resentment) and proceeding to show, in conjunction with (a), that such features are not merely empirically present in the virtue of justice but constitutive of it. My intention is to produce an account that is sufficiently plausible not to give rival explanations an easy time if its basic claims about the workings of justice are true.

ory (or, more modestly, account) of justice, as distinct from a normative or substantive theory.

Obviously, I need to be more specific about the kind of explanation I try to provide here. Now, socioeconomic factors clearly play an important part in the formation of a society's understanding and practice of justice, and such factors could be of relevance for an explanatory account of justice as well. Also of potential relevance are numerous cultural factors, always operating in connection with socioeconomic ones, that shape ideas of justice and help or hinder their realization. The explanatory account I offer in this book, however, is not of the socioeconomic or cultural kind. I focus instead on what may roughly be called the generic disposition toward, or sense of, justice. In choosing this focus, I am assuming that there is such a thing as a *generic* disposition toward justice, one that can be satisfactorily explained without reference to socioeconomic and cultural factors. This is a bold assumption, but instead of providing an explicit justification of it, I shall leave it to the unfolding of my arguments to show if an explanatory account of justice based on this assumption is capable of yielding worthwhile results. Socioeconomic and cultural factors are extremely important, of course, and I have no doubt that my account would be richer and more powerful if it could take such factors into account. Nevertheless, I believe that the arguments which make up this book will show that a study with a narrower focus can produce insights of a different, if more limited, kind.

I assume, further, that an explanatory account of justice of the kind provided here can be pursued independently of a normative theory of justice, for the reasons given earlier. In other words, the further assumption is that there are important things to be said about the disposition toward justice without reference to any substantive, normative conception of justice.[5] Indeed, it is only under this assumption that one can speak of a *generic* disposition toward justice in the first place. Here again, I do not systematically argue for this assumption but provide only occasional support for it, chiefly in Chapter 1. Although I believe that this assumption holds, at least in the sense that important insights can be produced under it, I do not find it necessary or helpful to steer clear of normative issues altogether.

5. In this sense, my account of justice may be said to be *normatively* unambitious in the way that, say, Hobbes's is. See, for example, Thomas Hobbes, *Leviathan*, ed. C. B. Macpherson (Harmondsworth: Penguin, 1968), chap. 15. As will be seen in Chapter 3, however, I have a more demanding view of the task of justice than Hobbes does. Thus, my account of justice is normatively unambitious in the sense of steering clear of substantive conceptions of justice, yet normatively quite demanding in terms of the task of justice that helps set the range of such substantive conceptions.

Nor do I believe that it is possible to draw a hard-and-fast line between the explanatory and the normative.[6]

As its title indicates, the main argument of the book is that justice has two "faces": the conditionality of interest and the unconditionality of morality. By the conditional face of justice I mean that the disposition to be just includes the willingness to follow certain norms, as defined in a given conception of justice, *provided that* other members of the relevant group act likewise. This *conditional willingness* reflects a principal aim of justice, namely, the *reciprocal* satisfaction of interests. It distinguishes justice from unconditional virtues on the one hand and from (rational) egoism on the other. But justice also has another face. Since no system of justice can rest securely on the basis of a general understanding of justice in terms of conditional motives and imperatives, the *institution* of justice exists to remove conditionality from the human willingness to be just, and thereby to counteract the otherwise contagious nature of breaches of justice. This means that justice has to be sustained through the social creation of *unconditional* imperatives and of a corresponding *unconditional* virtue of justice.

These two faces, the conditional and the unconditional, are equally true of justice, yet they seem contradictory. In this book, I seek a principled way of making unitary sense of these equally important yet apparently contradictory aspects of justice. In other words, I aim to develop an account of justice that captures the conditional nature of the disposition toward justice and at the same time makes sense of the way in which justice acquires the character of an unconditional imperative and an unconditional virtue. Such an account has to begin by understanding justice in terms of the conditional motives that are present in, or implied by, the circumstances of justice. It then has to render a plausible account of the social transformation of those motives into unconditional ones, a transformation that constitutes a qualitative leap from the circumstances of justice.

6. Brian Barry, in *Justice as Impartiality* (Oxford: Clarendon Press, 1995), p. 46, distinguishes three questions for a theory of justice,—namely: the motive or motives of just behavior, the criterion or criteria of just rules, and the relationship between the two. This set of questions captures quite well the scope of a theory of justice. In practice, however, theories of justice tend to devote considerably more attention to answering the second question than to answering the first and the third. If I were to characterize my study in terms of Barry's three questions, I would say that I focus on the first question, offering only occasional suggestions as to how the second and third might be answered in the light of my treatment of the first.

These two requirements—call them the requirement concerning *motivational continuity* (with the circumstances of justice) and the requirement concerning *motivational change* (from the circumstances of justice) —can be satisfied, I would suggest, only by attending to the *socialization* of justice. What I term the socialization of justice consists of the social establishment of justice as a property of institutions and the social inculcation of a corresponding virtue of justice on the part of individuals. The first of these processes is aimed at ensuring the unconditional *practice* of justice despite the intrinsically conditional motive of justice, while the second, going a step further, is designed to render the *motive* of justice itself unconditional. Yet even though the second, more ambitious process may succeed in removing the conditionality of justice from a just person's moral *consciousness,* that is, from a just person's self-understanding, the resulting disposition to be just retains elements of that conditionality. It does so, however, in a way that is not *directly* accessible to a just person's self-understanding, and thus the disposition to be just is both consciously unconditional and unconsciously conditional. This claim is not mere psychological speculation. For it is only by postulating this combination of conscious unconditionality and unconscious conditionality that we can account for certain basic features of the disposition to be just, such as a just person's proneness to resentment, his particular kind of reliance on potential legal sanctions against others as a motivational cushion for himself, his possession of a particular form and a high degree of moral consciousness, and, apparently in contradiction to all of these others, the unconditionality of a just person's actions and motivations as understood by the just person himself. Features such as these support, indeed require, the postulation of unconscious conditionality *despite* the just person's understanding of his or her own motives as unconditional.

Since such features arise from society's attempt to bridge the gap between the conditionality of interest and the unconditionality of morality, an attempt that lies at the heart of justice, they are not merely empirically present in the disposition toward justice but are constitutive of it. To be sure, justice is a social creation, and as such it is marked by considerable cultural and historical variability in terms of the principles or requirements that can make up a normative conception of justice. But justice is a social creation that is different from other social creations, such as unconditional virtues on the one hand and (rational) egoism on the other. The difference lies in the presence of the aforementioned features in the disposition toward justice and their absence for different reasons from unconditional virtues on the one hand and from (rational) egoism on the other.[7] In this sense, we can speak of a *generic* disposition toward justice as distinct from and independent of a normative conception of justice. It is necessary to make this distinction because the generic disposition toward justice is compatible, in principle, with all potential normative conceptions of justice, themselves identifiable as such by virtue of the fact that they are capable of being followed from such a disposition. The generic disposition toward justice thus has a greater, cross-cultural and trans-historical generality than any normative conception of justice, although it is no less a social construction than the latter. By the same token, the combination of conscious unconditionality and unconscious conditionality applies to justice in general regardless of differences between specific normative conceptions of justice.

In writing this book, I have two complementary aims. The first, already mentioned, is to provide an account of justice that both captures the conditional nature of the disposition to be just and explains how justice can acquire the character of unconditionality as an imperative and as a virtue. Since such an account is possible only by attending to the disposition toward justice, *whose generic features reflect the simultaneous conditionality and unconditionality of justice,* my second aim is to develop an account of the disposition toward justice. By pursuing these complementary aims, I hope to make *unitary* sense of a number of highly important aspects of justice, either as a property of social institutions or as a virtue of individual agents, such as those already mentioned. These aspects of justice are discussed here and there in the literature on justice, often insightfully, but to the best of my knowledge, they have not been brought together in one explanatory account. I believe that these aspects of justice are more likely to fall into place within a single unitary account.

This account, I hasten to add, is philosophical rather than sociological. When I investigate the socialization of justice, my objective is not to examine the empirical circumstances (such as the family or the educational environment) in which a just disposition is formed, important as these circumstances would be for a different, sociological account of the disposition toward justice. Rather, I am concerned with the *logic* of the socialization of justice, the *general rationale* of those social practices whereby the original, intrinsic conditionality of the motive of justice is transformed and made compatible with the unconditional practice of justice and often even with the just person's understanding of her own motivation as unconditional. I am concerned with the moral properties of the disposition that

7. See Chapter 1 for detailed discussion of justice as distinct from benevolence or egoism.

thereby emerges, and what these properties reveal about the moral status of justice as an individual virtue and the viability of justice as a property of social institutions.

Although I have formulated the main problems of this book from the vantage point of phenomena that may be especially salient in, or peculiar in degree or scale to, one society or another, my aim is to give a theoretical account of justice, not a treatment of phenomena or conceptions of justice characteristic of any particular society. The problems (or I should perhaps say problematics) that inform this book are general problems (or problematics), not ones unique to this or that society, and I take them up not because they happen to force themselves on our attention in the context of one society or another but because I believe they pertain to justice as such, and therefore studying them is important for understanding justice as such.[8]

Although to my knowledge no one has pursued these problems in the way I propose, many, past and present, have raised issues that in one way or another bear significantly on my inquiry. I develop my own views here through dialogue with and criticism of these scholars. Where such discussion is extensive, this is usually because I find it a helpful way of setting the stage for my own arguments (as in my treatment of Schopenhauer in Chapter 4) or of providing an illuminating contrast with them (as in my discussion of Habermas and Rawls in Chapter 1). Indeed, presentation of others' arguments (for instance, Brian Barry's in Chapter 6) often serves to provide a natural background against which my own arguments can emerge with particular clarity and relevance. At other times I am simply concerned with contrasting rival positions (such as those of Hume, Allen Buchanan, Rawls, and Habermas in Chapter 3) and choosing between them. In not a few cases, relatively lengthy treatment of other authors is further motivated by the fact that the views under discussion (such as those of Schopenhauer throughout the book and of the early Nietzsche in Chapter 12) are important, and important for my argument, and yet are

8. In view of this, and given the dearth of philosophical discourse on justice in the Chinese tradition, there need be nothing odd about the fact that I draw mainly on the Western philosophical tradition in dealing with these problems, and even, to some extent, in giving conceptual shape to these problems. There are deep social and cultural reasons for the dearth of philosophical treatment of justice in the Chinese tradition, although this is not the place to reflect on those reasons. Suffice it to say, approximately, that traditional China and Maoist China alike placed benevolence (and community) rather than justice (and individuals) at the center of their moral universe. The situation has begun to change in the past two decades or so, but philosophical discourse has yet to catch up with this new development.

relatively unfamiliar. I thus have different kinds of reasons for drawing on the work of others. But my aim is always to advance the book's argument rather than to provide scholarly exegesis.

It may appear strange that in a book of this kind I do not attempt to come to grips with the large body of work by psychologists on moral motivation. The main reason for this omission has to do with the nature of my undertaking. As I stressed earlier, my aim is not to examine the empirical circumstances, psychological or social, in which a just disposition is formed, although I see the importance of studying such circumstances in a different kind of inquiry. Instead, my concern is with the general rationale of those social practices whereby the two faces of justice, the conditional and the unconditional, combine to make justice a commendable yet "jealous" individual virtue, an impressive yet precarious social institution. For this more abstract kind of inquiry, I find moral psychology as practiced by Nietzsche, Schopenhauer, and Hume more relevant, and when I use the term "psychology" and its cognates, I do so largely with their types of work in mind. Besides, I have encountered numerous insights of a more or less psychological nature in the writings of contemporary moral philosophers, whether or not I agree with them. Some of them, such as Gabriele Taylor and Patricia Greenspan, have a special interest in moral psychology, while others, such as John Rawls, Jürgen Habermas, Brian Barry, Allan Gibbard, and Bernard Williams, raise issues of psychological relevance in otherwise not particularly psychologically oriented studies. In addition, and perhaps not very "respectably" by contemporary Anglo-American standards for a philosophical work on justice, I have occasionally found it helpful to discuss the psychological insights of religious thinkers such as Kierkegaard, Reinhold Niebuhr, and Paul Tillich.

It should be quite obvious, then, that although I draw extensively on Western intellectual discourse, I do not see myself as strictly a practitioner of a particular school of philosophizing. I make frequent references to Anglo-American work on specific topics of justice, and yet my way of thinking as a whole is more informed by "Continental" philosophers such as Nietzsche and Schopenhauer.[9] It should thus not be surprising that I often depart from the norms of moral and political philosophy in the analytic

9. Another source of inspiration, one that may be said to permeate this book but which precisely for this reason I have chosen to leave implicit, is the ancient Chinese text *Dao de jing*. One generally reliable English translation is in *A Source Book in Chinese Philosophy*, trans. and comp. Wing-tsit Chan (Princeton: Princeton University Press, 1963), pp. 136–176. It is tempting to make special mention of chap. 38, but insights of an extremely high (and elusive) order abound in the whole text.

tradition, especially in two respects. First, I do not always find it conducive to the aims of the book to follow a very neat line of argument. The ideas that make up my account do have a central thread running through them, as briefly described in the final section (which contains the only explicit, but necessarily inadequate, statement of my overall argument in one place). But I do not see this thematic thread in the form of one tidy and continuous line of argument. Rather, I develop a range of arguments, of varying degrees of generality, intended to illuminate diverse yet connected aspects of the disposition to be just and the two faces of justice reflected therein. Accordingly, I have adopted a style of composition that is sometimes more loosely structured, both within and across chapters, than is typical in analytic philosophy. This is designed to allow room for ideas that complicate and enrich the main themes of the book but nevertheless do not fall neatly into a straight line of argumentation either within a chapter or for the book as a whole. Of course, this messier or more flexible style also has its disadvantages, not the least of which is that sometimes the main lines of argument may appear less focused or structured than they could otherwise be. What I aim for is a reasonable balance between presenting the main thread of argument and finding room for other worthwhile if tangential insights. Although as a result the overall argument unfolds only slowly and cumulatively from one chapter to the next, it emerges, in this way, to best advantage, or so I believe.

Second, I operate with a somewhat different understanding of philosophical rigor from that which generally informs the analytic tradition. I understand rigor to mean a relentless yet sensitive probing that goes after the deepest insight rather than the tightest analysis—the kind of rigor most tellingly exemplified, in Western philosophy, by the best work of Nietzsche. Many ideas in moral and political philosophy, often of the more interesting and consequential kind, are not amenable to transparent presentation or strict proof. Where this is the case, I believe that a claim is sufficiently laid out if it is presented with a reasonable degree of clarity and precision. Even where this is not necessarily the case, I intend my arguments not so much to convince by proof as to push a familiar idea further here or provide a new perspective there, by means of metaphor and aphorism if necessary. According to this approach, an argument is not, in the first instance, an invitation to find counterevidence or a counterargument, but rather an invitation to share an insight or, where the reader disagrees, an incitement to come up with a different insight. A book carries an implicit claim to being a (connected) series of insights, and it is with these alone—not with this side point or that infelicity of formulation—that one agrees or disagrees in a deeply interesting and relevant way. I do not mean to claim, of course, that I have come anywhere near achieving the kind of philosophical rigor to which I aspire. My point is just that I would be happier to be found wanting by this standard of rigor than by norms to which the book is not designed strictly to conform.

None of this, however, is meant to take issue with the approach to moral and political philosophy that characterizes the analytic tradition. I have great respect for that tradition, and my indebtedness to its practitioners is evident on almost every page, even as I disagree with them. Indeed, for long stretches of the text, I have found it both possible and helpful to draw on means of argumentation perfected in the analytic tradition—not least in Chapter 1, where I take my point of departure from an essay by Peter Strawson, a truly inspiring analytic philosopher. But in the final analysis, for a variety of reasons, including intellectual temperament, cultural background, and the nature of my concerns, I have not produced a work that strictly fits the mold of analytic philosophy. There is no reason why I should. The book is perhaps best approached as a Chinese philosopher's critical dialogue with Western theories of justice—an act of philosophical appropriation from one point of view (in that I draw extensively on Western philosophical discourse) and an act of philosophical intervention from another (in that I bring to that discourse problematics that are of general significance and yet are particularly salient and thought-provoking in the Chinese context).

Finally, despite my misgivings about summing up the book's arguments too neatly, some rough indication of the main contents of the individual chapters may be helpful for the purpose of orientation. In Chapter 1 I lay out the various features of the disposition toward justice in a preliminary fashion. Before discussing these features in greater depth, in Chapters 2 and 3 I clarify the circumstances to which justice is a response, so as to determine both what kind of justice is necessary, given the objective circumstances of justice, and what kind of disposition toward justice is possible, given the subjective circumstances of justice. In Chapters 4 through 6 I attempt to ascertain what the disposition toward justice is *not,* that is, to rule out certain kinds of motives as either conceptually above or conceptually below the motive of justice, and to ascertain as well the kind of partially other-regarding motive that is appropriate to justice. By this point I will have laid the necessary groundwork for examining in greater depth the various elements of the disposition to be just first sketched out in Chapter 1. In Chapters 7 through 9, then, I develop a unitary explanatory account of reciprocity and resentment, the conditionality and the unconditionality of justice, and so on. In view of certain weaknesses or limitations of justice as revealed in these (and earlier) chapters, I proceed, in Chapters 10 and 11, to consider the possibility of the disposition toward justice being enhanced with higher virtues. In these two chapters I also discuss the more radical possibility of moving beyond (the conditionality of) justice—a response to the limitations of justice much as justice itself is a response to the problems inherent in the circumstances of justice. Finally, I conclude, in Chapter 12, with an analysis of justice as a mode of moral consciousness, in which are reflected both the achievements of justice and its costs, both its possibility and its limits. It is these characteristics of justice that make it an impressive yet precarious achievement as a virtue of individuals and as a property of social institutions.

1

Elements of a Just Disposition

My aim in this chapter is to give a general account of some defining elements of the disposition toward justice and of their relationship to one another. These elements include resentment, reciprocity or conditionality, reliance on legal sanctions, and, what seems to contradict all these, the appearance of unconditionality or autonomy. I have noted in the introduction that these features of the disposition to be just are connected in such a way that each of them can be properly understood only in relation to the rest. Thus any one of the dispositional features of justice could serve as a point of entry into the moral psychology of justice. Nevertheless, the close relationship among these features is something that is yet to be established, and until this is done, it is advisable to see the ineluctability of the dispositional features of justice as having different degrees of demonstrability and to begin this account with that feature whose demonstrability is particularly high.

Reactive Attitudes and the Reciprocity of Justice

A good place to begin is Peter Strawson's account of moral feelings.[1] What Strawson shows is that so long as we participate in human interaction, which we cannot avoid doing for long without losing our very humanity, we are prone to certain moral feelings, which he calls *reactive* attitudes. Specifically, in his account, the reactive attitudes that are ineluctable in any human interaction where the concept of justice plays a role are resentment, indignation (or disapprobation), and guilt. These attitudes are not

1. P. F. Strawson, *Freedom and Resentment* (London: Methuen, 1974), chap. 1. Another important account, albeit one whose focus is not on moral feelings, is given by Philip Pettit, *A Theory of Freedom: From the Psychology to the Politics of Agency* (Oxford: Oxford University Press, 2001), chap. 1.

just *empirically* present in any human interaction governed by the concept of justice. They are what one might call the structural or constitutive features of such interaction: a human interaction regulated by the concept of justice is what it is because of the presence of such features. The particular reactive attitudes of resentment, indignation, and guilt are to justice-governed human interaction what the reactive attitudes as a whole (as Strawson shows) are to any system of human interaction as such. Just as "in the absence of *any* forms of these attitudes it is doubtful whether we should have anything that *we* could find intelligible as a system of human relationships, as human society," so the absence of (the potential for) resentment, indignation, and guilt would render unintelligible any human interaction mediated by the notion of justice.[2]

From the reactive attitudes of resentment, indignation, and guilt discussed by Strawson, we can extrapolate a further dispositional feature of justice in the shape of reciprocity or conditionality. We can do this by assigning a certain priority to resentment among the three reactive attitudes. All three, as Strawson reminds us, are equally internal to the disposition toward justice. "In general, though within varying limits, we demand of others for others, as well as of ourselves for others, something of the regard which we demand of others for ourselves." Thus, "all three types of attitude alike have common roots in our human nature and our membership of human communities."[3] The fact that the three attitudes are on a par structurally and conceptually—necessarily "humanly connected," as Strawson puts it—does not mean, however, that they have to be on a par in terms of psychological salience or in terms of the sequence of their acquisition. There is, it seems, a sense in which our demands on others for ourselves, and hence our capacity for resentment, are experientially primary, and accordingly our demands on ourselves for others and on others for others, and hence our capacity for guilt and for indignation, are derivative. Strawson hints at this when he describes third-person attitudes like indignation and disapprobation as the "generalized or vicarious analogues of the personal reactive attitudes."[4] We might say that resentment is the

2. Ibid., pp. 23–24. It is worth noting that all the reactive attitudes are also what Scanlon calls "judgment-sensitive attitudes." As such, reactive attitudes have an epistemic dimension as well, for "judgment-sensitive attitudes constitute the class of things for which reasons in the standard normative sense can sensibly be asked for or offered." See Thomas Scanlon, *What We Owe to Each Other* (Cambridge, Mass.: Harvard University Press, 1998), pp. 20–21.

3. Ibid., pp. 15–16. See also Jürgen Habermas, *Justification and Application: Remarks on Discourse Ethics,* trans. Ciaran P. Cronin (Cambridge, Mass.: MIT Press, 1993), p. 40.

4. Strawson, *Freedom,* pp. 14–15.

experiential basis of guilt and indignation, although it does not fully qualify as resentment, that is, as a *moral* feeling, until the correlative feelings of guilt and indignation are also developed. Put another way, a sense of *in*justice (to oneself) is experientially prior to a sense of justice (to and on behalf of others), although here too the former is *fully* acquired only when the latter is also acquired.[5]

Even after this whole framework of attitudes is properly completed, it remains the case that the self-regarding demand is usually more insistent, and the corresponding capacity for resentment more easily mobilized. Given our natural partiality toward ourselves, we feel the sting of resentment keenly and effortlessly, and we may require prolonged moral training before we are able to muster enough sympathy and moral feeling to experience any deep sense of guilt or indignation—and even then we have a tendency to play down or explain away guilt and to be insufficiently motivated to act on indignation. To the extent that this is the case, there is a difference in motivational weight or psychological salience between our self-regarding and other-regarding demands, intrinsic and objectively necessary as both equally are to the structure of our moral experience. There is, in other words, a *motivational* asymmetry between our demands on others for ourselves and our demands on ourselves and on others for others, and hence between resentment on the one hand and guilt and indignation on the other, despite a perfect *structural* symmetry between them. The priority of resentment consists in this motivational asymmetry against the background of a structural symmetry.

It is important not to lose sight of either the motivational asymmetry or the structural symmetry. The concept of resentment points simultaneously to both and thus is indicative, more directly than guilt and indignation are, of a further constitutive feature of the disposition toward justice, namely (the demand for) reciprocity, which mediates between interests and norms in a way that is characteristic of justice.[6]

5. As Judith Shklar, expounding Rousseau's understanding of injustice, puts it, one could not come to terms with the rights of others without "the primary experience of injustice [to oneself] in the first place." That is why it is important to "teach children their rights first, so that they might eventually grasp their duties when they are ready to understand that other people also feel the stings of the sense of injustice, which is the natural ground of our rights." Judith N. Shklar, *The Faces of Injustice* (New Haven: Yale University Press, 1990), p. 88.

6. This is not to suggest that guilt or indignation cannot properly be the focus of an inquiry into moral psychology. What one chooses as one's focus depends on what it is one wants to illuminate. For a study centered on guilt, see P. S. Greenspan, *Practical Guilt: Moral Dilemmas, Emotions, and Social Norms* (New York: Oxford University Press, 1995).

Impersonal Norms and Personal Reciprocity

Needless to say, the fact that we make demands on others for ourselves does not by itself account for our capacity for resentment. Otherwise, our sense of justice would be no different from a sense of self-importance. In his comments on Strawson, Jürgen Habermas highlights the importance of our awareness of impersonal norms as a necessary condition of our ability to feel resentment: "Indignation and resentment are directed at a *specific* other person who has violated our integrity. Yet what makes this indignation moral is not the fact that the interaction between two concrete individuals has been disturbed but rather the violation of an underlying *normative expectation* that is valid not only for ego and alter but also for all members of a social group or even, in the case of moral norms in the strict sense, for all competent actors."[7] To be sure, this is quite true as an explanation of the *moral* character of resentment. Yet an equally important dimension of resentment is missing from Habermas's account, for it is not a sufficient condition of my resentment that someone, in hurting my interests, has violated a moral norm. It is also necessary—as long as I have enough sense of justice not to adopt double standards—that during the relevant stretch of time I have not violated that norm myself, particularly in relation to the person who has hurt my interests. Conversely, for me ordinarily to be in a position to feel guilt, it is necessary not only that I have acted contrary to a moral norm and in so doing hurt someone's interests, but also that that person has not, during the relevant period of time, done the same to me. Indeed, even the third-person emotion of moral indignation is typically experienced *against* someone who has hurt the interests of someone else in disregard of a moral norm, and experienced *on behalf of* the latter only provided that he or she has not done the same to the former.

That things are so is because our common (explicit or implicit) commitment to an impersonal norm is at the same time a personal commitment to one another in relation to that norm, such that each person's readiness to follow the norm is conditional on a similar readiness on the part of all concerned. The latter, personal commitment reflects, more directly than the former, the fact that we have personal interests which we seek to protect through our shared obligation to follow impersonal norms. It is this fact about the raison d'être of norms that makes our relationship to impersonal

7. Jürgen Habermas, *Moral Consciousness and Communicative Action,* trans. Christian Lenhardt and Shierry Weber Nicholsen (Cambridge, Mass.: MIT Press, 1990), p. 48.

norms *necessarily* also a reciprocal relationship among persons. Given the nature of norms as rooted in interests, any human relationship regulated by such norms is ipso facto a reciprocal relationship. The existence of impersonal norms does not suspend the reciprocity that is intrinsic to all human interaction involving interests but only transforms it into normatively regulated reciprocity.[8]

Thus reciprocity—that is, normatively regulated reciprocity—is where personal interests and impersonal norms meet, where personal interests are mediated by impersonal norms and in being so mediated cease to be mere "selfish" interests. Reciprocity is just the personal locus of impersonal norms. In committing ourselves to an impersonal norm, we at the same time form, for the protection of one another's legitimate interests, a personal relationship with all those who are similarly committed to that norm and whose commitment is a precondition of our commitment, as our commitment is a precondition of theirs, in the first place. It follows that every violation of an impersonal norm is at the same time a violation of someone's legitimate interests, and a violation of reciprocity. Accordingly, both norms and interests—that is, the violation thereof—play a role in causing resentment, and since they do so not separately but together, they may indeed be said to be the two faces of resentment.

The problem with Habermas's discussion of resentment is that while he rightly draws attention to the impersonal face of resentment to account for its moral character, he passes over the personal face of resentment. Although in resentment the impersonal dimension and the personal dimension always go hand in hand, what makes resentment the particular emotion it is—partly self-regarding, and thus different from the *purely moral* third-person attitude of indignation and continuous with the *nonmoral* desire for revenge—is the psychological salience of the personal over the impersonal dimension. What is psychologically salient in resentment is not "the violation of an underlying *normative expectation*" as such, which

8. The relationship between norms and interests, or the intrinsic reciprocity of norm-following, is well formulated by Hume in terms of "a general sense of common interest; which sense all the members of society express to one another, and which induces them to regulate their conduct by certain rules." Hume continues: "I observe, that it will be for my interest to leave another in the possession of his goods, *provided* he will act in the same manner with regard to me. He is sensible of a like interest in the regulation of his conduct. When this common sense of interest is mutually express'd, and is known to both, it produces a suitable resolution and behaviour." David Hume, *A Treatise of Human Nature,* ed. L. A. Selby-Bigge, 2nd ed., ed. P. H. Nidditch (Oxford: Clarendon Press, 1978), p. 490.

by itself can be a sufficient cause only of indignation, but precisely "the fact that the interaction between two concrete individuals has been disturbed," as this fact is apprehended in normative terms by the offended party.

It may indeed be suggested that when we are resentful, not merely indignant, the object of our moral reaction is not so much the violation of norms as the violation of our interests protected by the norms. It is the violation of our interests, rather than the violation of norms as such, that calls forth our resentment, although (needless to say) we perceive our interests as what they are, that is, as legitimate interests, only because of the relation in which they stand to the impersonal norms. In this sense, the violation of our interests, along with the perpetrator thereof, is the *direct* object of our resentment.

Insofar as we may be said to be resentful of the violation of norms, this is because we have invested in these norms through our commitment to a reciprocal relationship under them. Indeed, subscribing to impersonal norms *means* undertaking not to violate other people's interests sanctioned by these norms and thus giving up all our own nonlegitimate interests. As long as we abide by these norms, we may be said to have kept our part of the reciprocal relationship with others that we have contracted in binding ourselves to shared norms. If, however, other people violate the norms, they will have simultaneously violated the reciprocal relationship they have contracted with us, and it is the latter violation that we take *personally* and that is the *direct* object of our resentment. *Resentment is directed not at the violation of norms as such but at the unilateral violation of normatively regulated reciprocity.*

In this light, the ineluctability of resentment shows that reciprocity—the conditional willingness to abide by impersonal norms for the sake of mutual interests—is an equally ineluctable motivational component of justice. The thwarting of our legitimate self-regarding demands (say, in the form of rights) by others is capable of causing our resentment only because the (explicit or implicit) commitment of others to not thwarting them, in the form of a commitment to impersonal norms which render those self-regarding demands of ours legitimate, is an important reason why we have not thwarted similar self-regarding demands of theirs. Our resentment is at bottom a reaction to someone's rendering null and void an important motive behind our commitment to following the norms of justice. Where there is resentment, therefore, there must be, as conditions of its possibility, not only the recognition of impersonal norms but also, more saliently, the demand for reciprocity in relation to them. Thus, we may think of reciprocity as a *necessary motive* in the disposition toward justice, given that resentment is (as Strawson shows) a *necessary emotion* in the disposition toward justice, and vice versa.[9] It is impossible to deny that reciprocity is a motivational component of justice without also denying, incorrectly, that resentment is a reactive attitude of justice. All *substantive* conceptions of justice, to qualify as conceptions of justice and not of some more altruistic practice or virtue, have to contain a *formal* condition to the effect that one may reasonably be expected to comply with the norms of justice only provided that other people behave likewise. Such a formal condition reflects the ineradicability of reciprocity as part of the motivation of justice.

Justice as Distinct from Benevolence and Egoism

With the concept of reciprocity, we are able to set the upper and lower bounds for the disposition to be just—to explain the intuition that the virtue of justice is something intermediate between complete altruism and complete egoism. The disposition to be just is the willingness to perform certain kinds of actions, and particularly to refrain from certain other kinds of actions, as both kinds of actions are defined in a given substantive conception of justice, *provided that* other members of the community do likewise. By contrast, benevolence, as an example of a completely altruistic virtue, consists in the willingness to perform certain kinds of actions (some of them beyond what is required by a substantive conception of justice), as well as to refrain from certain other kinds of actions, *regardless of* whether the beneficiaries of those actions or abstentions do likewise. In this the benevolent person is closer to a saint than to a virtuous person normally conceived.

The difference between benevolence and justice has something to do with the range of actions involved, and the latter in turn has something to do with the essentially positive nature of benevolence as opposed to what is sometimes taken to be the negative nature of justice (that is, justice as

9. The motive of reciprocity is also relevant for explaining the "self-reactive" emotion of guilt, which is the converse of resentment in that I am the one who has unilaterally broken the reciprocal relationship under norms. In the case of the third-person emotion of indignation, though the motive of reciprocity is not directly at work with respect to me, my recognition of such a motive on the part of the injured party is an important reason for my indignation.

conceived chiefly in terms of negative duties, the abstention from harmful actions rather than the performance of beneficial ones). But the most crucial difference is that benevolence is independent of, while justice is dependent on, reciprocation by the beneficiary. Thus the disposition toward benevolence—a settled desire to promote the well-being of others for its own sake—differs from the disposition toward justice not only in covering a broader range of actions and abstentions but also, and more important, in having an unconditional willingness to perform such actions and abstentions. Even when the actions and abstentions motivated by benevolence happen to overlap with those motivated by a merely just disposition, they still spring from a qualitatively different motive, in that they would be performed even if the condition of reciprocity, a necessary condition of actions and abstentions that flow from a merely just disposition, were not met.[10] A merely just disposition, by contrast, is marked by a conditional willingness with respect to whatever actions and abstentions are enjoined by a substantive conception of justice, although, as we shall see later, the conditionality of such willingness is usually masked by the availability of legal redress and the prohibition of personal retaliation.

This conditionality does not, however, reduce justice to the level of (enlightened) egoism, because the condition is that of reciprocity rather than the one-sided satisfaction of self-interest. What distinguishes egoism from the disposition to be just is that it is not a sufficient condition for the egoist (to be willing) to perform or refrain from an action enjoined or prohibited by a substantive conception of justice even if the action in question is performed or refrained from by others. Thus (enlightened) egoism in its own way is also independent of considerations of reciprocity, in the sense that the egoist is not willing to do what the just person is willing to do even when the condition of reciprocity is fully satisfied. Regardless of how

10. Thus the crucial aspect of benevolence is its unconditionality, or lack of insistence on reciprocity. This need not prevent a benevolent person from apprehending, say, in a Kantian spirit, the duty of benevolence as having the universality of a moral law, which thereby necessarily includes the benevolent person himself as a potential beneficiary. Nevertheless, what makes his *motive* one of benevolence is his seeing himself as the subject of benevolence, and unconditionally so, rather than seeing himself equally as the object of benevolence and hence seeing benevolence as necessarily reciprocal. The benevolent person thus understood will not—at least, not as a necessary condition of his benevolence—entertain the thought that "by carrying out the duty of love to someone I put another under obligation; I make myself deserving from him." Immanuel Kant, *The Metaphysics of Morals,* trans. Mary Gregor (Cambridge: Cambridge University Press, 1991), p. 244. For Kant's emphasis on the universality of the duty of benevolence, see ibid., p. 245, "The Doctrine of Virtue," sec. 27.

other people act, the egoist will choose not to act in accordance with the impersonal norms of justice so long as he believes he can get away with it. Whereas what the law does for the just person is to force *other people* to be just (so that he or she can afford to be just), what it does to the egoist is to force *him* to act justly (since he would not do so otherwise).

In short, the just person insists on reciprocity for the sake of mutual benefit; the benevolent person (more an ideal than a reality) is willing not to demand reciprocity of others; and the egoist suspends reciprocity on his own part whenever possible, and he does so surreptitiously in order that his unilateral suspension of reciprocity will not cause a similar suspension by others or punishment by the state. By the same token, the disposition toward justice is distinguishable from benevolence on one side and from egoism on the other also in terms of the reactive attitude of resentment. Given that resentment is an emotion that reflects the motive of reciprocity, it is to be expected that where the motive of reciprocity is lacking, so too is the capacity for resentment. While the ability to feel resentment is intrinsic to the disposition toward justice, it is absent from benevolence in one way, in that benevolence is above the motive of reciprocity, and absent from egoism in another, in that egoism is below the motive of reciprocity.

The Conditionality of Justice

Once we agree that reciprocity, or the demand for reciprocity, is a necessary feature of the disposition toward justice in the sense I have described, we have to accept certain consequences that in my view have not been spelled out unequivocally enough in the literature and that, once fully clarified, seem to contradict some important notions frequently held or implied about the virtue of justice. These consequences arise because the reciprocity of justice implies the conditionality of justice, in the sense that a just person's willingness to be just is conditional on other people's showing the same willingness.[11] In Kantian terms, one might say that the imperative of justice has the character of a hypothetical as opposed to a cate-

11. This sense of conditionality is distinct from another sense in which we can describe certain norms of justice as conditional. In the first sense, the conditionality (of my compliance with a norm of justice) is a matter of whether others comply as well. In the second sense, the conditionality (of the application of a norm) is a function of the degree of stringency of the norm itself (for example, whether exceptions are permitted under special circumstances). I am concerned here with conditionality in the first sense only.

gorical imperative, and that the disposition to be just is a heteronomous rather than an autonomous disposition.[12]

It is well known that Kant has been charged with smuggling in a hypothetical imperative in the guise of a categorical one. Schopenhauer, one of those who have leveled this charge, singled out as his most telling proof this passage from Kant's *Metaphysics of Morals:* "For every man wants *to be helped*. If, however, he were to give utterance to his maxim not to want to help others, everyone would *be entitled* to refuse him assistance. Hence the selfish maxim contradicts itself."[13] In this passage Schopenhauer finds "expressed . . . in the clearest possible manner that moral obligation rests absolutely and entirely on assumed *reciprocity.* Consequently, it is utterly egoistic and obtains its interpretation from egoism. Under the condition of *reciprocity,* egoism cunningly acquiesces in a compromise." In this light, according to Schopenhauer, "when . . . it says in the *Foundations* . . . that 'the principle of always acting in accordance with the maxim whose universality as law you can at the same time will, is the only condition on which a man's will can never be in antagonism with itself,' then the true interpretation of the word *antagonism* is that if a will had sanctioned the maxim of injustice and uncharitableness, it would, if it *eventualiter* became the *passive part,* subsequently revoke it and thus *contradict* itself." Schopenhauer thus concludes that "that fundamental rule of Kant is not, as he incessantly asserts, a *categorical* imperative, but in fact a *hypothetical* one. For tacitly underlying it is the *condition* that the law to be laid down for my *action,* since I raise it to one that is *universal,* also becomes the law for my *suffering,* and on this condition I, as the *eventualiter passive* part, certainly *cannot will* injustice and uncharitableness."[14]

12. It is of course not a sufficient condition for an imperative to be a hypothetical one, in Kant's sense, that it has conditions attached to it. The conditions in question have to be of a kind that springs from the agent's inclinations or desires. Thus, in and of itself, even the condition that other people reciprocate in relation to the norms of justice is not one that necessarily makes the imperative I follow a hypothetical one in the Kantian sense. But, as I tried to show in my discussion of the relationship between impersonal norms and personal interests and of the distinction between justice and benevolence, the conditionality intrinsic to the disposition toward justice is indeed of a kind that is motivated in part by the desire, albeit a perfectly reasonable one, not to suffer unfair sacrifices in a scheme designed for mutual benefit. For this reason, the kind of conditionality insisted on by the just person does translate into the ability to act only in accordance with a hypothetical imperative of a specific kind.

13. Kant, *Metaphysics,* "The Doctrine of Virtue," sec. 30. The passage is cited in the form, including emphasis, in which it appears in Arthur Schopenhauer, *On the Basis of Morality,* trans. E. F. J. Payne (Indianapolis: Bobbs-Merrill, 1965), pp. 90–91.

14. Schopenhauer, *On the Basis of Morality,* p. 91.

I have quoted at length in order to show that the conditionality or reciprocity Schopenhauer supposedly detects in Kant is of a kind that occurs at the stage of deciding what maxims to adopt, that is, at the stage of fixing the content or substance of morality. Whether or not Kant is guilty of Schopenhauer's charge thus construed, he is clearly not in favor of conditionality at the subsequent stage of acting on the already chosen maxims.[15] To be sure, matters are complicated in *The Metaphysics of Morals* by Kant's distinction between the sphere of right and the sphere of virtue.[16] But even in this work Kant must be understood as ruling out for the duty of virtue any conditionality at the second stage. As far as the duty of virtue is concerned, *The Metaphysics of Morals* is continuous with the *Groundwork,* where Kant explicitly rules out any considerations of reciprocity when it comes to acting on the categorical imperative. This is most clear in a passage in the *Groundwork* where, presenting the categorical imperative in terms of the kingdom of ends, Kant makes a point that is equally germane to the present discussion. In that passage, having stated that "a kingdom of ends would actually come into existence through maxims which the categorical imperative prescribes as a rule for all rational beings, *if these maxims were universally followed,*" Kant goes on to say, by way of emphasizing the counterfactual status of this statement, that "even if a rational being were himself to follow such a maxim strictly, he cannot count on everybody else being faithful to it on this ground." This sober realization does not prevent Kant, however, from insisting that "in spite of this the law 'Act on the maxims of a member who makes universal laws for a merely possible kingdom of ends' remains in full force, since its command is categorical."[17]

What we have here, I suggest, is an all-important difference with respect to the *locus of conditionality.* The Kantian kind of conditionality, if it is that, is a function of determining whether a maxim can be an object of universal *willing* (that is, whether everyone can *will* it) and thus has to do with the justifiability of a maxim.[18] The other kind of conditionality, by

15. A similar distinction, between determining what one's duty is and acting on that duty, is drawn, though for a different purpose, in Thomas Hill, *Dignity and Practical Reason in Kant's Moral Theory* (Ithaca, N.Y.: Cornell University Press, 1992), p. 66.

16. For an illuminating discussion, see Thomas W. Pogge, "Kant's Theory of Justice," *Kant Studien* 79 (1988): 407–433, esp. pp. 410, 415.

17. Immanuel Kant, *Groundwork of the Metaphysic of Morals,* trans. H. J. Paton, in *The Moral Law* (London: Hutchinson, 1947), p. 106.

18. As Pogge puts it, in characterizing the "practical solipsism" in Kant's *Groundwork,* "Reason here merely demands *motivational* unity, separately within each individual: each

contrast, demands a universality of *performance* (that is, everyone will *practice* it) as a condition of one's own readiness to act on an already chosen maxim. It therefore is no longer a matter of a maxim's justifiability in the realm of reason but a matter of its practicability in the empirical realm of desires and interests. In the latter case, the reasons for an agent to be just are no longer independent reasons, in that an agent's having and acting on them is dependent not merely on whether other people *ought to* have and act on the same reasons, but on whether other people *actually* have and act on the same reasons.[19]

It is conditionality in the second sense—what we may call conditionality of performance or interest-based conditionality—that is regarded as a reasonable feature of the requirement of justice, and of the disposition toward justice, by modern theorists. This is then appended, as it were, to the maxims of justice in the form of the conditional clause "provided that other members of the relevant group act likewise." We should note that such a stipulation of reciprocity is not based on systemic or institutional considerations such as the Humean notion of justice as an artificial virtue (such that "a single act of justice, consider'd in itself, may often be contrary to the public good; and 'tis only the concurrence of mankind, in a general scheme or system of action, which is advantageous"),[20] but is based on individual psychological considerations falling under the rubric of what John Rawls calls "reasonable moral psychology." It is part of such a moral psychology that "when [citizens] believe that institutions or social practices are just, or fair (as the conception specifies), they are ready and willing to do their part in these arrangements *provided they have reasonable assurance that others will also do their part.*"[21] The demand for such assurance shows that the disposition to be just is cost-sensitive, to borrow a term used by Bernard Williams to describe the general disposition to cooperate.[22] As Williams remarks, such cost-sensitivity—the fact that the disposition toward cooperative interaction in general and toward justice in

person is to have a coherent, universalizable, and complete system of maxims" ("Kant's Theory," p. 410).

19. The term "independent reasons" is taken from Kurt Baier, *The Rational and the Moral Order* (Chicago: Open Court, 1995), p. 190. Baier rightly insists that justice is based, at least in part, on society-anchored, and hence nonindependent, reasons—a society-anchored reason being one that is "more or less dependent on others also having it, *and* following it when they have it."

20. Hume, *Treatise,* p. 579.

21. John Rawls, *Political Liberalism* (New York: Columbia University Press, 1993), p. 86, emphasis added.

22. Bernard Williams, "Formal Structures and Social Reality," in *Trust: Making and*

particular is "conditionalized"—"implies that the agent has other, in particular egoistic, motivations. Unless cooperation also, to some extent, serves those interests as well, the practices of cooperation will be unstable in the face of those other motivations."[23]

Autonomy, Heteronomy, and the Disposition toward Justice

Such a moral psychology fits well with—indeed, follows from—the nature of the disposition toward justice as I have described it. I do not dispute this moral psychology. What I want to argue, however, is that once we treat *interest-based* conditionality (or conditionality of performance) as part of the disposition toward justice, we must give up any attempt to conceive the desire to be just in terms of the Kantian notion of the categorical imperative and the correlative Kantian notion of the autonomous will. Interest-based conditionality, demanding as it does the satisfaction of (legitimate) interests,[24] divests the maxims of justice of the self-sufficiency or

---

Breaking Cooperative Relations, ed. Diego Gambetta (New York: Basil Blackwell, 1988), pp. 3–13; quotation from p. 4.

23. Ibid., p. 11.

24. It is important to stress that a just person demands, as the "return" for being just, the satisfaction not of her interests as such but only of her legitimate interests, that is, those sanctioned and protected by justice. It is thus confusing when Rawls describes the disposition to be just as consisting in part of the willingness to act on fair terms of social cooperation "provided others do, *even contrary to one's own interest.*" John Rawls, "Reply to Habermas," *Journal of Philosophy* 92 (1995): 132–180; quotation from p. 134, emphasis added. Justice, which exists to draw a line between legitimate and nonlegitimate interests, or a legitimate and a nonlegitimate way of pursuing interests, never demands the sacrifice of one's legitimate interests and always demands the forgoing of one's nonlegitimate interests. In this light, the clause "even contrary to one's own interest" is either trivially true, if interest is understood as nonlegitimate interest, or plainly false, if interest is understood as legitimate interest. Once we distinguish clearly between legitimate and nonlegitimate interests, we can see a built-in connection between any reciprocal practice, such as justice, and the satisfaction of (legitimate) self-interest. For a helpful discussion, see Lawrence C. Becker, *Reciprocity* (New York: Routledge, 1986), p. 126. Looking at the matter this way will help us avoid exaggerating the extent to which justice rises above self-interest or involves self-sacrifice. In this connection, one might also take issue with Dan Brock's characterization of "being a moral person, adopting the moral point of view" as involving "being prepared to do what morality requires not just when its requirements happen to coincide with one's self-interest, but *at all times.*" Dan W. Brock, "The Justification of Morality," *American Philosophical Quarterly* 14 (1977): 71–78; quotation from p. 73, emphasis added. Here, "at all times" gives the impression of a high degree of self-sacrifice when in fact it should simply mean giving up all nonlegitimate interests, which is the least that any morality or conception of justice must require. "At all times" does entail a high degree of self-sacrifice, beyond what justice requires, only when the morality in question does not have a conditional clause, as any conception of justice must.

categorical character on which Kant insists. It brings contingency and heteronomy into the disposition to act according to justifiable maxims, in a way that Kant's categorical imperative clearly does not.[25] Such heteronomy is completely at odds with Kant's insistence, which borders on the superhuman, that one "should think rather of the sacrifices which obedience to duty (i.e., virtue) entails than of the benefits he might reap from it, so that he will comprehend the imperative of duty in its full authority as a self-sufficient law, independent of all other influences, which requires unconditional obedience."[26] We have good reason, though, to free the term "heteronomy" of its negative connotations, inasmuch as autonomy in the strict Kantian sense is neither realistic nor perhaps wholly desirable. Once we do so, retaining for heteronomy its Kantian denotation without the Kantian connotations, we need have no hesitation in treating heteronomy as a characteristic of the disposition to be just.

As we have seen, interest-based conditionality is part of what Rawls rightly considers "reasonable moral psychology." It is no accident that the same interest-based conditionality is held to be a reasonable feature of justice by Habermas. Habermas spells out the underlying rationale even more clearly than Rawls does, insisting that "even morally well-justified norms may be warrantedly expected only of those who can expect that all others will also behave in the same way." For this insistence he adduces the argument that "only under the condition of a general observance of norms do reasons that can be adduced for their justification count."[27]

25. While I largely agree with Brian Barry when he follows Hill (*Dignity,* chap. 4) in charging Kant with "utopianism," I think it wrong for Barry to suggest, in *Justice as Impartiality* (Oxford: Clarendon Press, 1995), p. 244n, that "it was an idiosyncrasy of Kant's, not anything inherent in the idea of the Categorical Imperative, that led him to insist that one should determine what is the right thing to do on the assumption that everybody else will do it, whether or not they actually do." The stringency Barry complains about, with good reason, *is* a component of the categorical imperative itself, as Kant himself makes abundantly clear, for example, in the *Groundwork,* p. 106. Of course, one may be perfectly right to reject the Kantian stringency (as it applies to justice, say), but in so doing one is no longer in a position to retain the categorical imperative.

26. Immanuel Kant, "On the Common Saying: 'This May Be True in Theory, but It Does Not Apply in Practice,'" in *Kant's Political Writings,* ed. Hans Reiss, trans. H. B. Nisbet (Cambridge: Cambridge University Press, 1970), p. 64.

27. Jürgen Habermas, "Law and Morality," in *The Tanner Lectures on Human Values,* vol. 8, ed. Sterling M. McMurrin (Salt Lake City: University of Utah Press, 1988): 217–279; quotation from p. 245. See also Habermas, *Justification:* "A precondition of the general acceptance of any norm that passes the generalization test is that it should also be *actually* adhered to by everyone. . . [A]dherence to a valid norm is to be expected only of an individual who can be sure that all others will also follow the norm" (p. 155, emphasis added).

While this is a perfectly reasonable argument and one quite in keeping with the spirit of justice, there is nothing Kantian about it. For Habermas, the reasons adduced for the justification of norms have to be made good in the empirical realm for such reasons to count as good reasons for each individual—retrospectively as it were, or, what amounts to the same thing, prospectively only against a dependable background of legal deterrence and sanctions. These reasons are at least partly concerned with interests, as they have to be if justice is to remain distinct from some more altruistic disposition, rather than purely with the Kantian test of universalizability. If the desire to be just is cost-sensitive for Habermas, it is definitely not so for Kant.[28]

Habermas would be the last to deny this cost-sensitivity. This is clear from a passage in which he sheds a good deal of light on what he means by autonomy and what he takes to be the relationship between reason and self-interest, and in which he distinguishes justice from acts of supererogation in terms of legitimate self-interest. He writes:

> Autonomy can be reasonably expected *(zumutbar)* only in social contexts that are already themselves rational in the sense that they ensure that action motivated by good reasons will not of necessity conflict with one's own interests. The validity of moral commands is subject to the condition that they are *universally* adhered to as the basis for a general practice. Only when this condition is satisfied do they express what all could will. Only then are moral commands in the common interest and—precisely because they are equally good for all—do not impose supererogatory demands.[29]

This highly condensed passage contains not only a clear statement of the fact that, and of the sense in which, heteronomy is a constitutive feature of the disposition toward justice, but also a justification of why this should be. The only problem with the passage is that Habermas chooses to see the defining features of the disposition toward justice, themselves correctly and precisely identified, in highly questionable terms of autonomy. But for this invocation of autonomy, Habermas's account of the disposition toward justice would be one to which, in the final analysis, even Kant could have little reason to object, for it can be shown that what Kant takes

28. Kant, of course, recognizes no distinct virtue of justice but only a generic virtuous disposition that subsumes, as one instantiation of virtue among others, the willingness to follow principles of justice from a sense of duty. I will discuss this further presently, but for now this should not affect the point being made.

29. Habermas, *Justification,* p. 34.

to be merely empirical and "secondary" features of duty-following are in fact necessary and hence primary features *as far as justice is concerned.*

Now, Kant readily acknowledges the existence of "secondary notions and considerations which, through imagination, habit and inclination, accompany the concept of duty," going so far as to suggest that "perhaps no recognized and respected duty has ever been carried out by anyone without some selfishness or interference from other motives."[30] Predictably, Kant does not look deeply into such motives, for in his scheme of things they are but obstacles to be overcome on the difficult path to virtue. Yet from the fact that resentment and reciprocity are, as I have shown, *ineluctable* features of the disposition toward justice, we can infer that what Kant calls secondary motives, that is, motives having to do with the satisfaction of interests, are in fact primary, because necessary, components of the concept of justice. Thus, what Kant says is "perhaps" the case—namely, that "no recognized and respected duty has ever been carried out by anyone without some selfishness or interference from other motives" (where "*some* selfishness" may be taken to indicate that justice is both continuous with egoism and different from it)—is in fact necessarily the case as far as justice (conduct motivated by a merely just disposition) is concerned. Simply put, the disposition toward justice is not merely empirically heteronomous but *intrinsically* so.[31]

To be sure, Kant never said anything exactly to this effect, but this is arguably because his way of distinguishing between the sphere of right and the sphere of virtue makes it inappropriate to speak of a distinct motive of justice as opposed to a broad virtuous disposition that includes, as one instantiation of virtue among others, the willingness to follow the duties of right from a sense of duty.[32] What I have tried to show is that *if* Kant were to identify a distinct motive of justice, he too would be led to the view that the disposition to be just is a necessarily heteronomous one. As things actually stand, Kant's position on these matters hinges on the sharp

30. Kant, "On the Common Saying," p. 69. See also Kant, *Metaphysics,* p. 196.

31. This does not mean that conduct that meets the requirements of justice necessarily flows from a heteronomous will. The point is that where such conduct does not flow from a heteronomous will, it is necessarily motivated by a virtue higher than justice, whatever that may be, a virtue above resentment and reciprocity and hence a virtue whose motivating power does not stop at the causing of merely just conduct. This is precisely where someone with a *merely* just disposition would stop, in keeping with the intrinsic heteronomy of that disposition.

32. As Kant puts it, "There is only one virtuous disposition, the subjective determining ground to fulfill one's duty, which extends to duties of Right as well" (*Metaphysics,* p. 210).

distinction he draws between the spheres of right and virtue. With this distinction he is able, on the one hand, to treat the sphere of right as characterized by or at least compatible with heteronomy,[33] although, as we have seen, he fails to recognize the ineluctable rather than merely empirical character of such heteronomy. On the other hand, Kant is able to assign autonomy and the categorical imperative to the sphere of virtue alone. This move is of a piece with the fact that Kant does not speak of a distinct motive or virtue of justice.

Rawls and Habermas, for their part, do identify a distinct disposition toward justice. In so doing, however, they cannot also, as Kant does, treat autonomy as a feature of a sphere of virtue sharply separated from the sphere of right. Not that they would want to do any such thing, since they (rightly) regard general observance of norms of justice as a reasonable precondition of the duty of justice. In thus refusing to draw a hard-and-fast line between virtue and right, norms and interests, however, they are no longer in a position to deny that heteronomy in the Kantian sense is characteristic of the distinct virtuous disposition to be just. But this is something they do seem to deny, at least implicitly. On the one hand, in a non-Kantian fashion, they clearly acknowledge the interest-based and conditional nature of the disposition toward justice, as we have seen, as is only reasonable and indeed unavoidable. Yet on the other hand, in a recognizably Kantian spirit, they also bring in some notion of autonomy, which seems to be required if justice is to issue properly from the exercise of human reason and command the allegiance of every reasonable person. A certain tension thus arises in the position of Rawls and Habermas, since interest-based conditionality, with its sensitivity to cost, cannot square with autonomy in anything like a Kantian sense: autonomy in the Kantian sense is not cost-sensitive; only heteronomy is. This tension can be resolved only by abandoning the (Kantian) notion of autonomy, for we simply cannot give up the notion of interest-based conditionality as long as we are talking about justice.

It might be argued that Habermas does implicitly give up the strictly Kantian notion of autonomy when he proposes to treat autonomy not as a postulate of pure practical reason but as a product, however natural or immanent, of the empirical process of socialization.[34] Thus, according to a

33. See, e.g., ibid., p. 122.

34. Habermas uses the term *autonomy* in two related senses. The first, autonomy of will, is a function of whether one is "capable of acting from moral insight" (*Justification*, p. 14). This is the sense that resembles the Kantian notion of autonomy and is the one that is rele-

developmental view Habermas borrows in part from Lawrence Kohlberg, moral agents are supposed to move from cruder forms of reciprocity to the ideal form of reciprocity that is autonomy. And they are supposed to do so through a process of socialization that consists in a benign cycle of progressively refined mediation of norms and interests. By and large, this is also how Rawls attempts to solve the problem, treating autonomy and good will not as the moral-psychological prerequisites of a just society, as good will (or sympathy) is in utilitarianism, but as the predictable outcomes of a well-ordered society made possible in the first instance by lesser motives.[35]

There is a fundamental difference between this kind of autonomy, if we can call it that, and the Kantian kind. For Kant, autonomy, besides being independent of interest or inclination, is something one begins from, as a postulate of reason, whereas for Habermas and Rawls, autonomy, besides consisting in a certain mediation of norms and interests, is something one (it is to be hoped) ends up with, as the culmination of stages of moral development that are logically or developmentally antecedent. Habermas calls his own account of justice an "intersubjectivist version of Kant's principle of autonomy,"[36] but neither his account nor Rawls's actually fits this description. Since the notion of autonomy as used in their accounts is conditional on both interests and appropriate socialization, we can perhaps describe Habermas's and Rawls's kind of autonomy oxymoronically as *conditioned autonomy.* It can pass for autonomy in anything like the Kantian sense only when its conditionality, in the two senses just mentioned, is disguised or forgotten through fulfillment of the conditions in question.[37] In this way, the Kantian-sounding notion of autonomy takes its place, in the theories of Habermas and Rawls, only within an empirical developmental framework (a "progress of the sentiments," as Hume calls it) that is not Kantian but largely Humean. This calls into question the ap-

vant here. The other sense of autonomy, as in the notion of "personal autonomy," is defined in terms of its interrelation with solidarity, as part of a communicative conception of reason (see, e.g., ibid., p. 114). To make autonomy dependent on solidarity in this way is to use *autonomy* in a very different sense from that in which it contrasts with *heteronomy.* As paired with solidarity, autonomy means something like a viable individual identity.

35. For fuller discussion of Rawls and Habermas on these issues, see Chapter 7.

36. Jürgen Habermas, "Reconciliation through the Public Use of Reason: Remarks on John Rawls's Political Liberalism," *Journal of Philosophy* 92 (1995): 109–131; quotation from p. 109.

37. See the first section of Chapter 9 for further discussion.

propriateness of characterizing the disposition toward justice in terms of autonomy, especially the Kantian notion of autonomy.

There are important reasons for which it is necessary to show that the disposition toward justice is marked by heteronomy rather than autonomy—the same reasons why it is necessary to identify resentment, reciprocity, and interest-based conditionality as constitutive features of the disposition to be just. First, characterizing the disposition toward justice as heteronomous accords with the way, described earlier, in which justice is distinct from, and is a lesser virtue than, such unconditional, and in this sense properly autonomous, dispositions as benevolence. Second, and more important, it is only in terms of heteronomy that we can account for the continuity of the disposition to be just with the circumstances of justice, among them limited altruism. Finally, and most important, knowing why and in what way the disposition toward justice is marked by heteronomy gives us a more accurate idea of what we can expect of the disposition toward justice, even under idealized circumstances, in terms of what and how much it can, on its own, contribute to the establishment of reasonable norms and to the stability of a social order based on them.

As far as the establishment of reasonable norms is concerned, conceiving the disposition toward justice in terms of autonomy, as Habermas and Rawls do, has the effect of underestimating the difficulty of reaching agreement. One might say that Kant's notion of autonomy, with its exclusion of interests and desires from the determining grounds of moral legislation, eliminates from his theory the difficulty of reaching agreement only to leave it squarely in the empirical realm of conflicting interests and inclinations (which is not the concern of Kant's moral theory). Habermas and Rawls, by contrast, treat individual needs and interests as the very things with respect to which, indeed partly for the sake of which, agreement is to be sought. In so doing, they place the difficulty of reaching agreement at the heart of their theories rather than merely in the empirical realm of application.[38] On the whole, this is a more sensible conception of the moral enterprise. Once the difficulty arising from the conflict of interests is relocated in this way, however, the concept of autonomy, with its implication of freedom from determination by self-interest, belies the difficulty of reaching agreement.

More seriously, characterizing the disposition to be just in terms of au-

38. For a very helpful discussion of related issues, see Thomas McCarthy, *Ideals and Illusions* (Cambridge, Mass.: MIT Press, 1991), p. 210.

tonomy can give a misleading impression of how much such a disposition, even when generally present, as in a Rawlsian well-ordered society, can help ensure the stability of a just society. Not that either Habermas or Rawls necessarily has an exaggerated notion of how much a widespread disposition toward justice can accomplish in this regard. But their use of the notion of autonomy, with its almost unavoidable implications of moral independence and purity of purpose, does encourage such exaggerated notions. For treating the disposition toward justice as autonomous can easily lead one to suppose that it is capable of standing alone as a sufficient motive of just conduct, such that those with a just disposition require a background of legal sanctions only for their protection, and not as a necessary buttress for their willingness to be just. Such a belief in the self-sufficiency of a just disposition is surely false, and it will further our understanding of the disposition toward justice to see exactly why it is false.

Legal Coercion and the Motivation of the Just Person

Since the disposition toward justice is heteronomous, it leads to just conduct only conditionally, though not merely accidentally. Such conditionality is overcome, and the appearance of autonomy created, only through the introduction of law, which exists to compel the unjust to follow the norms of justice—even if only reluctantly—so that those with a just disposition can do so willingly, though conditionally. It is important to be clear about the role that legal coercion plays in this context. It is one thing to say that law is required to guarantee universal external freedom (Kant), or to annul an infringement of the right as right (Hegel), or according to commonsense conceptions, to deter and punish the unjust and protect the just. It is something altogether different to suggest, as Habermas does, that the role of law (or one of its roles) is to ensure that those with a just disposition can afford to be just.[39] As Habermas puts it, "The problem of the conditions under which moral commands are reasonable motivates the transition from morality to law."[40]

In this context, Habermas invokes Kant, who, according to him, "al-

39. Bernard Williams, in his game-theoretic discussion of the disposition to cooperate, speaks of an analogous "important difference in the possible role of sanctions, a difference relevant to political theory. The addition of sanctions may change the utilities for a basically egoistic agent, or they may provide assurance for an agent who is basically cooperative" ("Formal Structures," p. 4).

40. Habermas, *Justification,* p. 16, also pp. 155, 156; and Habermas, "Law," p. 245.

ready justified the transition from morality to state-sanctioned law in this way."[41] But this interpretation of Kant is only partially correct. In linking morality and law, Kant is concerned with the preservation of outer freedom, with "the possibility of connecting universal reciprocal coercion with the freedom of everyone,"[42] not with the provision of a legal cushion for those whose sense of duty is already a sufficient incentive to obey the law. Habermas, however, is concerned with the disposition toward justice itself, and therefore, for him to bring law into the picture to buttress the motivation of the just person is to say something about the nature of the motive of the just person in a way that Kant need not and would not. It is true of Habermas, but would not be true of Kant, that a background of legal coercion—namely, "the cognitive expectation that, if necessary, force may be brought to bear to ensure that everyone adheres to the individual legal norms"[43]—enters into the very motivation of those with a just disposition and becomes an element of their very willingness to be just.[44] In this way, the heteronomous nature of the disposition toward justice is confirmed by its intrinsic dependence on legal coercion.

This dependence on legal coercion follows not only from the motive of reciprocity but also, as one might expect, from the reactive attitude of resentment.[45] Reciprocity is to legal deterrence what resentment is to legal punishment. The motive of reciprocity that is part and parcel of a just disposition calls for potential punishment to deter people from violating the reciprocity of justice. When such deterrence fails, there arises on the part of the law-abiding the reactive attitude of resentment, which can be appeased only by the actual carrying out of punishment.

This situation can also be described in the Kantian terms of internal (or ethical) versus external (or juridical) lawgiving. For Kant, internal lawgiving is entirely independent, and so is virtue inasmuch as it is constituted by internal lawgiving. In Habermas's account of the virtue of justice, by contrast, although internal lawgiving plays a part, it is nevertheless dependent

41. Habermas, *Justification,* p. 155; see also pp. 87–88.

42. Kant, *Metaphysics,* p. 57, 47.

43. Habermas, *Justification,* p. 156. From the point of view of each individual with a just disposition, the cognitive expectation is that legal coercion will be used to bring everyone *else* into line.

44. See Diego Gambetta's instructive account, highly relevant to this discussion, of the relationship between cooperation, trust, and legal coercion in "Can We Trust Trust?" in Gambetta, *Trust,* pp. 213–237, esp. pp. 218–221.

45. See Strawson, *Freedom,* p. 22.

on the existence of external lawgiving directed at others. Thus, for Habermas, external lawgiving serves as a necessary background condition of internal lawgiving, which thereby ceases to be purely internal lawgiving. What external lawgiving does for the just is to force the unjust to comply, thus making human interaction mirror the built-in reciprocity that characterizes the disposition of the just. The problem is that the presence of external lawgiving as a dependable background against which the just can afford to be just obscures the precariousness of the reasonable moral psychology of justice *on its own*. Such precariousness comes to the fore once (as a thought experiment) we give up the assumption that reciprocity is guaranteed through effective legal enforcement.

It should be clear that I am not arguing against Habermas's moral psychology in favor of Kant's. I think Habermas's moral psychology by far the more reasonable of the two. What I am trying to show is that if we want to give up Kant's moral psychology, we should be clear about, and be prepared to accept, the philosophical implications of doing so. In this spirit, I want to suggest that Habermas is not in a position to draw a sharp line (which he may not want to draw anyway) between morality and self-interest, or between internal and external lawgiving, in that unlike Kant, he takes general observance of an impersonal norm to be a reasonable precondition of each individual's observance of it. This is indeed a reasonable precondition within the framework of justice, but it is also one that attenuates the independence of moral motives and blurs, though it certainly does not eliminate, the distinction between morality and self-interest, internal and external lawgiving, virtue and right. If we were to draw as sharp a line as Kant does between external and internal lawgiving and think of virtue as defined by internal lawgiving alone, we would be quite unable to explain such crucial features of justice as reciprocity and resentment in terms of virtue, for virtue, defined in terms of purely internal lawgiving, is incompatible with resentment and reciprocity. Therefore, as long as we treat justice as a virtue and at the same time recognize, as we must, reciprocity and resentment as characteristics of this virtue, we have no choice but to give up any attempt to draw a sharp distinction between internal and external lawgiving. And this means in turn that we must concede that the disposition toward justice, however reasonable, is not autonomous.

It is extremely important to recognize this Janus-faced character of the disposition to be just. What is important, in the first instance, is the fact that (not necessarily the precise way in which) justice consists in the mediation of norms and interests, such that the virtue of justice occupies an intermediate position between altruism and egoism. It is this mixed or intermediate character, however we may want to describe it precisely, that makes the disposition toward justice what it is, with its natural proneness to resentment, its ineluctable conditionality, and its intrinsic dependence on the availability of punishment for others in the event that they violate the reciprocity of justice. Beyond this, it is impossible to specify in advance the exact locus, as it were, of the intermediate position of the disposition toward justice. While this intermediate position, broadly construed, is intrinsic to the disposition toward justice as such, its precise locus is not pregiven but is a function of socialization. Between the poles of unconditional altruism and complete egoism, the process of socialization, itself always shaped by cultural and historical contingencies, determines where the disposition to be just is going to end up—say, closer to altruism or closer to egoism. As we shall see, however, successful socialization, or socialization carried out under relatively favorable subjective and objective circumstances, tends to push the disposition toward justice into the vicinity of the unconditional virtues, giving the disposition toward justice the appearance, which is not unimportant, of unconditionality and sometimes even the subjective feeling of unconditionality.

Unconditional Aspects of the Disposition toward Justice

Up to this point I have been concerned chiefly to bring out the generic conditionality of the disposition toward justice. But it is no less a psychological reality, something best captured by Kant, that a just person relates to the requirements of justice in the spirit of following a categorical imperative.[46] This apparently runs counter to the ineradicable conditionality of the motive of justice, which I have been at pains to demonstrate. What I want to argue is that both of these apparent features of justice are psychologically real and therefore have somehow to be squared in our account of the psychology of justice. It was in this sense that I suggested, in the introduction, that the task of an explanatory theory of justice is at once to account for the conditional nature of the disposition toward justice and to make sense of the fact that the requirements of justice (can) take the form of categorical imperatives in the psychology of a just person. I also suggested, without elaboration, that this twofold task is to be accomplished

46. See, e.g., Kant, *Groundwork,* p. 106. This is subject to the proviso, as noted earlier, that Kant identifies no distinct virtue of justice but only a virtuous disposition in general.

by examining the logic of those social practices whereby the original, intrinsic conditionality of the motive of justice is tamed and transformed.

Now, this conditionality of motive is tamed, in the first instance, in the sense that it is made compatible with the unconditional *practice* of justice, as indeed it has to be if the instituting of justice is to help maintain a stable society. This happens when the state, through its monopoly of the legal power of deterrence and punishment, makes itself solely responsible for safeguarding the reciprocity of justice and in so doing relieves individuals of the need and the power to do so. The state alone has the right to *act on* the premise that justice is reciprocal. In exchange for the state's enforcement of the reciprocity condition of justice, individuals have to practice justice *as if* it were an unconditional obligation, relying on the state to ensure that other people will do the same.

It should be emphasized that the achievement in this way of the unconditional practice of justice occurs entirely within the logic of justice itself, since individuals are prepared to practice justice unconditionally (in relation to other individuals) only on condition that the reciprocal nature of justice is preserved by the state (in relation to each individual). What happens is that justice is made unconditional as a practice in a manner that nevertheless accords with each individual's still conditional motive of justice. To the extent that the state succeeds in ensuring reciprocity, it may also succeed in time in creating on the part of individuals an understanding of justice in which the link between justice and reciprocity is no longer consciously perceived. But even this does not eliminate or transcend the original, conditional motive of justice. What happens is merely that the original motive, rooted in mutual advantage, is made redundant as a *conscious* motive of justice by circumstances in which mutual advantage is something to be taken for granted rather than to be struggled for.

No state, however, except in a utopian fantasy, can entirely succeed in creating and sustaining such favorable circumstances. When such circumstances are lacking, the *virtue* of unconditional justice, the willingness to be just in the absence of personal advantage, has to be developed to make up for them. In other words, the more the state fails to make good the connection between justice and mutual advantage in reality, the harder it will have to try to sever or weaken this connection in the consciousness of its citizens. To this end, the state needs an ideology of duty, whose function it is to transform justice from a conditional into an unconditional commitment, to create an unconditional commitment to justice on the basis of a conditional motive. Unlike the attempt to square the conditional motive of justice with the unconditional practice of justice, however, the attempt to render the motive of justice itself unconditional goes outside the logic of justice, and for that very reason is doomed to at least partial failure as long as the circumstances of justice obtain. The internalization of the ideology of duty, even as it succeeds in eliminating the conditionality of justice from *conscious* motivation, betrays that very conditionality in the continued, ever more refined ability to feel resentment.

Resentment is an affective or emotional correlate of conditional motives, and thus its very presence, with its frequent demand for punishment of the guilty, shows that the original, conditional motive of justice has not been transcended but has merely been suppressed—into the unconscious. Driven into the unconscious by the social inculcation of unconditional morality, the interest-based conditionality of justice finds expression no longer in any direct awareness of a conditional motive but only in the symptoms of such a motive. Resentment, as such a symptom, bespeaks the elimination of the conditionality of justice from consciousness but its simultaneous retention in the unconscious, thus suggesting that genuine autonomy is not possible within the confines of justice. Heteronomy, no longer visible, has merely receded from conscious awareness, whereby an appearance of autonomy is created.

Such a psychological state invites description in terms of "forgetting," Nietzsche's metaphor for capturing the mechanisms at work in the social production of justice as an unconditional virtue.[47] This description is particularly apt in that forgetting can involve at once the elimination of something from consciousness and its retention in the unconscious. In this sense, the idea of forgetting captures both the extent and the limit of the social production of justice as an unconditional virtue—both how far socialization can raise justice above the conditional motives implicit in the circumstances of justice and how even after such socialization the apparently unconditional virtue of justice remains tied to those very motives and circumstances.

Reciprocity under Reasonable Norms

In the explanatory account of justice presented here, the concept of reciprocity is used to answer not the question of what norms are justified but

47. Friedrich Nietzsche, *Human, All Too Human,* trans. R. J. Hollingdale, 2 vols. in 1 (Cambridge: Cambridge University Press, 1986), 1:92.

the very different question of the nature of the motivation for setting up norms and abiding by them. As an answer to the latter question, reciprocity or conditionality means a general willingness to enter into a reciprocal commitment to impersonal norms, whose content (a matter of the former question) is left open.

Nevertheless, not just any norms will do for this purpose. There are certain kinds of possible norms—norms that are either blatantly prejudicial to oneself or blatantly prejudicial to others—that are in principle incapable of being followed from a disposition that can properly be described as the disposition toward justice. *This follows from the nature of justice as an intermediate virtue between altruism and egoism.* That justice is different from (a misguided) altruism rules out accepting norms blatantly prejudicial to oneself, and that justice is different from egoism rules out accepting norms blatantly prejudicial to others. Within certain limits, of course, people may reasonably disagree as to whether a given norm is overly prejudicial, and it is precisely to allow for this possibility that I have disqualified, from the range of norms capable of being accepted from a just disposition, only those that are blatantly prejudicial to oneself or others—or that are, to borrow an expression from Stuart Hampshire, "extremely and evidently unjust."[48]

It is now possible to give a more precise meaning to the concept of reciprocity as a constitutive feature of the disposition toward justice. By reciprocity I mean the conditional compliance not with any norms whatsoever but with broadly reasonable norms, where the concept of the reasonable is to be construed, on the grounds I have suggested, in a fairly elastic way.[49] In short, reciprocity means: reciprocity under broadly reasonable norms.[50] This concept of reciprocity is neutral between rival substantive conceptions of justice. In the formulation "reciprocity under broadly reasonable norms," reciprocity is a constant, and reasonable norms a variable

48. Stuart Hampshire, *Justice Is Conflict* (Princeton: Princeton University Press, 2000), p. 85.

49. My concept of the *broadly* reasonable bears some resemblance to what Hampshire calls "a *rough* convergence of reflective human feeling" (ibid., p. 92, emphasis added). A defining feature of the reasonable, as Hampshire implies, is the element of reflection on proposed norms of justice. While I entirely agree with this view, developing it would take me beyond the scope of my main concerns.

50. This concept of reciprocity falls somewhere between what Hans Saner (*Kant's Political Thought,* trans. E. B. Ashton [Chicago: University of Chicago Press, 1973], p. 31) calls formal reciprocity and material reciprocity. Saner's is a helpful distinction, though it is not clear that Kant's notion of reciprocity is as formal as Saner makes it out to be.

that receives different content in the case of different substantive conceptions of justice. One might say, then, for example, that justice-as-impartiality, as a normative theory, means reciprocity under justice-as-impartiality, whereas justice-as-mutual-advantage, as another normative theory, means reciprocity under justice-as-mutual-advantage. Clearly, the disagreement here concerns the validity of norms, not the reciprocal nature of people's commitment to them.[51] The disposition to be just is compatible with following any one of a wide range of broadly reasonable substantive conceptions of justice, or norms derived therefrom, a range that includes both justice-as-impartiality and justice-as-mutual-advantage but is not exhausted by them.

The relationship between (substantive) norms and (formal) reciprocity may be expressed by saying that the norms around which a reciprocal relationship between agents is formed give normative content to reciprocity over and above such content as it already contains by virtue of its distinction from altruism on the one hand and egoism on the other. It is thus possible to identify a shared notion of the disposition toward justice and at the same time to allow that beyond its bare essentials the disposition toward justice is capable of assimilating, within the limits set by the intermediate nature of this disposition, different kinds of normative content as represented by rival substantive conceptions of justice. How else can we not only explain the continuity of justice over time, as a disposition of individuals and as a property of social institutions, but also account for the changes, sometimes profound, that justice as both can undergo?[52]

Such an explanatory advantage would be lost if we were to reject the

51. On the second issue but not the first, Rawls and Robert Nozick, say, or Brian Barry and David Gauthier could all agree, as they would have to if they were talking about justice as opposed to some more altruistic or more egoistic disposition.

52. This way of looking at the matter also allows for the possibility of sharp disagreement over substantive conceptions of justice and thus for the possibility that some may be morally enraged by what they regard as serious flaws in their society's norms of justice. This kind of moral indignation must be distinguished from a very different kind, which is caused by serious breaches of reciprocity against the background of general acceptance of a society's norms of justice as basically sound. In the first case, the injustice lies, in the eyes of those morally enraged, in the norms themselves, such that effective compliance and implementation would only make things worse, whereas in the second case, the injustice results from the failure of some to comply with just norms or, worse, from the failure of the state to enforce such norms seriously. My account, neutral as it is between different substantive conceptions of justice within the range of the broadly reasonable, deals with the second type of case only, leaving the first type to be explained within the framework of some normative account of justice.

distinction between the descriptive and the normative, between a minimal (or minimally substantive) notion of reciprocity and the norms around which a reciprocal relationship between agents is formed. Those who do reject such a distinction would insist that only compliance with norms based on certain substantive considerations—say, impartiality—can count as genuine reciprocity. But this would be to turn reciprocity into a thoroughly substantive concept, indistinguishable from the content of the norms by which it is fleshed out. The result would be a significant loss of explanatory power, unless it could be shown that justice-as-impartiality, say, cannot be practiced from the disposition toward justice conceived in terms of a minimally substantive notion of reciprocity, as I have described it, but only from some *preexisting* motive that already contains the normative content of justice-as-impartiality.

There is no reason to think that this kind of one-to-one correspondence is at work. Instead, it seems more appropriate to understand the formation of the disposition toward justice as involving the social production of norms and the socialization of agents in accordance with them. The arena of socialization is one marked by enormous flexibility, albeit subject to limits set by the broadly reasonable. The socialization of agents into embracing a society's principles of justice consists in instilling, firmly though seldom irrevocably, specific normative content over and above a minimally substantive disposition toward justice characterized by reciprocity. To be sure, this minimally substantive disposition toward justice is itself to some degree the product of socialization. But here socialization does not have the same degree of flexibility that applies to the inculcation of specific norms. This is because reciprocity itself cannot be socialized away, as it were, in favor of either unconditional altruism or egoism without doing away with the disposition toward justice altogether. Indeed, as a minimally substantive concept that is intrinsic to the disposition toward justice as such, reciprocity constrains all potential full-fledged substantive conceptions of justice.

Yet precisely because of its *minimally* substantive character, the disposition toward justice as such can be—and indeed has to be—fleshed out by one substantive conception of justice or another, with justice-as-impartiality one among several possibilities. There is thus a two-way influence between the disposition to be just as such and any substantive conception of justice: the former constrains the latter, while the latter in turn shapes and enriches the former. It is only out of this two-way process that any actual—that is, culturally and historically specific—disposition toward justice can emerge. Such an actual disposition toward justice is more than the generic disposition toward justice, but it will always bear its mark, just as it will always assume the shape of a particular substantive conception of justice.

Reciprocity and Impartiality

In view of some of the issues raised in the preceding section, it is worth saying more to clear up some common confusions regarding the status of reciprocity and impartiality in the disposition toward justice. I do so here with particular reference to Brian Barry's writings on the subject.

In the literature on justice, justice-as-impartiality is sometimes contrasted with justice-as-reciprocity, as if these were mutually exclusive. The conceptions of justice typically so designated are indeed opposed, but this is because the terms "justice-as-impartiality" and "justice-as-reciprocity" are used to refer to two rival normative theories of justice. A normative theory of justice is centrally concerned with what should count as the most reasonable or defensible principles of justice. When justice-as-impartiality and justice-as-reciprocity are treated as rival conceptions of justice, as for example by Barry,[53] they are so treated, in the first instance, as different answers to this normative question.

This normative question is one of several questions faced by a theory of justice. Barry identifies three such questions, which concern, respectively, the motivation of just conduct, the criteria of norms of justice, and the connection between the two. When Barry argues against justice-as-reciprocity in favor of justice-as-impartiality, he is clearly treating both as comprehensive theories of justice, each designed to answer all three questions.[54] The problem is that understanding justice-as-impartiality in this comprehensive sense seems to have prevented Barry from seeing that his first question, the one concerning the motivation of agents rather than the justifiability of norms, has to be answered at least in part in terms of the minimally substantive concept of reciprocity. As we saw earlier, reciprocity, as a minimally substantive concept within the disposition to be just, is something on which a full-fledged substantive conception of justice, such as justice-as-impartiality, can be superimposed, but which, given the na-

53. See Brian Barry, *Theories of Justice* (Berkeley: University of California Press, 1989), and *Justice*. Yet a third substantive conception of justice discussed by Barry is justice-as-mutual-advantage.

54. This is true of both *Theories of Justice* and *Justice as Impartiality*.

ture of the disposition toward justice, cannot be displaced by any such conception.

This becomes even clearer if we bring in Barry's distinction between first-order and second-order impartiality. "What the supporters of impartiality [Barry himself included] are defending," he writes, "is second-order impartiality. Impartiality is here seen as a test to be applied to the moral and legal rules of a society: one which asks about their acceptability among free and equal people. The critics are talking about first-order impartiality—impartiality as a maxim of behaviour in everyday life."[55] This distinction enables Barry to say, largely correctly, that "justice as impartiality does not require, and is indeed inconsistent with, a rule of universal first-order impartiality."[56] In other words, first-order impartiality, as a universal requirement, is both unnecessary and undesirable and therefore should not be treated as the proper motive of everyday just conduct, that is, as the right answer to Barry's first question. Second-order impartiality, by contrast, has to do with the justifiability of norms rather than the motivation of norm-following agents and thus pertains to Barry's second question rather than the first. Clearly, if Barry were to keep his distinction between first-order and second-order impartiality firmly in mind and relate this distinction to his three questions for a theory of justice, he should not be in a position to reject outright, as he mistakenly does (explicitly) in *Justice as Impartiality* and (implicitly) in *Theories of Justice,* the concept of reciprocity as (part of) an answer to his first question.

Not surprisingly, despite his refusal to answer the first question in explicit terms of reciprocity, some notion of reciprocity does creep into Barry's understanding of the motive of justice. To his first question for a theory of justice, his answer is that the motive of just conduct is the "desire to behave fairly." Thus, "if I am motivated by a desire to behave fairly, I will want to do what the rules mandated by justice as impartiality require *so long as enough other people are doing the same.*"[57] What happens here is that the norms of justice are determined by standards of impartiality (Barry's second question), but the motive to comply with such norms (Barry's first question) is not very different from what I have been calling reciprocity under broadly reasonable norms, or from what Allan Gibbard calls fair reciprocity.[58] This is quite evident from Barry's introduction of an

55. Barry, *Justice,* p. 194.

56. Ibid., p. 213.

57. Ibid., p. 51, emphasis added.

58. Allan Gibbard, "Constructing Justice," *Philosophy and Public Affairs* 20 (1991): 264–279.

explicit conditional clause regarding other people's readiness to abide by the same norms of justice. Although Barry takes issue with Gibbard's conception of justice-as-fair-reciprocity *as a whole*,[59] his own conception of justice-as-impartiality differs from Gibbard's conception not on the first question but only on the second. This concurrence on the first question, though not acknowledged by Barry,[60] is only to be expected, since the motive of reciprocity under broadly reasonable norms is a constitutive feature of the disposition toward justice as such.

It is revealing, in this connection, that Rawls's theory, which Barry regards as a conception of justice-as-impartiality, operates with a notion of "reasonable moral psychology," one of whose chief features is reciprocity. Barry explains this apparent inconsistency by suggesting that "two theories of justice can be found in John Rawls's *A Theory of Justice*."[61] It is, in my view, just as plausible to see these apparently conflicting parts of Rawls's theory as perfectly compatible answers, within a single theory, to the first and second questions of justice, respectively. On this view, Rawls's theory can indeed be properly regarded as a conception of justice-as-impartiality, but this applies only to his answer to the second question. This need not prevent Rawls from answering the first question in terms of the concept of reciprocity, as indeed he does.[62] Only if there is reason to think that the first and second questions have to be answered both in terms of impartiality, or both in terms of reciprocity, do we have to treat the apparently conflicting parts of Rawls's theory as evidence that he advances two distinct theories. But there is no reason to think that the two questions, though they must be answered coherently within a single theory, must be answered in the same terms. As I suggested earlier, the disposition toward justice is compatible with a fairly broad range of substantive conceptions of justice, a range that includes justice-as-impartiality but is not exhausted by it. In other words, the same minimally substantive disposition toward justice can motivate compliance with a wider range of norms than those

59. Barry, *Justice*, pp. 48–50.

60. Barry does concede, in his earlier *Theories* (p. 361), that "there is absolutely no question that this [reciprocity or mutual advantage] is at any rate a part of justice. Reciprocity is a core element in every society's conception of justice."

61. Ibid., p. 179.

62. Rawls himself distinguishes clearly between "reciprocity . . . as a principle giving its content and as a disposition to answer in kind." John Rawls, *Justice as Fairness*, ed. Erin Kelly (Cambridge, Mass.: Harvard University Press, 2001), p. 196. What he calls "reciprocity . . . as a principle giving its content" is a substantive conception of justice and, despite its name, clearly qualifies as a conception of justice-as-impartiality, as Barry notes in speaking of one of Rawls's "two theories of justice."

that pass the stringent test of impartiality. One key component of such a minimally substantive disposition toward justice is a minimally substantive concept of reciprocity under broadly reasonable norms, and therefore it is in terms of such a concept of reciprocity that Barry's first question for a theory of justice has to be answered. It is a separate, and open, issue whether his second question is to be answered in terms of a fully substantive conception of justice-as-impartiality.

2

The Subjective Circumstances of Justice

In an explanatory, as in a normative, account of justice, one of the first things to be clarified is what we take to be the circumstances of justice.[1] This is because a conception of the circumstances of justice is a conception both of the problems to be solved by justice and of the available motivational capacities for solving them. In both regards, once we begin with a certain conception of the circumstances of justice, we will be drawn into a certain way of thinking about justice. Of this Hume remains perhaps the foremost example. His theory of justice—proceeding from an account of the circumstances of justice in terms of limited benevolence under conditions of material scarcity to a conception of justice as the distribution of property rights—furnishes a compelling demonstration of the fact that what we regard as the circumstances of justice will largely determine how we conceive of the domain and role of justice as well as the nature of the virtue of justice.

It is common to distinguish two kinds of circumstances of justice, the subjective and the objective. This distinction is especially necessary for my account, since I want (in this chapter) to defend a modified Humean conception of the subjective circumstances of justice but at the same time (in the next chapter) to reject, at least in part, the Humean conception of the objective circumstances of justice. Hume's conception of both sets of circumstances is most succinctly summed up in that famous passage where he writes that "'tis only from the selfishness and confin'd generosity of men, along with the scanty provision nature has made for his wants, that justice

1. The term "circumstances of justice" is taken from John Rawls, *A Theory of Justice,* rev. ed. (Cambridge, Mass.: Harvard University Press, 1999), p. 109. The idea itself, as Rawls says, is of course Hume's.

derives its origin."[2] I try to show, in this chapter, that the Humean understanding of the subjective circumstances of justice in terms of egoism or lack of altruism (which is what "the selfishness and confin'd generosity of men" amounts to) is neither mistaken nor antiquated by modern conditions, although it needs to be complemented by the idea of competing conceptions of the good. It is important to show this because it is an increasingly common view that scarcity of altruism is not among the necessary conditions of the need for justice, and because this view obscures, I believe, both the nature of the need for justice and the kinds of motives that can be relied on to make justice possible.

Subjective and Objective Circumstances of Justice Defined

Following Hume's account of our "outward circumstances" and our "natural temper," Rawls distinguishes between the objective and the subjective circumstances of justice.[3] While adopting this general distinction, I do not stick exactly to Rawls's way of drawing it. What I count among the subjective circumstances of justice are those motives and dispositions that make justice both necessary and possible. In these motives and dispositions we see the limits of justice as a virtue and by implication as a social practice, limits that can be transcended only to the extent that the circumstances of justice themselves are transcended. By the objective circumstances of justice I mean certain vital needs common to all human beings, along with those external features of the human condition that render the satisfaction of such needs difficult or impossible without the instituting of justice. In the case of Hume, for example, one such vital need is that of subsistence, and the corresponding feature of the human condition is material scarcity. I have deliberately, at this stage, left vague the content of the human needs involved, as well as the corresponding features of the human condition, because to specify them is already to be committed to a particular conception of the objective circumstances of justice.

There is a sense, though, in which the problems to be solved by justice are presented by the objective circumstances of justice. It is true that such problems might disappear if the subjective circumstances of justice did not obtain. But what justice is chiefly designed to secure, say, respect for per-

2. David Hume, *A Treatise of Human Nature,* ed. L. A. Selby-Bigge, 2nd ed., ed. P. H. Nidditch (Oxford: Clarendon Press, 1978), p. 495, with italics removed from the original.

3. See Rawls, *Theory,* pp. 109–110.

sons or protection of property rights, depends on one's view of what constitute the most important objective circumstances of justice. In this sense I see the problems of justice—or the domain of justice—as determined by the objective circumstances of justice, although the need for justice arises equally from the subjective circumstances.

No matter how the problems of justice are conceived, the motivational capacities for dealing with them are contained in the subjective circumstances of justice. These subjective circumstances help make justice necessary in the first place. For better or for worse, these same subjective circumstances also contain all the motivational capacities which, unlike the altruistic or benevolent virtues whose abundance (according to Hume) would obviate the need for justice, can be relied on (in the sense of being presumed to exist to a sufficient degree) for making justice possible.

Thus, by and large, I treat the problems to be solved by justice and the motivational capacities for solving them as residing in the objective and the subjective circumstances of justice, respectively. When I nevertheless discuss, from time to time, how the subjective circumstances help give rise to the problems faced by justice, I do so because, as I have said, the problems of justice would not arise in the absence of such subjective circumstances. In addition, I do so with a view to gauging by inference the motivational capacities that can be presumed available for coping with such problems. In the end, the distinction as I draw it is in part a stipulative one, its adequacy a matter of what we are able to say with it.

Hume's Conception Modified; or, Rawls's General Conception

The need for justice, it is generally agreed, arises from the presence of conflict between individuals or groups. Traditional accounts of such conflict, for example, those of Hobbes, Hume, and Schopenhauer, explain it in terms of a clash of self-interests. That interests can come into conflict is a function, according to Hume's famous treatment of the subject, of a twofold scarcity, the scarcity of goods and the scarcity of altruism. It follows that justice is a remedial virtue, something that would not be needed in a (hypothetical) society where either of these circumstances of justice did not obtain.

Such an understanding of justice—both of the nature of the need for justice and of the nature of justice as a remedial virtue—has increasingly been called into question. Modern theorists of justice have generally come to hold that the problems of justice are best conceived instead in terms of competing conceptions of the good or, more simply put, pluralism. This has led to nothing less than a new conception of the circumstances and raison d'être of justice. The new conception is most influentially presented by Rawls, who distinguishes between a general and a special version. According to the general conception, the subjective circumstances of justice arise from the fact of pluralism as such, that is, the simple fact that members of a society pursue different and conflicting conceptions of the good, regardless of the further question of whether any or all of such conceptions are reasonable. In the special conception, the fact of pluralism is further stipulated as one of reasonable pluralism.[4]

It is noteworthy that in the general conception the role of egoism or limited altruism is more or less bracketed, with no firm conclusion drawn as to whether it plays any part in making justice necessary or possible, and, if so, what part. Despite this, there is already a significant shift in the vocabulary and thrust of explanation—from self-interests to conceptions of the good, from clash between self-interests to conflict between conceptions of the good. In the special conception, by contrast, egoism is explicitly denied as the right kind of explanation, still less a necessary explanation, for the need for justice.[5] Given this significant difference, the general and special conceptions have to be considered separately. In both cases, the main question is what, if anything, is lost in terms of explanatory power if we are to give up the idea that egoism is among the chief subjective circumstances of justice.

While Rawls usefully identifies the general conception, Stuart Hampshire spells out the rationale for it with greater force and clarity. As Hampshire sees it, "Hobbes, and most theorists in the social-contract tradition, misidentify the central problem of morality when they ask under what conditions persons can reasonably be expected to live together given that they have conflicting appetites and interests, and given that they have a drive to dominate in order to satisfy their appetites." This is because "ferocious appetites and interests are more easily reconciled by rational calculations within a society than ferocious conceptions of the good and of right and wrong. No games theory, no ingenious mechanisms of rational

4. As Rawls puts it, "These latter [subjective] circumstances are, in general, the fact of pluralism as such; although in a well-ordered society of justice as fairness, they include the fact of reasonable pluralism." John Rawls, *Political Liberalism* (New York: Columbia University Press, 1993), p. 66.

5. See ibid., pp. 55–56, 58.

choice, can help in moral conflicts as they might with competing appetites and interests."[6]

This is a salutary corrective of the less sophisticated view, to the extent that such a view has been held, that justice exists to solve the conflict between naked or unmediated self-interests.[7] Hampshire draws attention to an important truth, namely, that the pursuit of self-interest, whether interest in the self or, neutrally speaking, interest of a self, generally takes the form of the pursuit of a conception of the good.[8] In any case, it is in this form that different people's self-interests come into the kind of acute conflict that stands most in need of justice for its resolution. If it is self-interests that clash, it is not simply *as* self-interests that they do so. For the self-interests between which serious and prolonged conflict is most likely are themselves moralized self-interests, interests as conceived and articulated in a conception of the good. The kind of conflict to which people seek a moral solution through justice tends to take a moral form itself.[9]

There is thus a lot to be said for thinking about the need for justice in terms of competing conceptions of the good rather than *simply* in terms of conflicting egoisms.[10] This way of understanding the problem comes closer to how people actually see their pursuit of interests and see those

6. Stuart Hampshire, *Innocence and Experience* (Cambridge, Mass.: Harvard University Press, 1989), p. 141. A similar view is expressed by Rawls, *Political Liberalism,* p. 4.

7. A different kind of corrective is provided by John Dunn, who identifies "moral error," "conflict of interests," and "partiality of judgment" as distinct explanatory categories where a less nuanced view would conflate them in one way or another. See John Dunn, *The Cunning of Unreason* (New York: Basic Books, 2000), pp. 19–47. It should be noted, though, that Dunn is concerned not with the nature of the need for justice but with the somewhat different question of why there is politics.

8. See discussion of the relationship between ideas and interests in Jürgen Habermas, *The Theory of Communicative Action,* vol. 1, *Reason and the Rationalization of Society,* trans. Thomas McCarthy (Boston: Beacon Press, 1984), pp. 187–194.

9. Already, in *A Theory of Justice,* Rawls sometimes replaces the Humean phrase "the selfishness and confin'd generosity of men" with reference to competing conceptions of the good. This is a perfectly legitimate move, even within the Humean framework, in that Rawls does not here conclude, from the new locution, that universal altruism is compatible with (the need for) justice. For Rawls, a conception of the good is but the form that self-interest takes, although the interest need not always be in the self. Therefore, and this is important, justice can still be regarded as a remedial virtue. See, e.g., Rawls, *Theory,* pp. 110–112.

10. An equally appropriate way of thinking about this would be to see the need for justice in terms of conflicts involving "structured" desires rather than atomistic ones. See Raymond Geuss, *History and Illusion in Politics* (Cambridge: Cambridge University Press, 2001), p. 23.

situations in which such pursuit leads to conflict with others. More important, the kind of conflict that occurs between interests which are themselves moralized does present different, and much more intractable, problems than the kind of conflict that is attributable to what may be called unadorned egoism, that is, such egoism as is not mediated by a conception of the good (if such egoism exists). For these reasons, we may regard an account such as Hampshire's as exhibiting a higher level of sophistication than the Hobbesian or Humean account.

This more sophisticated account of the subjective circumstances of justice should not, however, be taken to mark a complete break with the traditional account. Rather than invalidating the Humean idea that egoism, or scarcity of altruism, is a necessary condition of the need for justice, it serves only to make more exact the sense in which this idea is true. It is worth noting that from the fact that a conflict *takes the form of* a clash between different conceptions of the good, it does not follow that what gives rise to the conflict and makes justice necessary for resolving it is the fact of difference as such. Instead, when people with different conceptions of the good do come into conflict, what makes justice necessary is at bottom not the mere fact that their conceptions of the good happen to be different, but the egoism that makes some people prepared to pursue their conception of the good, whatever it may be, without due respect for other people's right to pursue their conception of the good.

This becomes even clearer when we ask what it is that is overcome or curbed when justice is imposed.[11] It certainly need not be the disparate conceptions of the good themselves, nor the differences between them; rather, it is the tendency to pursue one's own conception of the good without due respect for or at the expense of others. It is this tendency, above all, that justice is designed to counteract. Such a tendency or desire can quite accurately be characterized as egoism, as long as we remember that it is egoism mediated—legitimated and sometimes made fanatic—by some conception of the good. This is not to suggest that egoism somehow forms the substance of one conception of the good or another, although it is possible for conceptions of the good to amount to little more than rationalizations of self-interest. But the willingness to pursue a conception of the good, whatever its substance, without due consideration for others is

11. See Hampshire, *Innocence,* pp. 71–72; and Immanuel Kant, *Critique of Practical Reason,* in *Critique of Practical Reason and Other Writings in Moral Philosophy,* trans. and ed. Lewis White Beck (Chicago: University of Chicago Press, 1949), p. 181.

no less a form of egoism. It is chiefly on account of this kind of egoism that people pursuing different conceptions of the good can come into conflict and in so doing give rise to the need for justice.

This modification of Hume's understanding of the subjective circumstances of justice need pose no serious problem for Rawls's *general* conception. For Rawls could quite easily account for the kind of conflict sketched here by saying that some or all of the conceptions of the good that happen to be in conflict are unreasonable, and, if pressed, would readily agree that the unreasonable typically involves one form or another of excessive egoism.[12] After all, there is nothing particularly challenging about explaining the need for justice in terms of the phenomenon of pluralism *as such,* that is, explaining *unreasonable* disagreement. To questions such as what needs to be overcome for the sake of justice in a situation of pluralism as such, and what limits exist to the motivational capacities available for such overcoming, the answer could in principle be a very simple one: egoism, or unreasonableness, in both cases probably in the form of some conception of the good. In this way, within Rawls's general conception, we can easily retain the core of Hume's understanding of the subjective circumstances of justice, raised now to a higher level of sophistication through combination with the idea of conceptions of the good. According to the revised Humean conception, then, the subjective circumstances of justice consist of competing self-interests in the form of conflicting conceptions of the good. This way of keeping egoism as among the subjective circumstances of justice is especially important for the purpose of maintaining an undimmed awareness of the intrinsic limits to the motivational capacities that can regularly be mobilized for the cause of justice.

Egoism and Reasonable Pluralism; or, Rawls's Special Conception

Does the line of reasoning I have suggested apply to the special conception of the subjective circumstances of justice?[13] The special conception is

12. "We do not," says Rawls, "of course, deny that prejudice and bias, self- and group interest, blindness and willfulness, play their all too familiar part in political life" (*Political Liberalism,* p. 58).

13. For another explicit formulation of the special conception, see John Rawls, *Justice as Fairness,* ed. Erin Kelly (Cambridge, Mass.: Harvard University Press, 2001): "We take this [reasonable] pluralism to be a permanent feature of a democratic society, and view it as characterizing what we may call the subjective circumstances of justice" (p. 84).

Rawls's unique invention, and, as I said earlier, unlike the general conception, it allows no explanatory role for egoism, even egoism in the form of some conception of the good. Rawls stipulates, for his special conception, that *all* the conceptions of the good that happen to be in conflict are reasonable, where both the reasonableness and the conflict are treated in turn as a function of "burdens of judgment," that is, "the sources, or causes, of disagreement between reasonable persons."[14] Instead of pluralism as such, we have (somewhat) by stipulation a situation of reasonable pluralism, and the question is whether reasonable pluralism is exclusive of egoism in the context of understanding the need for justice and, especially for my purposes, in the context of gauging the limits to the motivational capacities that can be presumed available for making justice possible.

There is something about Rawls's special conception I will *not* challenge, and that has to do with the normative use to which it is put. Rawls's idea is that once we recognize the burdens of judgment, we will accept a democratic principle of toleration as setting limits to the legitimate exercise of political power in a constitutional regime.[15] The resulting notion of the reasonable seems *normatively* beyond reproach, although it is an open question whether, and to what extent, the reality of the kind of constitutional regime Rawls has in mind approximates to the ideal of reasonable pluralism.

It is a very different question, and one that concerns us here, whether the idea of burdens of judgment is sufficient for *explaining* the possibility of justice-necessitating conflict within reasonable pluralism, that is, of conflict among conceptions of the good when all of them are reasonable. Rawls does say, though not without some ambivalence, that "the burdens of judgments *alone* can account for the fact of reasonable pluralism."[16] It all depends on how "account for" is to be construed: in the sense of underpinning reasonable pluralism for normative purposes, or in the sense of (exhaustively) explaining the nature of the conflicts that are possible within reasonable pluralism.[17] If the former, as seems the more plausible

14. Rawls, *Political Liberalism,* p. 55.

15. See ibid., pp. 54, 58.

16. Rawls, *Justice as Fairness,* p. 36, emphasis added.

17. Thus, it is rather confusing when Rawls says that "an *explanation* of the right kind is that the sources of reasonable disagreement—the burdens of judgment—among reasonable persons are the many hazards involved in the correct (and conscientious) exercise of our powers of reason and judgment in the ordinary course of political life" (*Political Liberalism,* pp. 55–56, emphasis added).

interpretation in the relevant context, I do not take issue with it, as I said earlier. If the latter, however, Rawls's claim would seem to be highly questionable.

With respect to the latter, there is perhaps no more revealing question than whether people in a situation of reasonable pluralism need to overcome egoism for the sake of justice. The answer should clearly be in the affirmative, and from this we can infer that egoism (in the form of various conceptions of the good) is part of reasonable pluralism together with the burdens of judgment. Rawls asks, "Why does not our conscientious attempt to reason with one another lead to reasonable agreement?" and offers the noncommittal yet (in the context) thought-provoking observation that "it seems to do so in natural science, at least in the long run."[18] One explanation for this kind of difference between science on the one hand and morality and politics on the other is, as Bernard Williams suggests, that the unity of interest between prereflective self and reflective self is easier to maintain in theoretical, including scientific, deliberation than in moral or practical deliberation, and therefore scientists have an easier time being "disinterested" and "objective" within the confines of their strictly scientific endeavors.[19]

If this is correct, and it does seem essentially correct (though this need not be the whole story), we can account for the possibility of justice-necessitating conflict or disagreement within reasonable pluralism in terms of people being subject to burdens of judgment *and* being partial (though not extremely so) to themselves.[20] This moderate degree of egoism is quite compatible with all parties to a conflict being reasonable, and yet it is clearly something to be overcome if justice is to be possible. Being reasonable here means just the ability to accomplish such overcoming on a regular basis by proposing and abiding by fair terms of cooperation.[21] This says something not only about the sources of the need for justice within reasonable pluralism but also about the motivational capacities available therein for the cause of justice. Something important is at stake here: Knowing that there is something there *for us to overcome,* aside from those

18. Ibid., p. 55.

19. See Bernard Williams, *Ethics and the Limits of Philosophy* (Cambridge, Mass.: Harvard University Press, 1985), p. 69.

20. This claim is pursued further in my discussion of altruism and reasonable pluralism later in this chapter.

21. For analysis of related issues, see my discussion in Chapter 6 of an other-centered concept of impartiality.

burdens of judgment for which we cannot in any way be held responsible, gives us a more sober or less complacent picture of the moral capacities of the parties in conflict and hence of the very considerable difficulty of proposing and abiding by fair terms of cooperation even in a situation of reasonable pluralism.[22]

Thus, for explanatory, as distinct from normative, purposes, there is no need to regard the burdens of judgment as exclusive of egoism's being a source of justice-necessitating conflict within reasonable pluralism. To hold that the burdens of judgment alone are the sources of conflict and disagreement within reasonable pluralism—Rawls comes close to saying this at times—would be to remove, by sheer stipulation, one major source of the need for justice and of the difficulty of achieving justice, or else, if reasonable pluralism is treated as an empirical prospect, to indulge in an unrealistic utopia. In either case, if there were nothing about us we needed to overcome for the sake of justice, then we would all be saints, and it is arguable that saints would not need justice.[23]

Egoism, Altruism, and the Problem of Imposition

With regard to the general conception of the subjective circumstances of justice, matters are complicated by the fact that sometimes the ostensible substance of one's conception of the good is the well-being of others, a fact that may appear to make the imposition of that kind of conception of the good more acceptable than it would otherwise be. This is a perennial problem in moral and political philosophy, to which there are essentially two kinds of response. One response, the older of the two, is to see some disguised form of egoism in the very act of imposing a conception of the good on others. The other response, in part a rejection of the first, treats altruism as compatible with acts of imposition and hence as standing in equally strong need of limitation in the interests of justice. What is at issue, for our purposes, is whether egoism is a necessary component of the subjective circumstances of justice. In my discussion of reasonable pluralism thus far, I have argued for treating egoism as one component among others but have stopped short of claiming that egoism is a *necessary* component, a component in the absence of which all other components would be

22. The difficulty presented by egoism, while analytically distinct, is in practice mixed up with the difficulties caused by some, if not all, of the burdens of judgment.

23. See the final section of this chapter.

insufficient to cause a need for justice. This further claim is a very strong one, implying as it does that altruism is somehow incompatible with the need for justice, and that some form of egoism must be lurking behind, or mixed up with, any other component in the subjective circumstances of justice if the latter is to give rise to the need for justice. I will pursue this claim in the remainder of this chapter, in effect arguing against the second response in favor of the first.

I begin by discussing one major exponent of the second response. Thomas Nagel holds that "altruism by itself generates as many conflicting standpoints as there are conceptions of the good," citing as his example "those who wish to limit my religious freedom . . . with my own best interests in mind."[24] Nevertheless, he finds it necessary to add a footnote, in which he cautions that "*in real life* one must always be skeptical about this."[25] As I see it, this cautionary concession does not go nearly far enough. How much further we need to go is best suggested by John Locke, whose *Letter Concerning Toleration* Nagel himself cites in this context. Locke is rightly categorical about the incompatibility *in principle* between altruism and imposition on others when he writes:

> Let them not call in the Magistrate's Authority to the aid of their Eloquence, or Learning; lest, perhaps, whilst they pretend only Love for the Truth, this their intemperate Zeal, breathing nothing but Fire and Sword, betray their Ambition, and shew that what they desire is Temporal Dominion. For it will be very difficult to persuade men of Sense, that he, who with dry Eyes, and satisfaction of mind, can deliver his Brother unto the Executioner, to be burnt alive, does sincerely and heartily concern himself to save that Brother from the Flames of Hell in the World to come.[26]

In this Locke is echoed by, among others, Kant, according to whom "I cannot do good to anyone in accordance with *my* concepts of happiness (except to young children and the insane), thinking to benefit him by forcing a gift upon him; rather, I can benefit him only in accordance with *his* concepts of happiness."[27] In this way we can distinguish the all too rare

24. Thomas Nagel, *Equality and Partiality* (New York: Oxford University Press, 1991), pp. 163–164.

25. Ibid., p. 164, emphasis added. See also Rawls, *Theory*, p. 110.

26. Cited in Nagel, *Equality*, p. 164n.

27. Immanuel Kant, *The Metaphysics of Morals*, trans. Mary Gregor (Cambridge: Cambridge University Press, 1991), p. 248.

virtue of altruism from the all too common tendency to justify egoism, indeed domination, in the name of truth or morality or other people's well-being.

It is worth extending, or clarifying, this classic line of thought by emphasizing that altruism has both moral and epistemic properties, themselves integrally connected, without either of which (it is the epistemic properties that typically get neglected) it ceases to be altruism worthy of the name. Thus, whenever one's alleged desire to promote other people's good is not matched by an equally strong desire to view their good on their terms (provided that these terms are morally permissible) instead of one's own, one betrays an epistemic shortsightedness that is ultimately a form of moral shortsightedness, that is, egoism. Altruism, on this view, is at once a moral and an epistemic accomplishment, in which the ability to understand other people's point of view is a function of a genuine desire to promote their good, and where the realization of that desire is in turn dependent on epistemic insight.[28] Epistemic shortsightedness, unless explainable in terms of objective constraints (for example, in terms of the lack of such information regarding others as no one can reasonably be expected to have access to, even after due effort), is invariably traceable to lack of altruism, even when what is ostensibly promoted is not one's own good but other people's. An altruist has no reason to hide behind the unwarranted separation of morality and knowledge, concern and insight.

We ought therefore to take it as axiomatic that altruists will not impose their conception of the good on others—or if they do, they are doing it for themselves, as both Locke and Kant rightly imply, in which case they are acting not altruistically but only in the name of altruism. It is only by denying this axiom, as Nagel seems to do, that one could locate the need for justice in the existence of multiple conceptions of the good *as such*, even on the part of altruists, instead of seeing, as I have tried to argue, the need for justice as arising from the presence of egoism over and above the mere fact of difference or pluralism. A variation on this theme is the attempt to show that justice would be needed even in a (hypothetical) society made up *entirely* of altruists. Steven Lukes has given perhaps the most lucid and powerful articulation of this idea, and it is worth examining whether he succeeds, and why.

28. For a critique of a line of thought that appears to make such epistemic insight impossible, see Michael J. Sandel, *Liberalism and the Limits of Justice* (Cambridge: Cambridge University Press, 1982), pp. 172, 181.

Altruism and Reasonable Pluralism

Lukes presents this idea mainly through a critique of Hume. He sets up the target of his critique and puts forward the main lines of that critique as follows:

> Hume mistakenly thought that if you increase "to a sufficient degree the benevolence of men or the bounty of nature . . . you render justice useless by supplying its place with much nobler virtues, and more favourable blessings" . . . But even under conditions of co-operative abundance and altruism, there will, if conceptions of the good conflict, be a need for the fair allocation of benefits and burdens, for the assigning of obligations and the protection of rights; but we should then need them in the face of benevolence rather than the selfishness of others. Altruists, sincerely and conscientiously pursuing their respective conceptions of the good, can certainly cause injustice and violate rights. For every conception of the good will favour certain social relationships and ways of defining individuals' interests—or, more precisely, certain ways of conceiving and ranking the various interests that individuals have. It will also disfavour others, and in a world in which no such conception is fully realised, and universally accepted, even the non-egoistic practitioners of one threaten the adherents of others: hence the need for justice, rights and obligations.[29]

It is clear from this passage that Lukes's argument that justice would be needed even in a society of universal altruism stands or falls on the correctness of two claims. The first claim, nowhere stated but obviously implied, is that different conceptions of the good would, or at least could, arise among complete altruists. The second claim, presupposing the correctness of the first, is that given the existence of different conceptions of the good, altruists would be quite capable of imposing their conception of the good on other altruists who happened to favor a different conception of the good. If both claims are true, they should constitute a powerful case against the view that justice would be superfluous in a society of universal altruism.

In order to assess the first claim, we cannot avoid broaching the genealogical question of how conceptions of the good come to be formed, or

29. Steven Lukes, "Taking Morality Seriously," in *Morality and Objectivity*, ed. Ted Honderich (London: Routledge & Kegan Paul, 1985), pp. 98–109; quotation from p. 104.

what they are a function of. Otherwise we would beg the question of whether, and how, different conceptions of the good could arise among people who are completely benevolent and altruistic.[30] Answers to this latter question are not the kind of thing we can directly extrapolate from human society as we empirically know it, if only because all actually existing societies are made up of people of whom the vast majority would not qualify as altruists. With regard to such societies, we cannot rule out the possibility that the diversity of conceptions of the good springs from the fact that all or most conceptions of the good originate from needs and interests, conscious or not so conscious, that are largely self-centered or self-regarding (in the sense of interests *in* a self). Therefore, if it is claimed that similarly altruistic people can develop different conceptions of the good, this is something that needs to be shown, not just assumed. Instead of looking into the genealogy of conceptions of the good, however, Lukes proceeds almost as if a conception of the good could exist apart from and prior to interests and desires. Since he does not address the genealogical question, it may be instructive to revisit Rawls's idea of reasonable pluralism—the coexistence of reasonable but incompatible conceptions of the good—inasmuch as this idea can be construed in such a way as to provide support for Lukes's first claim.

The idea of reasonable pluralism is important for Rawls, as noted earlier, because it serves to ground the democratic principle of toleration. In this context, Rawls emphasizes the reasonableness of reasonable pluralism. His account of what he calls the burdens of judgment, or the sources of reasonable disagreement, is designed to show that different agents can be committed to conflicting conceptions of the good while nevertheless all being reasonable.[31] This may be persuasive for normative purposes, as I granted earlier, but in emphasizing the reasonableness of reasonable pluralism, Rawls fails to see (or at least to say) that the diversity of reasonable yet conflicting conceptions of the good may stem from those involved being *self-interested in a reasonable fashion*. That a particular interest is reasonable makes it worthy of protection in a just society, but that a particular interest should be protected does not rule out its being a self-interest (that is, a self-interest in the strict sense of an interest *in* the self). Thus, Rawls's

30. The same criticism could be made of Nagel, who simply assumes that "altruism by itself generates as many conflicting standpoints as there are conceptions of the good" (*Equality*, 164). See also Allen E. Buchanan, *Marx and Justice: The Radical Critique of Liberalism* (Totowa, N.J.: Rowman and Littlefield, 1982), pp. 157, 167.

31. See Rawls, *Political Liberalism*, p. 58.

distinction between pluralism as such and reasonable pluralism can translate, at least partly, into the difference between conflicting self-interests per se and conflicting reasonable self-interests. This would allow us to say that when the pursuit of different yet reasonable self-interests gives rise to diverse conceptions of the good, the result is reasonable pluralism.

The problem is that Rawls does not distinguish between self-interest and reasonable self-interest in this context and is therefore forced to dismiss out of hand *any* explanation of reasonable pluralism in terms of egoism as too easy and not of the right kind.[32] In bending over backwards to avoid such explanation, Rawls makes it appear that unless we explain reasonable pluralism in terms completely other than those of egoism, we shall be guilty of mistakenly supposing that "all our differences are rooted solely in ignorance and perversity, or else in the rivalries for power, status, or economic gain."[33] This is an unnecessarily stark contrast, for once we distinguish between self-interest and reasonable self-interest, or between pursuing self-interest and pursuing self-interest in a reasonable fashion, it is clearly possible to explain reasonable pluralism in terms of people pursuing different yet reasonable self-interests, or pursuing different self-interests in a reasonable fashion.[34] By the same token, the idea of reasonable pluralism is entirely compatible with the pursuit of reasonable self-interest—call it *reasonable egoism*—being one source of the diversity of conflicting yet reasonable conceptions of the good. When Rawls says that reasonable pluralism is the "long-run outcome of the work of human reason under enduring free institutions,"[35] one plausible interpretation of this rather vague claim is that reasonable pluralism arises (in part) from the pursuit of self-interest within the limits of reason. Accordingly, to the question "Why should free institutions lead to reasonable pluralism[?]"[36] one plausible answer is that this is because free institutions leave it to individuals to pursue whatever interests they see fit—including self-interests in the strict sense—as long as they do so within the limits set by justice.

There is some reason to conclude, then, that the idea of reasonable pluralism, understood precisely, confirms rather than disproves the link between some form or degree of egoism and the diversity of conceptions of

32. See ibid., p. 55.

33. Ibid., p. 58.

34. Such a possibility is quite consistent with the fact that Rawls's idea of reasonable pluralism lays down only "rather minimal necessary conditions" (ibid., p. 37n).

35. Ibid., p. 129.

36. Ibid., p. 55.

the good. Not that Lukes's first claim can be refuted decisively. It is sufficient, for our purposes, to have cast serious doubt on it, especially since his second and more directly important claim is also open to doubt. It is just as important, for the overall argument in this chapter, to have shown (as I hope I have) that reasonable pluralism can be understood in terms of, or at least as compatible with, what I have called reasonable egoism.

Altruism and Justice

Lukes's (implied) first claim is presupposed by his (stated) second claim, namely, that given the diversity of conceptions of the good, altruists are capable of imposing their conception of the good on fellow altruists whose conceptions of the good happen to be different. It is thus a serious objection to his argument as a whole that the first claim is open to serious doubt. Suppose, however, for the sake of argument, that the first claim is valid. It would then need to be shown, in support of the second claim, that altruists who happen to be pursuing different conceptions of the good and yet acting *for the sake of others* (since they are all altruists) could be doing so in ways that call for regulation by rules of justice as opposed to mere operational rules. As we saw earlier, the fact that two conceptions of the good are different is not by itself a sufficient condition for them to come into conflict and give rise to the need for justice. Given the fact of difference (as distinct from conflict), and given such further facts as limitations on human knowledge and ability, there would clearly be a need for what Tom Campbell calls educative and informative rules, organizational rules, or cooperative rules.[37] Such rules, however, are "devices for enabling altruism to express itself rather than ways of minimising the harmful effects of selfish actions,"[38] and as such they differ from the coercive rules of justice.[39] What has to be shown, therefore, is that over and above noncoercive operational rules, coercive rules of justice are required even in the face

37. See Tom Campbell, *The Left and Rights* (London: Routledge & Kegan Paul, 1983), pp. 44–46, 49–51, 57.

38. Ibid., p. 51.

39. Lukes mentions, among the conditions necessitating justice, "lack of perfect rationality, information and understanding" ("Taking Morality Seriously," p. 105). But where understanding is not perfect but intention is, what seems to be needed is better information rather than sanctions against action based on less than perfect information. Even when the best information and the best effort at understanding prove to be of no avail, so that potential benefactor and potential beneficiary fail to agree on what the latter needs or ought to need, the worst that could happen, given the altruist's avoidance of paternalism, is nonaction rather than imposition.

of genuine altruism, that is, altruism that meets the standard of moral and epistemic unity set out earlier.

Not surprisingly, in trying to make good this claim, Lukes operates with concepts that clearly pertain, in the first instance, to our existing, less than fully altruistic society—concepts such as benefits and burdens, claims on common resources, enforcement of respect for others' interests and views, and so on.[40] Applying such concepts to the hypothetical society of complete altruists, he creates a picture of altruists who are not very different from the nonaltruists or half-altruists we are familiar with in our existing societies. The problem is that such resemblance is assumed rather than proved, and for this reason it undercuts the very argument it is designed to support, namely, that even a radically different society, one consisting entirely of altruists, stands in need of justice.[41] This is a very understandable failure of the imagination, the failure to do justice to the radical difference between a society of altruists that exists only in the imagination and the actually existing societies we know from experience, which cannot but form our point of reference even when we picture what an ideal society would look like. After all, the object of imagination in this case is a form of society radically different from any known to us, and the attempt to picture its hazy contours can only be a dizzying exercise.

The lesson to be drawn from this failure, however, is not one that should encourage us or would enable us to picture the utopian society with greater accuracy than Lukes has achieved. For it is in the nature of a hypothetical and radically different form of society that we are simply not in a position to have any but the vaguest inkling of what it would be like. Lukes's mistake lies not in failing to achieve more accuracy than he has but in conducting his argument as if such accuracy were possible. Indeed, such a mistake can confuse the imaginary with the actual, as when Allen Buchanan, in making an argument similar to Lukes's, treats as a "fact" the wholly imaginary situation in which "there can be conflicts of interest or of ideals, which, though nonegoistic, are nonetheless serious enough to require the use of principles of justice."[42] How can we know this for a fact—how can we know that "even a society of perfect altruists . . . may

40. See ibid., pp. 104, 105.

41. The same criticism applies to Buchanan. His list of reasons why rights backed up by sanctions are necessary in a society of altruists (*Marx*, p. 165), with the possible exception of the fifth item, reads too much like a list of problems facing our existing societies—where egoism in various guises is ever present—to be convincing as a description of the radically different society of complete altruists.

42. Ibid., p. 157.

have throat-cutting disagreements over what the common good is"[43]—unless what we have in mind are in fact figures that are all too familiar from our actual world, those self-proclaimed altruists or saviors of humankind who go about trying to achieve their aims in the name of the common good and are not above cutting people's throats in the process?[44] Although Lukes stops short of mistaking the imaginary for the real, he too presents his argument regarding the hypothetical society of complete altruists with a degree of certainty or confidence that is out of place in thinking about a radically different form of society.

After all, we *are* talking about a society that is supposedly very different from our existing societies, and as long as we are doing so, it seems advisable to give more weight to its being different from our existing societies than to its being similar to them. To proceed otherwise is to run the risk of importing notions of our existing societies into our picture of the imaginary society of altruists and hence misconstruing the latter. To be sure, it would be reasonable to assume that any future human society, simply by virtue of being *human* society, will resemble our present societies in important respects. Insofar as such an assumption extends to the need for justice, however, it is perhaps most plausibly construed not as implying that even a society of complete altruists would sufficiently resemble our existing societies to require justice, but rather as implying that any future society would resemble our existing societies in falling short of universal altruism and hence in standing in perpetual need of justice. This latter interpretation is just the commonplace belief that the circumstances of justice constitute a permanent feature of human society.

Such a belief, whether as formulated by Hume in terms of the scarcity of altruism being part of human nature in general or as formulated by Rawls in terms of the permanence of reasonable pluralism in the special case of a democratic society,[45] can serve as a response to those who devalue justice on the grounds that the circumstances of justice will eventually disappear (say, with the advent of communism). The alternative response is to argue

43. Ibid.

44. Similarly, when Buchanan refers to "the fact that nonegoists and even perfect altruists can be in serious conflict over what the common good is or how to achieve it, and that those who are committed to achieving the common good *as they perceive it,* and *by the means they deem appropriate,* are often willing to use their authority to do so" (ibid., p. 175, emphasis added), the "perfect altruists" are lifted straight from our knowledge of the imperfect or seeming altruists in our existing societies.

45. See Rawls, *Political Liberalism,* pp. 129, 216–217.

that justice would be needed even under conditions of universal altruism. Lukes favors the latter response, because treating limited altruism and limited resources as among the circumstances of justice, as Hume and John Mackie have done, produces, in his view, undesirable consequences for our moral beliefs and attitudes.[46] Among such consequences is "the altogether disastrous tendency of marxism, and certain other forms of socialist and communitarian thinking, to take a hostile view of 'justice,' 'rights' and the morality of duty and to look forward to a withering away of this kind of morality . . . in a more communitarian society which has overcome, or greatly diminished, scarcity and egoism, and in which 'nobler virtues, and more favourable blessings' will prevail—a community beyond justice and rights."[47]

This has indeed been a disastrous tendency, as has been the tendency to believe that a society beyond justice can be achieved by means that go against justice. But these tendencies are disastrous, I would argue, for reasons other than those adduced by Lukes. Where Marxists go wrong is not, as he suggests, in failing to see that justice would be needed even in an ideal society, but in being so confident that such a society can ever come about and, worse, that such a society can be brought about by means that show a cavalier disregard for justice. Here, given the radical difference between an ideal society and any existing one, the burden of proof is on those who claim that such an ideal society can be brought about, and that the circumstances of justice as comprising limited altruism and limited resources will eventually be transcended. To place the burden of proof on Marxists in this regard is to give prima facie credibility to Rawls's counterclaim that the circumstances of justice, as expressed, say, by the idea of reasonable pluralism (in conjunction, as I have argued, with that of reasonable egoism), constitute, or should be allowed to constitute, a permanent feature of human society. This should be sufficient, I would argue, to engender the respect for justice on which Lukes rightly insists. This too is a way of taking justice seriously, whereas Lukes believes that the only way of doing so is to make good the claim that justice would be necessary even in a condition of universal altruism.[48] As far as *this* claim is concerned, the burden of proof, as I have tried to show, is not on Marxists but on Lukes and like-minded theorists, and proof is not forthcoming. For this reason,

46. See Lukes, "Taking Morality Seriously," pp. 107–108.
47. Ibid., p. 108.
48. Ibid., p. 109.

Marxists—and Humeans, for that matter—should not be faulted for treating limited altruism as among the circumstances of justice. Nor should they be faulted for inferring from such circumstances the moral limits of justice, for displaying what Lukes calls "the inclination to see justice as a merely 'remedial virtue.'"[49]

Whether justice is a remedial virtue depends on the moral status of what is to be overcome through the imposition of justice. If what needs to be overcome is the absence or scarcity of something that is of higher moral status than justice itself, namely altruism, then it follows that justice is a remedial virtue, a virtue whose function is to make up for the lack of a higher virtue.[50] It follows too that the motives that can be presumed available for bringing about justice are also ones that fall below those virtues the lack of which makes justice necessary in the first place. Therefore, not to treat egoism as a necessary condition of the need for justice and consequently not to treat justice as a remedial virtue is at once to misconceive the nature of the need for justice and to misconceive or exaggerate the moral status of the virtue of justice and, more important, the kinds of motivational capacities that can be presumed available for making justice possible. It says a great deal about the sobriety of Marx that he was not guilty of either misconception, though he was far from sober in looking forward with confidence to the day when the circumstances of justice and hence justice itself would be transcended. Such sobriety is still salutary today.[51] Indeed, Marx's utopian stance on this matter is not entirely misguided either. For one can glean from it the insight that the best way to achieve justice is to push back the frontiers of the circumstances of justice.[52] This need not lead to the devaluation of justice, as Lukes fears, if to the Marxian insight we add the sobering Humean or Rawlsian realization—a reasonably safe bet given the locus of the burden of proof—that these frontiers are unlikely, and some of them should not be made, ever to disappear.

It is worth noting, perhaps as an afterthought, that Lukes is picturing a hypothetical society of *universal* altruism, one in which *everyone* is an altruist. What I have tried to show is that it is far from proven that justice would be necessary in such a society. This is very different from arguing

49. Ibid., p. 108.

50. For an illuminating discussion of the view of justice as a remedial virtue and the implications of such a view, see Sandel, *Liberalism,* pp. 31–35.

51. See Buchanan, *Marx,* p. 178.

52. Something like this insight seems to be (at least) implicit in Sandel, *Liberalism,* pp. 32, 34.

that an altruist, merely by virtue of being an altruist, does not need to be restrained by justice in any circumstances whatsoever. For the problems facing an altruist are altogether different in a society that is characterized, as all actual societies are, by the presence of various forms of egoism and the evils that result from them. In such a society, one difficulty for an altruistic or benevolent person is that, as Rawls puts it, "the love of several persons is thrown into confusion once the claims of these persons conflict . . . Benevolence is at sea as long as its many loves are in opposition in the persons of its many objects."[53] To this may be added an even more intractable problem: in such a society a person deeply committed to promoting other people's good could become sorely frustrated and driven to intolerance and even fanaticism, not unlike the kind found among certain well-intentioned communists. If this is the case, then an altruist could easily face a dilemma of ends and means, and for this reason he or she may well need to be restrained by justice with regard to means, besides being subject to the requirement of moral and epistemic unity.

None of this contradicts the idea that egoism is a necessary condition of the need for justice. What the case of the altruist in a partially egoistic society shows is that the egoism need not issue from the altruist herself for her, along with the egoists of her society, to need restraint by justice. If we add to the fact of partial egoism the further fact that egoism tends to be mediated by some conception of the good, then it will indeed be the case, as Nagel puts it, that "the most intellectually difficult problem regarding an acceptable partition of motives arises not from conflicts of interest but from conflicts over what is truly valuable."[54] One must be careful, however, not to extend such a problem to a situation in which it may well not belong, namely, a condition of universal altruism. It seems reasonable to imagine that a society of universal altruism would be a society of at least relative happiness for everyone. If so, an altruist—one who not only promotes other people's good but also sees their good as much as possible from their point of view—would be free of the kind of dilemma and frustration that characterize the situation of an altruist in a partially egoistic society with its many evils. An altruist would thus no longer need to be intolerant or fanatic *on other people's behalf.* In a (hypothetical) society where most are relatively happy and none desperately unhappy, only those need restraint by justice who are promoting not other people's good but their

53. Rawls, *Theory,* p. 190.
54. Nagel, *Equality,* p. 154.

own good, whatever the guise may be, at other people's expense. It cannot therefore be said of such a society, as Nagel says of it, that "members of a society *all* motivated by an impartial regard for one another will be led into conflict by that very motive if they disagree about what the good life consists in, hence what they should want impartially for everyone."[55] So once again, egoism turns out to be a necessary condition of the need for justice. To realize this is to know the limits beyond which one cannot reasonably argue, and others should have no reason to accept, that one is promoting other people's good, or even that one is pursuing a conception of the good which is more than the rationalization of one's narrow self-interest.

55. Ibid., emphasis added.

3

The Objective Circumstances of Justice

I turn in this chapter to the objective circumstances of justice and consider, especially, the implications of adopting one particular conception of such circumstances rather than another. I begin with an account of how Hume conceives the role of justice narrowly in terms of the distribution of property rights and argue that this understanding of the role of justice follows from a prior, equally narrow conception of the objective circumstances of justice in terms of the scarcity of external goods. Against Hume's position, I discuss three accounts of "subject-centered" justice whose guiding idea is some kind of equality of respect. John Rawls and Allen Buchanan in different ways espouse a concept of subject-centered justice that is radically opposed to Hume's property-centered concept of justice. I argue, however, that neither Rawls nor Buchanan properly grounds subject-centered justice in a prior, equally subject-centered conception of the objective circumstances of justice. As a result, their concept of subject-centered justice, highly attractive in itself, is compromised by an explicit (Rawls) or implicit (Buchanan) understanding of the objective circumstances of justice that bears a close resemblance to Hume's. I then try to show how this flaw is overcome in Habermas's conception of the objective circumstances of justice, with its focus on the fragility of personal identity and the corresponding need for respect. Finally, I address certain complications, not noted by Habermas, that any adequate conception of the objective circumstances of justice, such as Habermas's, will cause for our understanding of the *subjective* circumstances of justice.

Hume on the Role of Justice

As in the previous chapter, it is helpful to begin here with Hume, this time because Hume's account contains a conception of the objective circumstances of justice that still needs to be argued against, and yet his account exhibits a consistency (between this conception and the implications Hume derived from it regarding the domain and role of justice) that is nevertheless highly instructive. On both counts, Hume's position throws into sharp relief the strengths and weaknesses of the other positions I will consider.

The chief objective circumstance that makes justice necessary, according to Hume, is material scarcity. Hume says, in a famous statement covering both the subjective and the objective circumstances of justice, that "'tis only from the selfishness and confin'd generosity of men, along with *the scanty provision nature has made for his wants,* that justice derives its origin."[1] On this view, justice has to do with possessions, or what Hume calls "external goods," that is, "such possessions as we have acquir'd by our industry and good fortune."[2] Of the three kinds of goods available to human beings—"the internal satisfaction of our mind, the external advantages of our body, and the enjoyment of such possessions as we have acquir'd by our industry and good fortune"—only the last, external goods, "are both expos'd to the violence of others, and may be transferr'd without suffering any loss or alteration; while at the same time, there is not a sufficient quantity of them to supply every one's desires and necessities. As the improvement, therefore, of these goods is the chief advantage of society, so the *instability* of their possession, along with their *scarcity,* is the chief impediment."[3]

It follows that the removal of this impediment is the chief function of justice, which serves to "bestow stability on the possession of those external goods, and leave every one in the peaceable enjoyment of what he may acquire by his fortune and industry."[4] Accordingly, the *domain* of justice,

1. David Hume, *A Treatise of Human Nature,* ed. L. A. Selby-Bigge, 2nd ed., ed. P. H. Nidditch (Oxford: Clarendon Press, 1978), p. 495; the entire quotation is italicized in the original.

2. Ibid., pp. 489, 487.

3. Ibid., pp. 487–488. Alasdair MacIntyre, who uses the term "external goods" in a sense very similar to (though somewhat more elastic than) Hume's, remarks of external goods: "It is characteristic of what I have called external goods that when achieved they are always some individual's property and possession. Moreover characteristically they are such that the more someone has of them, the less there is for other people. This is sometimes necessarily the case, as with power and fame, and sometimes the case by reason of contingent circumstance as with money. External goods are therefore characteristically objects of competition in which there must be losers as well as winners." Alasdair MacIntyre, *After Virtue,* 2nd ed. (Notre Dame, Ind.: University of Notre Dame Press, 1984), p. 190.

4. Hume, *Treatise,* p. 489.

what Hume calls the *object* of justice, is property, and the *role* of justice is to regulate the disposition of property, to "make a partition of goods."[5] Indeed, justice exists to make property possible in the first place, for without the concepts of justice and injustice, Hume says, the idea of property itself would be altogether unintelligible.[6] Given this conception of the circumstances of justice, Hume is not overstating his conclusions when he claims: "No one can doubt, that the convention for the distinction of property, and for the stability of possession, is of all circumstances the most necessary to the establishment of human society"—so much so that "after the agreement for the fixing and observing of this rule, there remains little or nothing to be done towards settling a perfect harmony and concord."[7]

By the same token, the circumstances of justice also determine what kind of virtue justice is and what kind of vice it is meant to overcome. It follows from Hume's understanding of the scarcity of external goods as the chief objective circumstance of justice that the primary vice to be subdued through cultivating the virtue of justice is greed. "This avidity alone, of acquiring goods and possessions for ourselves and our nearest friends, is insatiable, perpetual, universal, and directly destructive of society . . . So that upon the whole, we are to esteem the difficulties in the establishment of society, to be greater or less, according to those we encounter in regulating and restraining this passion." It is characteristic of Hume's way of thinking that the vice of greed, a vice pertaining to the domain of external goods, is to be overcome, at least in the first instance, not with anything superimposed from some other (say, spiritual or independently moral) domain, not even with the help of the instinct of sympathy with which Hume explains the approbation of justice, but with something from within the domain of external goods itself: "There is no passion . . . capable of controlling the interested affection, but the very affection itself, by an alteration of its direction." What overcomes greed is merely enlightened greed, in the form of the knowledge that "the passion [of avidity] is much better

5. David Hume, *An Enquiry Concerning the Principles of Morals,* ed. J. B. Schneewind (Indianapolis: Hackett, 1983), p. 21. See also the discussion on this issue in Annette C. Baier, *A Progress of Sentiments: Reflections on Hume's Treatise* (Cambridge, Mass.: Harvard University Press, 1991), pp. 221–226; Barry Stroud, *Hume* (London: Routledge & Kegan Paul, 1977), pp. 202–203; and Knud Haakonssen, "The Structure of Hume's Political Theory," in *The Cambridge Companion to Hume,* ed. David Fate Norton (Cambridge: Cambridge University Press, 1993), pp. 182–221, esp. pp. 198–199.

6. See Hume, *Treatise,* p. 489.

7. Ibid., p. 491.

satisfy'd by its restraint, than by its liberty, and that by preserving society, we make much greater advances in the acquiring of possessions."[8] Since justice thus consists in the *self*-transformation of greed, it can be no more than what Hume calls a "cautious, jealous virtue."[9] No virtue confined in its motivation and function to the domain of external goods could be otherwise.[10]

Hume does not say, of course, that the distribution of property rights, or the control of greed, is the *ultimate* purpose of justice. The goal of justice and property rights, as of every human convention, is, according to him, "the interest and happiness of human society." In making such general references to the purpose of justice, however, Hume seems to have in mind not much more than the subsistence of society and the material well-being of individuals.[11] Beyond this, his arguments for justice turn extremely vague. Yet in the overall scheme of Hume's understanding of justice, this vagueness need not be a weakness at all. Given his conception of the objective circumstances of justice, there is simply no room for any notion of human happiness, *which justice can help promote,* that is beyond the secure possession and full enjoyment of external goods. Thus the lack of any such notion only goes to show that Hume's understanding of justice is all of a piece. He begins with a conception of the circumstances of justice and proceeds to work only with those notions that are consistent with it—notions regarding the domain and role of justice and regarding the nature of the virtue of justice and its corresponding vice.

At first sight, it may seem easier to embrace Hume's conception of the objective circumstances of justice, as Rawls for example does, than to accept his understanding of the role of justice as confined to the establishment and distribution of property rights, as Rawls for example does not (to the same degree). Nevertheless, as long as we subscribe to Hume's conception of the objective circumstances of justice, we have no choice, except at the cost of inconsistency, but to accept what such a conception entails about the domain and role of justice as well as the nature of the virtue of justice. Annette Baier puts the point well: "The story about the sup-

8. Ibid., pp. 491–492.

9. Hume, *Enquiry,* p. 21.

10. Thus Hume goes so far as to say, regarding the origin of justice, that "whether the passion of self-interest be esteemed vicious or virtuous, 'tis all a case; since itself alone restrains it: So that if it be virtuous, men become social by their virtue; if vicious, their vice has the same effect" (*Treatise,* p. 492).

11. Hume, *Enquiry,* pp. 30, 32.

posed 'origin' of justice is told to make clear, first, what problem it is that justice is invented to solve. Once limited generosity over transferable good is seen to be the problem, the general lines of the solution follow immediately."[12] In this regard, Hume's understanding of justice exhibits a degree of internal consistency that still offers valuable lessons.[13] There may of course be good reason, as many now believe, to reject Hume's property-centered understanding of the function of justice.[14] If that is the case, we must also reject the conception of the objective circumstances of justice that underlies Hume's narrow understanding of the role of justice in the first place.

Subject-Centered Justice

A clearly articulated challenge to the Humean understanding of justice comes from Allen Buchanan, who attributes to Hume what he calls the "reciprocity thesis," namely, "the claim that only those who do (or at least can) make a contribution to the cooperative surplus have rights to social resources."[15] This attribution is based on a passage in section three of the *Enquiry,* where Hume speculates, in Buchanan's words, that "creatures otherwise like us but powerless to harm us can at most hope to be treated mercifully, but cannot be treated justly."[16] More important, but this is not noted by Buchanan (I will come back to the significance of this oversight later), the reciprocity thesis is one that can be naturally and consistently derived from Hume's conception of the objective circumstances of justice.

In opposition to the reciprocity thesis, also called "justice as reciprocity," Buchanan offers a conception of subject-centered justice, which he defines in terms of "the fundamental moral equality of persons." According to him, "this way of looking at questions of justice is radically different from the perspective of justice as reciprocity. It focuses upon the needs and nonstrategic capacities of the person and upon our collective ability to help satisfy those needs and develop those capacities."[17] While in broad

12. Baier, *Progress,* p. 226.

13. A similar consistency is found in David Gauthier, *Morals by Agreement* (Oxford: Clarendon Press, 1986), pp. 113–116.

14. See, e.g., Judith N. Shklar, *The Faces of Injustice* (New Haven: Yale University Press, 1990), pp. 117–118.

15. Allen Buchanan, "Justice as Reciprocity versus Subject-Centered Justice," *Philosophy and Public Affairs* 19 (1990): 227–252; quotation from p. 230.

16. Ibid., p. 227.

17. Ibid., pp. 231, 233.

agreement with his position, I believe that Buchanan's critique of the reciprocity thesis and his affirmation of subject-centered justice do not go far enough, since he does not question the Humean conception of the domain and role of justice, still less the Humean conception of the objective circumstances of justice underlying it. In fact, he does not directly invoke any conception of the circumstances of justice. But since the domain of justice is for him that of access to material resources, and since this domain is determined by the Humean conception of the objective circumstances of justice, he is committed, if unwittingly and at the cost of inconsistency with his other notions of justice, to the Humean conception of the objective circumstances of justice.

The point of showing that Buchanan (implicitly) follows the Humean conception of the objective circumstances of justice is that a particular conception of the objective circumstances of justice determines the domain and role of justice (that is, the nature and scope of the problems to be solved by it).[18] And a particular conception of the domain and role of justice, in turn, rules out certain normative conceptions of justice (that is, proposals for solving the problems of justice) as unsuitable for or even irrelevant to the problems of justice. Therefore, once we *begin with* Hume's non-subject-centered conception of the objective circumstances of justice, explicitly or implicitly, we are trapped in a certain non-subject-centered way of thinking about *the rest of justice.* Unless we abandon the Humean conception of the objective circumstances of justice altogether, we can escape that trap, as Buchanan seeks to do with his concept of subject-centered justice, only at the cost of inconsistency and confusion.

A case in point is that when Buchanan challenges the reciprocity thesis, he does so with the argument that it is "blind to the prior question of which cooperative institutions will produce *just conditions for membership in the class of contributors.*"[19] This argument is not without merit, but the question of contribution, though prior to the question of distribution, still leaves us in the very domain of justice where the reciprocity thesis is most at home.[20] For contribution, as defined by Buchanan, is no less *to* social resources than distribution is *of* them. As correlative notions, contribution and distribution share the same domain. While Buchanan is right to say,

18. See John Rawls, *A Theory of Justice,* rev. ed. (Cambridge, Mass.: Harvard University Press, 1999), p. 109.

19. Buchanan, "Justice," p. 238.

20. Here, despite his criticism of Gauthier, Buchanan's understanding of the domain and role of justice is not fundamentally different from Gauthier's in *Morals* (e.g., pp. 114, 116).

"Given that the capacity to be a contributor is socially determined, then it is clear that questions of justice arise not only with respect to relations among contributors but also at the deeper level of what sort of cooperative institutions we ought to have, insofar as the character of these institutions will determine in part who can contribute,"[21] he fails to situate this issue of membership at an even deeper level of considerations—those that underpin subject-centered justice—in terms of which the question of the "just conditions for membership in the class of contributors" itself ought to be framed. Although Buchanan elsewhere touches on such considerations, he bypasses them in this argument.

It is these deeper considerations that pertain *directly* to subject-centered justice *before* they determine or shape answers to questions of contribution and distribution. Subject-centered justice, having to do with whatever it is that is considered most fundamental to the human subject, is not distributive, and hence is not concerned with access to resources *in the first instance*. If subject-centered justice should serve as a basis for distributive justice, it is not distributive justice itself.[22] We may think of the domain with which subject-centered justice is directly concerned as *the primary domain of justice* and treat distributive justice (understood here as covering both the question of distribution and the prior question of contribution) as *the secondary domain of justice*.[23] The point of drawing this distinction is that the status of subject-centered justice has to be established first before it can be used to ground a conception of distributive justice. The main problem with Buchanan's account of subject-centered justice, then, is that for the most part he skips over the primary domain of justice and treats subject-centered justice as if it had to do *directly* with the secondary domain of justice, that is, with the contribution to and distribution of resources, or at best with the issue of membership regarding both. What is conspicuously lacking in his account is any conception of the objective circumstances of justice that can give sense to the notion of subject-centered justice.

The result is a serious mismatch between the kind of justice Buchanan espouses and the domain of justice in which he operates. On the one hand,

21. Buchanan, "Justice," p. 238.

22. Walzer puts it well when he says that self-respect is "the deepest purpose of distributive justice." Michael Walzer, *Spheres of Justice* (New York: Basic Books, 1983), p. 278.

23. This distinction bears some general resemblance to Rawls's division of the social structure into two domains governed by separate, lexically ordered principles. But I draw this distinction with particular reference to how we should conceive of the objective circumstances of justice. For discussion of Rawls's distinction, see the next section.

justice is concerned, for Buchanan, with "the fundamental moral equality of persons." Yet on the other hand, the domain of justice is allowed to be determined by the Humean question of "basic rights to resources,"[24] with the role of justice defined accordingly as the equitable distribution thereof. This inconsistency is worth noting because as long as one subscribes, if only implicitly, to the Humean conception of the objective circumstances of justice and treats the (primary) domain of justice in terms of the contribution to and distribution of resources, one is conceptually too close to the reciprocity thesis to mount any fundamental challenge to it. Something like the reciprocity thesis is natural, indeed unavoidable, given the Humean conception of the objective circumstances of justice and the domain of justice that follows from it. The Humean conception leaves no room for anything that could serve as an effective rationale for subject-centered justice. Therefore, in order to give subject-centered justice a clear articulation and a firm basis, we must step outside the Humean domain of justice, indeed outside the Humean conception of the objective circumstances of justice, altogether. The point of departure for subject-centered justice needs to be located elsewhere, in a radically different conception of the objective circumstances and, as follows from this, of the domain and role of justice. Before I consider what such a conception should look like, I want to bring into focus some further dimensions of the mismatch or incompatibility between subject-centered justice and the Humean conception of the objective circumstances of justice, this time with particular reference to Rawls's treatment of the main issues.

If Buchanan does not explicitly invoke the Humean conception of the circumstances of justice, Rawls, an exemplary proponent of subject-centered justice in Buchanan's view, undoubtedly does. As a matter of fact, Rawls finds Hume's account of the circumstances of justice "especially perspicuous," saying that his own account "adds nothing essential to [Hume's] much fuller discussion." According to Rawls's formulation of Hume's essential points, "the circumstances of justice obtain whenever persons put forward conflicting claims to the division of social advantages under conditions of moderate scarcity." For Rawls, the importance of specifying the circumstances of justice lies in the fact that the circumstances of justice and the requirements they generate "define the role of justice." Since Rawls follows Hume in his conception of the circumstances of justice, it is only

24. Buchanan, "Justice," p. 231.

natural that he should also see the role of justice in an essentially Humean spirit. The role of justice, as Rawls puts it, is the selection of "principles . . . for choosing among the various social arrangements which determine this division of advantages and for underwriting an agreement on the proper distributive shares." Not surprisingly, the circumstances of justice have implications not only for the role of justice but also, as Rawls realizes in common with Hume, for the nature of the virtue of justice. Unless the circumstances of justice exist, according to Rawls, "there would be no occasion for the virtue of justice."[25] If Rawls were to spell out the nature of the virtue of justice, he would have to follow Hume in regarding justice as a cautious and jealous virtue.[26]

What is striking is that if Rawls sets out with a Humean conception of the circumstances of justice, he nevertheless ends up on an unmistakably Kantian note, invoking "the value of persons that Kant says is beyond all price" and treating self-respect as "the most important primary good."[27] Given this inconsistency, it is not surprising that this most important primary good has a status in Rawls's account that is often uncertain or otherwise problematic. We catch a glimpse of such uncertainty when Rawls at one point leaves some room for doubting that self-respect is the most important primary good. *"Perhaps,"* he writes in one place—only perhaps!—"the most important primary good is that of self-respect."[28] I would not attend to this note of hesitation, Rawls being a cautious thinker throughout, but for the fact that such ambivalence is expressed elsewhere in the *Theory* in a more substantive fashion.

This is particularly obvious in the case of Rawls's *general* conception of justice,[29] which does not distinguish self-respect from other social primary goods, treating all of them as commensurable: "*All* social values—liberty and opportunity, income and wealth, *and the bases of self-respect*—are to be distributed equally *unless an unequal distribution of any, or all, of these values is to everyone's advantage*. Injustice, then, is simply inequalities that are not to the benefit of all."[30] What is problematic here is that Rawls lumps

25. Ibid., pp. 109–110.

26. This at least seems true of *A Theory of Justice,* if not of much of Rawls's later work.

27. Rawls, *Theory,* pp. 513, 386.

28. Ibid., p. 386, emphasis added.

29. For a perspicacious discussion of the distinction between Rawls's general and special conceptions of justice, especially of problems with the special conception, see Thomas W. Pogge, *Realizing Rawls* (Ithaca, N.Y.: Cornell University Press, 1989), pp. 122–148.

30. Rawls, *Theory,* p. 54, emphasis added.

income and wealth together with the bases of self-respect. Insofar as income and wealth do not constitute the basis of self-respect—or beyond the point that they do—it is arguable that they should be "distributed equally unless an unequal distribution of any, or all, of these values is to everyone's advantage." But it would be difficult to maintain that any unequal distribution of the bases of self-respect could ever be to *everyone's* advantage, least of all to the advantage of those whose unfortunate situation forces them to accept some loss in self-respect (the most important primary good) in exchange, say, for some increase in their meager income (a lesser good). In other words, it would be difficult to see how an unequal distribution of the bases of self-respect could be justified *within* a conception of justice whose chief primary good is self-respect—even under less than favorable conditions.

It is precisely to avoid this kind of self-defeating unequal distribution that Rawls proposes a *special* conception of justice for societies that enjoy reasonably favorable conditions.[31] In the special conception, the importance of self-respect is reflected in the division of the social structure into two domains and in the lexical priority of the principle of equal basic liberties over the difference principle.[32] Thus: "The best solution is to support the primary good of self-respect *as far as possible* by the assignment of the basic liberties that can indeed be made equal, defining the same status for all. At the same time, *relative shares of material means are relegated to a subordinate place.* Thus we arrive at another reason for factoring the social order into two parts as indicated by the principles of justice. While these principles permit inequalities in return for contributions that are for the benefit of all, the precedence of liberty entails equality in the social bases of respect."[33] It is presumably this special conception that causes Buchanan to regard Rawls's theory of justice as a paradigm of subject-centered justice. Interestingly, there is no trace in this special conception of the Humean understanding of the objective circumstances of justice. For

31. It is not very clear, though, what reasonably favorable conditions exactly are. My argument, however, does not require me to be more precise on this question than Rawls is.

32. See Rawls, *Theory,* pp. 53–54. The difference principle is of course only part of Rawls's second principle of justice, which also includes the principle of fair equality of opportunity. Strictly speaking, the first principle, that of equal basic liberties, is lexically prior to the second principle, within which the principle of fair equality of opportunity is lexically prior to the difference principle. For our purposes, though, we may leave the principle of fair equality of opportunity out of account.

33. Ibid., p. 478, emphasis added.

given the Humean conception, justice is concerned not with self-respect but with the merely practical business of the distribution of resources and advantages (and the securing of social peace), and if so, there is no rationale for relegating distributive justice, as Rawls proposes to do, to a subordinate place. Thus Rawls's leap from the Humean conception of the objective circumstances of justice to the Kantian attachment of supreme importance to self-respect is accomplished at the cost of a fundamental inconsistency or ambivalence.[34] Rawls's sympathies seem largely Kantian, and yet such sympathies are apparently not enough to produce a clean break with the Humean conception of the objective circumstances of justice. Such ambivalence in turn is reflected in contradictions within Rawls's special conception of justice itself. As Rawls sees it, an unequal distribution of the social bases of self-respect can be avoided to the extent that the bases of self-respect are kept separate from the distribution of resources and social advantages—to the extent, as Rawls puts it, that "self-respect is secured by the public affirmation of the status of equal citizenship for all" so that "the distribution of material means is left to take care of itself in accordance with pure procedural justice regulated by just background institutions." But Rawls realizes that "it is quite possible that this idea cannot be carried through completely. To some extent men's sense of their own worth may hinge upon their institutional position and their income share."[35] If this is the case, then we must confront the fact that the conflict to which distributive justice is proposed as a solution involves not merely claims to things that facilitate the pursuit of conceptions of the good but, more important, claims to things that are part of the very basis of self-respect. Rawls's solution to problems arising from this fact is quite idealistic, in that he envisions a society in which self-respect, as guaranteed by the principle of equal basic liberties, is entirely independent of income and status, those things which it is the function of the difference principle to regulate. This is the point of the lexical order of the two principles of justice.

This idealistic solution has an important consequence, however, that ap-

34. Such an inconsistency also exists between the original position and the circumstances of justice, and hence within the original position itself inasmuch as the circumstances of justice are known to the deliberating subjects in the original position. Since the lexical ordering of principles of justice is determined within the original position, there is a mismatch between the original position, which assigns priority to the principle of equal basic liberties, and the objective circumstances of justice, which only call for principles regulating resources and advantages.

35. Rawls, *Theory,* p. 478.

parently eludes Rawls: namely, to the extent that such a society is realized, the difference principle no longer has as crucial a function to perform as Rawls seems to assign it. For once income and status and things of that sort are severed from the most important primary good, self-respect, there is significantly less incentive to fight over them and accordingly less need for any principle of distributive justice, such as Rawls's difference principle, to regulate their distribution. A major part of what is at stake in conflicts involving income and status is the connection, itself socially engendered, between such things and self-respect.

This is well illustrated by the case of the Stoic. Though greatly mistaken in severing external goods or "natural advantages" from self-respect and functioning,[36] the Stoic is perfectly logical in concluding, from the premise that self-respect is independent of external goods, that there is no need to fuss over external goods. Rawls quite correctly holds that there is such a need, and hence the need for a principle of distributive justice, such as the difference principle, to regulate the distribution of income and other external goods. But as the case of the Stoic reminds us, the very acknowledgment of such a need, particularly if we attach to it the kind of importance that Rawls does, is at the same time an acknowledgment that external goods do form a significant part of the basis of self-respect, whether we like it or not. Thus the very need for something like Rawls's difference principle, along with the importance of such a principle, is evidence of the kind of situation in which people, each fighting for a larger share of external goods, are at bottom "at odds with one another in the pursuit of their self-esteem."[37] This is not "a great misfortune" that happens only under extraordinary circumstances, as Rawls believes, but part of our normal condition.

If this is the case, it is not at all clear that Rawls's difference principle, or some such principle serving a distributive function, is necessarily less important than the principle of equal basic liberties—and this because of, not in spite of, the fact (or belief) that self-respect is the most important primary good. Instead of deciding in advance, and once and for all, on a lexical order for the principles of justice, as Rawls does, one should perhaps leave the issue to be settled with reference to the relative weight that liberty and economic equality happen to carry as the bases of self-respect. In any case, it does not seem possible to lay down in advance, even for those

36. See Martha C. Nussbaum, *The Therapy of Desire: Theory and Practice in Hellenistic Ethics* (Princeton: Princeton University Press, 1995), pp. 505–506.

37. Rawls, *Theory*, p. 478.

societies that enjoy reasonably favorable conditions, the relative importance of liberty and economic equality as the bases of self-respect. If it were possible to do this, it would by the same token also be possible, by treating equal basic liberties as the *sole* basis of self-respect (as Rawls does), to reduce the importance of any principle governing the distribution of external goods to a degree hardly imaginable in our existing societies. Put another way, either equal basic liberties form the sole basis of self-respect or they do not. If they do, the difference principle, having no connection with the most important good of self-respect, is of relatively little consequence. If not, then the lexical order does not strictly hold. Thus, and speaking at a higher level of generality, we can say that *either* Rawls's lexical order, or any other fixed order of principles of justice for that matter, lacks a good rationale; *or* Rawls's difference principle, or any other conceivable principle of distributive justice for that matter, is of far less importance than it is usually made out to be.

We should note, however, an additional complication. Rawls's ambivalence regarding the status of self-respect also results, it seems, from an attempt to come to grips with a tricky methodological problem. The problem, as Rawls puts it, is that "while the principles of justice will be effective only if men have a sense of justice and do therefore respect one another, the notion of respect or of the inherent worth of persons is not a suitable basis for arriving at these principles. It is precisely these ideas that call for interpretation." In constructing a theory of justice, therefore, even a subject-centered theory of justice, we cannot, says Rawls, start out from such ideas. Rather, our theory should proceed from something conceptually more basic, then "once the conception of justice is on hand, . . . the ideas of respect and of human dignity can be given a more definite meaning."[38] Hence the need for a device like the original position. Hence also, presumably, the need to begin from the Humean conception of the circumstances of justice.

Yet even to ground respect and dignity in this fashion, rather than to have respect and dignity ground everything else from the outset, is to have at least an unsystematic notion of the prime importance of respect and dignity. Indeed, as Rawls makes clear at the very beginning of *Theory* in discussing the role of justice,[39] some such intuitive notion lies at the heart of the entire Rawlsian project. What is therefore problematic is that *Rawls's conception of the objective circumstances of justice does not take ac-*

38. Ibid., p. 513.
39. Ibid., pp. 3–4.

count of such a notion at all. It may be the case, as he believes, that "there is no way to avoid the complications of the original position, or of some similar construction, if our notions of respect and the natural basis of equality are to be *systematically* presented."[40] Nevertheless, as long as we are keen, as Rawls apparently is, to attach the highest importance to such notions, if only at the end of a normative inquiry, this already presupposes that the ensuring of respect and dignity rather than the distribution of resources and advantages must take its place from the start as the most important problem to be solved by justice. This means, in turn, that we need a different conception of the objective circumstances of justice from the Humean one that Rawls takes over uncritically. If we are to have any chance of ending up with a coherent conception of subject-centered justice, we have to begin with a conception of the objective circumstances of justice that is consistent with it.

Jürgen Habermas does precisely that, providing a conception of the objective circumstances of justice from which subject-centered justice follows as a natural conclusion. Like Hume and Rawls, he begins with a scene of conflict (a scene that also contains the possibility of agreement and cooperation), as anyone must in order to account for the need for justice. But he sees in this conflict something far more important at stake than access to resources for the pursuit of conceptions of the good, more important even than security. According to Habermas, "the basic facts"—that is, the circumstances that make justice necessary—"are the following: Creatures that are individuated only through socialization are vulnerable and morally in need of considerateness." This is because in the process of becoming individuated the subject simultaneously and necessarily "becomes entangled in a densely woven fabric of mutual recognition, that is, of reciprocal exposedness and vulnerability. Unless the subject externalizes himself by participating in interpersonal relations through language, he is unable to form that inner center that is his personal identity." This "almost constitutional insecurity and chronic fragility of personal identity" is of greater importance than access to material resources and social advantages. Indeed it is "antecedent to cruder threats to the integrity of life and limb."[41] This is

40. Ibid., p. 513, emphasis added.

41. Jürgen Habermas, *Moral Consciousness and Communicative Action,* trans. Christian Lenhardt and Shierry Weber Nicholsen (Cambridge, Mass.: MIT Press, 1990), p. 199. See also his *Philosophical-Political Profiles,* trans. Frederick G. Lawrence (Cambridge, Mass.: MIT Press, 1985), pp. 122–123; and *Justification and Application: Remarks on Discourse Ethics,* trans. Ciaran P. Cronin (Cambridge, Mass.: MIT Press, 1993), pp. 130–131, 154, 174.

not to say that such cruder threats do not fall under the rubric of injustice. They certainly do, but first and foremost in a sense that goes beyond the inflicting of bodily harm, grave though that is. Schopenhauer, whose influence is much in evidence in Habermas's account, captures this sense when he defines wrong *(Unrecht)* as "breaking through the boundary of another's affirmation of will."[42] Thus, "the sufferer of the wrong feels the transgression into his own body's sphere of affirmation through the denial of this by another individual, as an immediate and *mental* pain. This is *entirely separate and different from* the physical suffering through the deed or annoyance at the loss, which is felt *simultaneously* with it."[43] It is in this deep sense that what Schopenhauer calls the fundamental principle of justice, namely "Neminen laede" (injure no one),[44] is to be understood, that is, in the sense of not only not causing physical harm but also, and more important, not damaging anyone's self-respect.[45] This, and nothing short

42. Arthur Schopenhauer, *The World as Will and Representation,* trans. E. F. J. Payne, vol. 1 (New York: Dover, 1969), p. 334.

43. Ibid., p. 355, emphasis added; see also pp. 337, 338.

44. Arthur Schopenhauer, *On the Basis of Morality,* trans. E. F. J. Payne (Indianapolis: Bobbs-Merrill, 1965), p. 149. Once we take this deeper view of justice, we can see that Philip Mercer misses the point when, objecting to Schopenhauer's understanding of the fundamental principle of justice, he proposes, "If one had to formulate [the fundamental principle of justice] then perhaps something like 'Treat everyone alike' would be more satisfactory. So long as we made no exception (including ourselves) we could *with justice injure everyone.*" Philip Mercer, *Sympathy and Ethics* (Oxford: Clarendon Press, 1972), p. 131, emphasis added. To be sure, justice contains the idea of treating everyone alike, but not alike in any manner whatsoever—certainly not, as Mercer allows, injuring everyone alike. Given a conception of the objective circumstances of justice such as that advanced by Habermas and prefigured in Schopenhauer, the role of justice is to injure no one, and this already implies treating everyone alike, but doing so in the right fashion, namely, treating everyone with equal respect. Thus, Mercer's view of justice is problematic because we can imagine no circumstances of justice which would make sense of it.

45. On this point Schopenhauer has close affinities with Kant and particularly with Hegel (despite Schopenhauer's contempt for the latter). In *The Metaphysics of Morals* (trans. Mary Gregor [Cambridge: Cambridge University Press, 1991], p. 244), for example, Kant defines respect as "the *maxim* of limiting our self-esteem by the dignity of humanity in another person." When he goes on to say that the duty of respect is "*analogous* to the duty of Right not to encroach upon what belongs to anyone" (emphasis added), one is supposed to understand the two as merely analogous but not identical, since what separates them is the deep divide between virtue and Right. It is only in the sphere of virtue that one person can be just to another in the sense—that is, Schopenhauer's sense—I have been talking about. Hegel is even more explicit about what it is that is the object of injustice. "It is only the will existent in an object that can suffer injury," and hence a crime is what it is because it implies a "negatively *infinite* judgment in its full sense" in that the criminal implicitly asserts a *complete* incompati-

of this, should be treated as the principal role of justice, given that what is violated by injustice is at bottom self-respect.[46] Accordingly, an unjust distribution of resources and advantages is ultimately unjust for reasons that involve failure to render respect where respect is due. Only this way of understanding justice is adequate to explain the depth of resentment against injustice, distributive or otherwise, which a mere sense of material loss or even bodily harm cannot account for.[47] By the same token, only this way of understanding justice captures the psychology of the truly just person, one who is concerned not to injure (or, better still, to help preserve) the identity and self-respect of another person, as well as the psychology of the truly unjust person, one who is totally devoid of such concern.[48]

In this regard, Habermas's understanding of justice is continuous with Schopenhauer's. For Habermas, the domain of justice is "the subjective freedom of inalienable individuality," and accordingly *the role of justice* is to "instruct us on how best to behave in situations where it is in our power

---

bility between his victim and any capacity for rights. In this sense, injustice, of a serious kind, is "an infinite injury." See G. W. F. Hegel, *Hegel's Philosophy of Right,* trans. T. M. Knox (Oxford: Clarendon Press, 1952), paras. 96 (p. 68), 95 (p. 67, emphasis added), and 218 (p. 140), respectively; the entire section "C. Coercion and Crime," pp. 66–73, is highly relevant.

46. Schopenhauer's understanding of justice has behind it an ontology (regarding the phenomenal world) of the will to self-affirmation. This will is already beyond the will-to-live narrowly understood, since the mere will-to-live would imply a conception of justice limited to the prevention of physical harm. Indeed, the will to self-affirmation, what one might call a robust version of the will-to-live, is continuous with what Nietzsche was to call the will to power. As this reference to Nietzsche reminds us, however, the idea of *equal* respect, as contained, for example, in the maxim "Injure no one," is not entailed by the proposition that self-respect, that is, the will to self-affirmation or the will to power, is the domain of justice. Justice in the sense of equal respect or equal affirmation of will is exactly what Nietzsche opposes. But even in opposing it, Nietzsche is right about the domain of justice and about the source and nature of resentment as having to do with power or self-respect.

47. Shklar links the sense of injustice with rage and sees the harm of rage as immeasurable: "Nothing is more painful or soul-destroying than rage. If we cause rage by arousing a sense of injustice, we cannot measure the harm we do by simply taking the tangible deprivation into account. We must also add the psychological harm we inflict and especially the lasting anger we inspire. One need only consider the injuries of racial discrimination to recognize that it is not only unjust to deprive people of their social rights but it is also unjust to make them feel the fury and resentment of being humiliated" (*Faces of Injustice,* p. 49).

48. The majority of people seem to fall somewhere in between, in that their concern with justice, however scrupulous, has something superficial about it and generally does not extend much beyond respect for other people's socially prescribed rights. For a characterization of the unjust person, see Schopenhauer, *World,* p. 363.

to counteract the extreme vulnerability of others by being thoughtful and considerate. In anthropological terms, morality is a safety device compensating for a vulnerability built into the sociocultural form of life."[49] In this way Habermas breaks completely with the Humean conception of the domain of justice in terms of resources, and of the role of justice as the regulation or distribution thereof. There is nothing directly distributive about justice so conceived, since by definition distribution applies to goods of which, notwithstanding the variability of scarcity,[50] there is a limited overall amount (at any given point in time) such that some people having more will necessarily mean other people having less. Personal identity or self-respect, Habermas's domain of justice, is not such a good, something of which one can reasonably prefer a larger to a lesser share, as Rawls says of material resources and social advantages. Given this understanding of the domain and role of justice, it is structurally impossible for justice to be fully achieved in any social setting which is shot through with the spirit of competition, that is, a social setting in which people, each preferring a larger share of whatever it is that justice is supposed to regulate, practice justice in the spirit of what Hume calls a cautious and jealous virtue. To do other people justice in this grudging fashion is not to do them justice enough in the sense intended by Habermas, since to be just is to show concern for other people's identity and self-respect.[51]

What is needed above all, accordingly, is not the justice of institutions as such but the compassion of members of society, however essential a role institutions may play in inculcating and sustaining such compassion. This is why Habermas turns to "moral philosophies of sympathy and compassion," which "have discovered that this profound vulnerability [of persons individuated through socialization] calls for some guarantee of mutual consideration. This considerateness has the twofold objective of defending the integrity of the individual and of preserving the vital fabric of ties of mutual recognition through which individuals *reciprocally* stabilize their fragile identities."[52] Given Habermas's conception of the objective cir-

49. Habermas, *Moral Consciousness,* pp. 200, 199.

50. See Gauthier, *Morals,* p. 114.

51. This concern has an epistemic dimension as well, in that "human beings are capable of assessing reasons and justifications, and proper respect for their distinctive value involves treating them only in ways that they could, by the proper exercise of this capacity, recognize as justifiable." Thomas Scanlon, *What We Owe to Each Other* (Cambridge, Mass.: Harvard University Press, 1998), p. 169.

52. Habermas, *Moral Consciousness,* p. 200.

cumstances and of the domain and role of justice, the notion of compassion (sympathy or empathy) is foundational for his conception of justice in a way that it is not, say, for Rawls's. This does not preclude Habermas from taking account of the importance of institutions; but the importance of just institutions comes from their role in creating just people, people who are just from compassion.[53]

Another way of making the same point is that justice is *necessarily and from the very beginning* only one side of a coin of which the other side, what Habermas calls solidarity, is equally necessary and important. That this is so follows from Habermas's conception of the circumstances of justice: "Since moralities are tailored to suit the fragility of human beings individuated through socialization, they must always solve *two* tasks at *once*. They must emphasize the inviolability of the individual by postulating equal respect for the dignity of each individual. But they must also protect the web of intersubjective relations of mutual recognition by which these individuals survive as members of a community. To these two complementary aspects correspond the principles of justice and solidarity respectively. The first postulates equal respect and equal rights for the individual, whereas the second postulates empathy and concern for the well-being of one's neighbor."[54] I have cited this passage from Habermas not only because it serves to sum up his conception of justice but also because it helps to explain, better than any other account known to me, the otherwise puzzling and seemingly overblown notion, despite its long history in religious thought, of the unity of justice and love (solidarity).

Paul Tillich is a case in point, in that he wrote eloquently and insightfully on the interdependence of justice and love and yet in the end somehow failed to get his point across. Despite his many forceful arguments, a statement such as "Justice is just because of the love which is implicit in it"[55] seems to invite an exclusively religious interpretation and may leave unmoved those who do not share his religious outlook. Now, once we spell out the circumstances of justice in a Habermasian or Schopenhauerian fashion, such a statement need no longer be read as presenting an exclusively religious view of justice. And as such a conception of the cir-

53. Akin to this way of thinking, in spirit if not in substance, is what G. A. Cohen has to say about the importance of personal attitude as an intrinsic part of a just basic structure in *If You're an Egalitarian, How Come You're So Rich?* (Cambridge, Mass.: Harvard University Press, 2000), esp. chaps. 8, 9.

54. Habermas, *Moral Consciousness,* p. 200.

55. Paul Tillich, *Love, Power, and Justice* (London: Oxford University Press, 1954), p. 15.

cumstances of justice leads naturally, as in the case of Habermas, to the notion of the interdependence of justice and love (synonymous with solidarity in this context), so conversely whenever justice and love are regarded as somehow interdependent, as in the case of Tillich, this must imply a corresponding, antecedent view of the circumstances of justice. Rather than adding a touch of sentimentality to the Humean notion of justice, the fusion of love and justice signals a domain and a role of justice qualitatively different from distributive justice.[56] In secular terms, this fusion can be translated into the idea that given the inherently fragile nature of human beings' identity, justice calls for a certain respect that is owed to each and every human being for his or her *generic* identity, that is, *as a human being*. This sense of respect, owed as it is to a human being as a human being, is entirely nondistributive and noncomparative, and the term "love" in the expression "the unity of justice and love" refers to, or hints at, just this kind of solicitous respect.[57]

Thus Tillich's notion of the unity of justice and love turns out to be quite comprehensible, indeed compelling, once we make clear the corresponding and prior conception of the objective circumstances of justice. When Tillich says, "All the implications of the idea of justice, especially the

56. Some such conception of the domain and role of justice is implicitly held by anyone who believes, like Abraham Heschel, that "the logic of justice may seem impersonal, yet the concern for justice is an act of love," or, like Agnes Heller, that "justice and benevolence are not two separate virtues." See Abraham J. Heschel, *The Prophets* (New York: Harper and Row, 1962), p. 201, also p. 220; and Agnes Heller, *Beyond Justice* (Oxford: Basil Blackwell, 1987), p. 55. Statements like these are not romantic exaggerations regarding the domain of justice but quite precise expressions of the view, best articulated by Habermas, that *the concern for justice is a concern for another's identity,* a concern that amounts to love.

57. This sense of respect is distinct from the potentially distributive or comparative sense in which one can respect X more than Y for being more excellent with regard to a *particular* identity, say, for being a virtuoso violinist. Although these two senses of respect are analytically distinct, respect for a human being in the generic (and hence nondistributive and noncomparative) sense may require some degree of respect also for his or her particular identity, for one's generic identity is to a large degree expressed and maintained through one's particular identity.

See Walzer, *Spheres,* pp. 273–275 for the distinction between self-esteem and self-respect. Much of what is true of this distinction must also be true of the distinction between esteem and respect, although Walzer (rightly) resists direct translation from esteem and respect into self-esteem and self-respect (see pp. 272–273). The notion of respect that emerges in this way is close to what I mean by respect for the generic identity of a human being. As Walzer points out, "the practice of respecting oneself isn't a competitive practice" (p. 275). The same can be said of the practice of respecting others.

various forms of equality and liberty, are applications of the imperative to acknowledge every potential person as a person,"[58] Habermas's account of the circumstances of justice explains why. In this way, Tillich's intuitively appealing ideas begin to make more systematic sense once we spell out the circumstances of justice to which they are a response, because they are comprehensible and compelling only to the extent that the underlying conception of the objective circumstances of justice is itself comprehensible and compelling. If Tillich's ideas about the interdependence of love and justice can seem mere assertions or sentimental exaggerations, it is only because the conception of justice from which they spring is truncated by the lack of an adequate conception of the objective circumstances of justice. The very considerable merit of Habermas's account is that in it such a lack is made good—not simply for Tillich's notion of justice but for subject-centered conceptions of justice in general.

Habermas and the Subjective Circumstances of Justice

One consequence of adopting a Habermasian conception of the objective circumstances of justice is that the corresponding role of justice requires the introduction of motives, such as a high degree of empathy or compassion, whose lack or scarcity is precisely what constitutes the most important subjective circumstance of justice. In other words, the requisite degree of empathy or compassion is not among those subjective circumstances that are available to make justice *possible*. This fact does not invalidate Habermas's conception of the objective circumstances of justice, but it does create a motivational problem that has to be overcome if the role of justice as dictated by Habermas's conception of the objective circumstances of justice is to have any chance of being carried out.

A conception of the circumstances of justice is at the same time a conception of the motivational capacities that can be presumed available for fulfilling the role of justice as necessitated by those circumstances, that is, for solving the problems presented by the circumstances of justice. It is here that Habermas, with his deeper conception of the objective circumstances, faces a problem that is less acute for Hume. We may formulate this problem in terms of the compatibility, or lack thereof, between the objective and the subjective circumstances of justice or, more precisely, between

58. Paul Tillich, *Morality and Beyond* (New York: Harper and Row, 1963), p. 38; see also Tillich, *Love,* pp. 60, 63, 85.

those objective circumstances that make justice necessary and those subjective circumstances that are available to make justice possible.

Hume, with his shallower conception of the objective circumstances of justice, requires for the solution of the problems presented by these circumstances no motivational capacities that are inconsistent with his conception of the subjective circumstances of justice. The Humean notion of justice as reciprocal respect for property rights relies on enlightened self-interest for the establishment of justice, and therefore it need postulate no motivational capacities that in any way exceed what Hume identifies as the subjective circumstances of justice, namely, scarcity of altruism. As Annette Baier puts it, in Hume's picture of the origin of justice, those engaged in conflict "not only know the theoretical recipe for ending it, but require no psychological conversion to put that recipe into effect."[59] Hume does draw on the problematic notion of sympathy, but he does so only for explaining the approbation of justice, as opposed to its original motive. Even if a modicum of good will is presupposed as a cognitive element in the original motive of justice (that is, for correctly identifying one another's needs in order to make the mutual satisfaction of self-interest possible), the degree and quality of the good will presupposed can still be consistent with the subjective circumstances of justice, in that such circumstances involve the lack, not the complete absence, of altruism or good will.

With Habermas, the situation is altogether different. To be sure, he does not explicitly invoke anything like the Humean conception of the subjective circumstances of justice, speaking only of a "motivational weakness" characteristic of post-traditional morality (and in consequence an increased reliance on law).[60] But some such circumstances have to obtain, in addition to the objective circumstances of justice, if justice is to be necessary in the first place. Although Habermas nowhere denies this, there is little doubt that the subjective circumstances of justice, and the motivational problems they present, are somewhat obscured in his account of the type of action that embodies the values of justice and solidarity, namely, communicative action, with practical discourse as its reflexive form.

In defining communicative action as "action when actors are prepared to harmonize their plans of action through internal means, committing

59. Baier, *Progress*, p. 228. See also Stroud, *Hume*, p. 209.

60. See Jürgen Habermas, "Law and Morality," in *The Tanner Lectures on Human Values*, vol. 8, ed. Sterling M. McMurrin (Salt Lake City: University of Utah Press, 1988), pp. 217–279; quotation from p. 245.

themselves to pursuing their goals only on the condition of an agreement—one that already exists or one to be negotiated—about definitions of the situation and prospective outcomes,"[61] Habermas does not make entirely clear what kind of interests each brings to communicative action—self-interest, the interest of others, or the interest of the community. It is not enough to say, as Habermas does, that communicative action occurs when people pursue their goals only on condition of an agreement reached through practical discourse. One also needs to know whether the goals pursued in communicative action are the same mostly self-interested ones pursued in strategic action.[62] Presumably, given that an agreement "allows alter to link his actions to ego's,"[63] the interests pursued in communicative action cease to be either purely self-regarding or purely other-regarding and community-regarding interests. Through communicative action the boundary between self-regarding goals and other-regarding goals is blurred, just as in a society where communicative action is the order of the day, the boundary between self and other, between autonomy and solidarity is blurred. But the point of justice, as Habermas is at pains to show, is precisely to prevent the blurring from becoming complete, especially since complete blurring can easily serve as a pretext for domination. Thus, "nothing better prevents others from perspectivally distorting one's own interests than actual participation."[64] If this is the case, however, then at least part of what each individual brings to communicative action or practical discourse is his own interest strictly conceived (though, needless to say, socially constituted), that is, self-interest of a kind that no one else can be relied on to represent properly.[65] Only for this reason is it important to insist on what Habermas calls principle (U), namely: "For a norm to be valid, the consequences and side effects that its *general* observance can be expected to have for the satisfaction of the particular interests

61. Habermas, *Moral Consciousness,* p. 134.

62. The situation is not clarified but only compounded by the fact that needs and interests, however individualistically pursued, always presuppose some shared social framework of understanding and evaluation. For this fact, as we saw in the last chapter, does not eliminate the conflict of self-interests but only gives such conflict a particular, usually more intractable form. In this discussion, therefore, I disregard this complication. For a forceful yet sympathetic critique of Habermas on related issues, see Thomas McCarthy, *Ideals and Illusions* (Cambridge, Mass.: MIT Press, 1991), chap. 7.

63. Habermas, *Moral Consciousness,* p. 134.

64. Ibid., p. 67.

65. See McCarthy, *Ideals,* p. 210, for a comparison of the place of interests in Habermas's moral philosophy and in Kant's.

of *each* person affected must be such that *all* affected can accept them freely."[66]

Given this understanding of interest as robustly (if not exclusively) individual, it seems wrong, or at least odd, for Habermas to suggest that "it follows *directly* from (U) that anyone who takes part in argumentation of any sort is in principle able to reach the same judgments on the acceptability of norms of action." For (U) implies that "the individual is the last court of appeal for judging what is in his best interest," and there is no guarantee, even in principle, that all the individual courts of appeal will issue the same verdict unless a further condition, one that is not already present in (U), is introduced, namely, a significant degree of consideration for or identification with others. Only under this further condition can practical discourse achieve its aim of serving "as a warrant of insightful will formation, insuring that the interests of individuals are given their due without cutting the social bonds that intersubjectively unite them." Thus the same self-interest that is the last court of appeal is also the self-interest that has to be forfeited or modified in favor of a common interest. After all, "participants in a practical discourse strive to clarify a common interest" instead of trying "to strike a balance between conflicting particular interests."[67] But since the requirement of justice sees to it that only the individuals themselves are entitled to give up their own self-interest, thus ruling out altruism by proxy as it were, each individual will actually do so only if he or she is already morally and epistemically equipped in the right way.

Not surprisingly, Habermas readily acknowledges that something like empathy or altruism is one of the normative presuppositions of practical discourse: "The agreement made possible by discourse depends on two things: the individual's inalienable right to say yes or no and *his overcoming of his egocentric viewpoint.* Without the individual's uninfringeable freedom to respond with a 'yes' or 'no' to criticizable validity claims, consent is merely factual rather than truly universal. Conversely, *without empathetic sensitivity by each person to everyone else, no solution deserving universal consent will result from the deliberation.*"[68] Another way of saying this is that practical discourse is not a purely cognitive undertaking. The cognitive operations required by practical discourse, as Habermas puts it in no un-

66. Habermas, *Moral Consciousness,* p. 120.

67. Ibid., pp. 121 (emphasis added), 67, 202, and 72, respectively.

68. Ibid., p. 202, emphasis added. See also Habermas, *Justification,* pp. 154, 175.

certain terms, are "*internally* linked with motives and emotional dispositions and attitudes like empathy. Where sociocultural distance is a factor, concern for the fate of one's neighbor—who more often than not is anything but close by—is *a necessary prerequisite* for the cognitive operations expected of participants in discourse." It is therefore only the "*integration* of cognitive operations and emotional dispositions and attitudes in justifying and applying norms" that characterizes "the *mature* capacity for moral judgment."[69]

Habermas's account of the relationship between empathy and cognitive insight is a cogent one as far as it goes. The problem is that the empathetic motives are presupposed rather than shown to exist. Indeed, these are precisely the motives the *lack* of which constitutes the subjective circumstances of justice. It is these subjective circumstances that, along with the objective circumstances, give rise to the very need for practical discourse as well as for justice. Yet in Habermas's account, the possibility of practical discourse and of justice is built on normative presuppositions that are incompatible with the subjective circumstances of justice. Holding these normative presuppositions to have significant effect in practical discourse is tantamount to saying that the subjective circumstances of justice do not obtain. In this way, the presence of egoism to a considerable degree (hence the need for justice) and the overcoming of egoism to a considerable degree (hence the possibility of justice) are simultaneously presupposed by practical discourse.

It needs to be emphasized that in Habermas's account the overcoming of egoism must be understood in a sense that goes beyond the mere overcoming of *unenlightened* egoism. For the overcoming of unenlightened egoism is sufficient only for the purpose of compromise. Since practical discourse is oriented toward reaching agreement as distinct from compromise, it depends on the presupposition that egoism can be overcome in a moral rather than a prudential sense. Only under this strong presupposition can it reasonably be expected that "anyone who takes part in argumentation of any sort is in principle able to reach the same judgments on the acceptability of norms of action."[70] But by the same token, such a strong presupposition cancels the subjective circumstances of justice and in so doing removes the need for justice altogether. In the end, Haber-

69. Habermas, *Moral Consciousness,* p. 182, emphasis added except for the word "mature."

70. Ibid., p. 121.

mas's conception of practical discourse, by invoking a degree of empathy sufficient for the moral (as distinct from the prudential) overcoming of egoism, simply presupposes the solution of the most difficult problem that makes justice and practical discourse necessary in the first place.

To find a way out of this paradox, we need to reconstruct Habermas's account by foregrounding the role of socialization and thereby reconceiving the normative presuppositions of practical discourse in an empirical rather than an a priori manner. Habermas provides a clue when he suggests that in order for the normative presuppositions of practical discourse to be actually lived up to, "there has to be a modicum of congruence between morality and the practices of socialization and education . . . In addition, there must be a modicum of fit between morality and sociopolitical institutions."[71] This condition carries the all-important implication that empathy or altruism need not be present *from the start* in the subjective circumstances of justice. Instead, empathy can be presupposed only empirically, as it were, that is, only in the sense that it may be treated as a natural product of socialization and therefore as something that can be reliably predicted of "anyone who has grown up in a reasonably functional family, who has formed his identity in relations of mutual recognition, who maintains himself in the network of reciprocal expectations and perspectives built into the pragmatics of the speech situation and communicative action."[72] In this sense, the capacity for empathy and altruism is presupposed as the culmination of a developmental process rather than as its inception or point of departure.

What is it, then, in the way of motives that can be presupposed as the point of departure? Habermas suggests, following Lawrence Kohlberg, that the empirically available point of departure is a rudimentary form of reciprocity—reciprocity "in the form of authority-governed complementarity and interest-governed symmetry."[73] Clearly, such reciprocity is a far cry from the ideal role-taking that for Habermas characterizes the developed sense of justice. In the process of successful socialization, however, it will develop into higher forms, first "the reciprocity of behavioral expectations that are linked together in social roles," next "the reciprocity of rights and obligations that are linked together in norms,"[74] and finally the reciprocity of respect, the kind of reciprocity required by subject-cen-

71. Ibid., pp. 207–208.

72. Habermas, *Justification*, p. 114.

73. Habermas, *Moral Consciousness*, p. 163.

74. Ibid.

tered justice. While the initial form of reciprocity is on a par with the Humean conception of the objective circumstances of justice, the final form of reciprocity rises to the level of the Habermasian conception of the objective circumstances.

This account of reciprocity can thus accommodate two levels of objective circumstances of justice and two corresponding levels of conceptions of justice. Since these two levels are situated at different points in a process of development, they are not mutually exclusive, as they would have to be if we were forced to choose between them in a nondevelopmental account. Instead, they simply represent two levels of moral achievement. On the one hand, justice as mutual advantage, the initial form of reciprocity that is required by the Humean conception of the objective circumstances of justice, draws on motivational capacities that are already present in the subjective circumstances of justice. Subject-centered justice, on the other hand, the final form of reciprocity that is consonant with the highly demanding Habermasian conception of the objective circumstances of justice, presupposes motivational capacities that are not present in the original subjective circumstances of justice but that can become available in the course of successful socialization.

In this sense, subject-centered justice represents a higher moral achievement than justice as mutual advantage, but for this very reason it is a conception that is much harder to realize. Indeed, being at second remove from the original subjective circumstances of justice, a conception of subject-centered justice depends for its realization on the prior achievement of justice as mutual advantage. The claim I am working toward here, to be fleshed out in later chapters, is that the achievement of justice as mutual advantage may, through its creation of mutual trust and good will, gradually improve the subjective circumstances of justice sufficiently to furnish not only the cognitive insights needed to grasp the Habermasian conception of the objective circumstances of justice but also the moral motives for carrying out a conception of subject-centered justice that is dictated by such circumstances. It is only after this that we may at last find ourselves in subjective circumstances of justice that are on a par with the Habermasian conception of the objective circumstances of justice and that can supply the necessary motives for realizing Habermas's (or any other) conception of subject-centered justice. Such subjective circumstances, unlike the Humean ones, are not given but represent a moral achievement. Given its discontinuity from the original subjective circumstances of justice, a conception of subject-centered justice has no other chance of being realized.

4

The Idea of Voluntary Justice

In the last two chapters I have tried to determine both what kind of justice is needed, given the objective circumstances of justice, and what motives are available for realizing this kind of justice, given the subjective circumstances of justice. Against this background, I mean to rule out, in this chapter and the next, certain kinds of motives or dispositions as either conceptually above or conceptually below the motives compatible with justice. This exercise in deciding what to rule out *at both ends* is necessary because justice is an intermediate virtue, occupying as it does a middle position somewhere between the two poles of altruism or benevolence on the one hand and prudence or rational egoism on the other. It is this broadly intermediate position that makes justice the virtue it is and helps explain its workings and its limits. For this reason it is important, for both normative and explanatory accounts of justice, to find a relatively precise way of distinguishing justice equally from both poles, though in practice theorists of justice may be motivated by their specific concerns to see a greater need for separating justice from one pole than from the other.[1]

In this context, I examine in this brief chapter Schopenhauer's concept of "voluntary justice" *(freie Gerechtigkeit)*. To be sure, the concept is embedded in a rather idiosyncratic philosophical system, one whose central ethical category is compassion and whose central metaphysical category is the distinction between appearance and reality in terms of representation and will. In spite of this, the concept of voluntary justice itself reflects a common view and presents problems that need to be confronted by any psychological account of justice. It is especially helpful to address these

1. See, for example, Brian Barry, *Theories of Justice* (Berkeley: University of California Press, 1989), p. 372; and John Rawls, *Political Liberalism* (New York: Columbia University Press, 1993), pp. 16–17.

problems with reference to Schopenhauer, because in his work the idea of voluntary justice is formulated with exceptional clarity, and as a result the problems, as they exist for any explanatory or psychological account of justice and not merely for Schopenhauer's own, are thrown into sharp relief. Schopenhauer's account is, I believe, largely mistaken, but it is mistaken in ways that remain illuminating. By showing why it is mistaken, I hope to shed some new light on the intermediate status of justice, particularly on the mistake of using other-regarding motives *alone* to explain this status. Along the way I will deal with a number of concepts and issues, most significantly the distinction between the active and passive points of view with regard to justice, a distinction that will also be useful in later chapters.

The Active and Passive Points of View of Justice

While some philosophers, such as Hume with his understanding of justice as a cautious and jealous virtue,[2] are concerned to distinguish justice from other-regarding virtues, Schopenhauer is more interested in explaining how justice is different from disguised egoism or the mere appearance of justice. It is not hard to see why Schopenhauer wants to do this. The concept of justice is so commonly applied, in Schopenhauer's day as in our own, to actions attributable at least in part to motives that have little to do with the intrinsic desire for justice—motives that in one way or another come under the rubrics of seeking reward or avoiding punishment—that those who treat justice as a virtue and virtue as a matter of intention find it necessary to distinguish the intrinsic desire for justice from the mere appearance of justice. The specific concept used by Schopenhauer to mark this distinction is "voluntary justice." By a "just" person Schopenhauer means not merely someone whose actions, however motivated, happen to accord with the requirements of justice but only "the man who voluntarily recognizes and accepts that merely moral boundary between wrong and right, even where no State or other authority guarantees it, and who consequently, according to our explanation, never in the affirmation of his own will goes to the length of denying the will that manifests itself in another individual."[3] For Schopenhauer, the boundary between right and

2. See David Hume, *An Enquiry Concerning the Principles of Morals,* ed. J. B. Schneewind (Indianapolis: Hackett, 1983), p. 21.

3. Arthur Schopenhauer, *The World as Will and Representation,* trans. E. F. J. Payne, vol. 1 (New York: Dover, 1969), p. 370; see also p. 371.

wrong is *merely* moral in the sense that it is action-guiding for the just person regardless of whether it happens to coincide with the boundary between legality and illegality, prudence and imprudence.

This idea of voluntary justice, as distinct from Schopenhauer's presentation of it, may not seem particularly novel. Indeed, it bears a striking resemblance to Kant's notion of internal or ethical lawgiving, whereby a sense of duty is sufficient as a motive for action. As we saw in Chapter 1, however, Kant recognizes no distinct virtuous disposition toward justice but only one general virtuous disposition, though this general disposition covers duties of justice.[4] By contrast, as we also saw in Chapter 1, philosophers such as Jürgen Habermas and John Rawls do identify a distinct disposition toward justice, but it falls short of the Kantian criteria for a perfectly virtuous disposition in that it exhibits a heteronomous concern with reciprocity. What makes Schopenhauer's concept of voluntary justice different is that, as we shall see, he regards it as a disposition that is *both distinct and entirely virtuous.* It is this understanding of the virtue of justice that creates problems of a highly revealing kind. Such an understanding springs in part from a particularly sharp distinction Schopenhauer draws between morality and egoism. Thus, by way of leading up to the most interesting part of Schopenhauer's position, namely, the problems and implications of his concept of voluntary justice, I first need to give a sketch of Schopenhauer's somewhat less interesting account of the distinction between morality and egoism. Fortunately, it is a terminological, if not a substantive, invention of Schopenhauer's that the distinction between morality and egoism, between other-regarding and self-regarding motives, is formulated in terms of the more useful distinction between what he calls the active and the passive points of view of justice (and of morality in general). Even though the substance of this distinction is commonplace, Schopenhauer's formulation of it is novel and illuminating.

A desire for a state of affairs describable as just can issue from two radically different points of view, according to Schopenhauer, because "in determining a maxim for general observance, I must necessarily regard myself not merely as the always active part, but also as the *eventualiter* and sometimes *passive*."[5] The passive point of view is at work when "my *egoism* decides for justice and philanthropy not because it desires to *prac-*

4. See Immanuel Kant, *The Metaphysics of Morals,* trans. Mary Gregor (Cambridge: Cambridge University Press, 1991), p. 210.

5. Arthur Schopenhauer, *On the Basis of Morality,* trans. E. F. J. Payne (Indianapolis: Bobbs-Merrill, 1965), p. 89.

tice these virtues, but because it wants to *experience* them."[6] It is simply the desire to *receive* justice, in the sense of benefiting from it. If justice is apprehended from the passive point of view alone, it is not really justice but egoism, and even when one *practices* justice from this point of view—that is, when one practices justice in order to receive justice or as a condition for receiving justice—one merely elevates egoism to "enlightened" egoism. The passive point of view reduces justice to prudence, turning it into the mere appearance of justice. By contrast, voluntary justice is marked by the active point of view, whereby one's concern in being just is not to cause harm, rather than merely, as is the case with the passive point of view, not to suffer it.[7] For Schopenhauer, voluntary justice is the only motive besides benevolence that possesses genuine moral worth, and as such it is characterized by "the exclusion of that class of motives whereby all human actions are otherwise prompted, namely, those of *self-interest* in the widest sense of the term."[8] The crucial stipulation here is "in the widest sense of the term," and it is this stipulation that gives Schopenhauer's distinction between voluntary justice and the mere appearance of justice an unusual sharpness and his idea of egoism a particular stringency.

By egoism "in the widest sense of the term," Schopenhauer means "everything done with respect to reward or punishment." Such actions necessarily involve an "egoistic transaction"—the display of virtue in return for reward or avoidance of punishment—and are totally devoid of moral value even when they produce, as they often do, socially desirable consequences.[9] By this standard, a great deal of what ordinarily passes for justice is merely disguised or enlightened egoism.[10] "For example," he writes, "if a man is firmly persuaded that every good deed is repaid to him a hundredfold in a future life, then such a conviction is valid and effective in precisely the same way as a safe bill of exchange at a very long date, and he can *give from egoism* just as, from another point of view, he would *take from egoism*." What makes an act of giving a moral act, on this view, is not

6. Ibid.; see also p. 204, and Schopenhauer, *World*, pp. 345–346.

7. See Schopenhauer, *World*, pp. 345–346.

8. Schopenhauer, *On the Basis of Morality*, p. 139; see also p. 140. I use the more common term "benevolence" instead of "philanthropy" or "loving-kindness." What is important for my purposes is the area of meaning such terms share rather than any subtle differences among them. D. W. Hamlyn, for one, uses the term "benevolence" interchangeably with "philanthropy" in his *Schopenhauer* (London: Routledge & Kegan Paul, 1980), pp. 134–135.

9. Schopenhauer, *On the Basis of Morality*, p. 56; see also pp. 66, 142.

10. See ibid., pp. 122, 125, 152.

the benefit to the recipient but the motive from which it issues. Thus, giving need not be an act of justice or benevolence, and when an act of giving is performed from self-regarding motives, it is no different from taking. The resulting paradox—that one can, as Schopenhauer memorably put it, "give from egoism"—divides moralists into those purists for whom it drastically narrows the range of moral goodness and those realists for whom it supplies the recipe for morality, less stringently conceived, and for moral education.[11]

That recipe, Schopenhauer suggests, is nowhere more effectively put to work than in what on a less stringent view would count as one of the great sources of moral goodness, namely, Christianity. What sets Christianity apart from unmediated egoism is its farsightedness in delaying the return for good deeds to a future life and, owing to this farsightedness, its effectiveness in inducing apparently moral behavior and sustaining it over time, indeed, over a lifetime. This may be a reason for attaching instrumental value to the Christian otherworldly realm as the most effective, and the best-disguised, locus of "egoistic transaction." Yet, when it comes to a person's moral worth, "it is immaterial . . . whether he makes donations to the destitute, firmly persuaded that he will receive everything back tenfold in a future life, or spends the same sum on improving an estate that will bear interest, late certainly, but all the more secure and substantial . . . For these are *anxious only about themselves, about their egoism*."[12] If such a view, with its disconcertingly hard-and-fast line between what is morally commendable and what is at best morally indifferent though practically useful, is uncongenial to the moral and intellectual temper of our day (for reasons we need not go into here), perhaps even more so is the understanding of human nature that underlies it. For Schopenhauer, "there are generally only *three fundamental incentives* of human actions, and all possible motives operate solely through their stimulation": these are *egoism,* which "desires one's own weal," *malice,* which "desires another's woe," and *compassion,* which "desires another's weal"—in each case for its own sake. With this understanding of human motivation, Schopenhauer is able to give a psychological account of the origin of justice and injustice in terms of one or another of the three fundamental incentives. What is responsible for injustice is either egoism or malice; what is responsible for the appearance of justice is egoism; and what is responsible for voluntary justice is

11. Schopenhauer, *World,* p. 295, emphasis added.
12. Ibid., pp. 368–369, emphasis added.

compassion, and compassion alone. As far as the last is concerned, "the effect of compassion is that it opposes and impedes those sufferings which I intend to cause to others by my inherent antimoral forces . . . Thus there arises . . . the maxim, *Neminem laede,* i.e., the fundamental principle of *justice.* Only here does this virtue have its origin—genuine, purely moral, and free from all admixture—and nowhere else, since then it would have to rest on egoism."[13]

Justice, Benevolence, and Degrees of Compassion

If compassion is the sole psychological origin of voluntary justice, as Schopenhauer holds, how is one to distinguish voluntary justice from the higher virtue of benevolence? According to Schopenhauer, what sets the two virtues apart and makes benevolence a nobler virtue is only the *degree* of compassion involved. Thus, "there are two clearly separate degrees wherein another's suffering can directly become my motive, in other words, can determine me to do or omit to do something. In the first degree, by counteracting egoistic and malicious motives, compassion prevents me from causing suffering to another and hence from becoming myself the cause of another's pain, and thus from bringing about something that does not yet exist. In the second place, there is the higher degree where compassion works positively and incites me to active help."[14] This is highly questionable. To be sure, people may differ in their capacity for compassion, but there is little evidence to suggest that such difference takes the form of the neat compartmentalization of compassion into two degrees, still less two exact degrees corresponding to justice and benevolence, respectively. It is only because Schopenhauer treats voluntary justice as distinct from egoism on one side and from benevolence on the other—an entirely valid move in itself—and because moreover he treats compassion as the only motive of genuine moral worth—a rather questionable move—that he has to postulate something like compassion of "the first degree" in order to account for voluntary justice as he defines it. The result is a philosophical fiction: a kind of person whose disposition is "susceptible to compassion up to that degree" which corresponds exactly to justice[15]—neither more nor less.

13. Schopenhauer, *On the Basis of Morality,* pp. 145, 149.

14. Ibid., p. 148; see also pp. 149, 163, 192.

15. Ibid., p. 149.

I am not denying, of course, that there are those whose general tendency is to act justly but neither more nor less. I am only denying that such a tendency can be plausibly explained in terms of a fixed degree of compassion. In other words, I am saying, on the one hand, that a relatively fixed tendency to act justly—neither more nor less—may be real, and yet a fixed degree of compassion corresponding to and accounting for it is a philosophical fiction.[16] On the other hand, I am not ruling out the possibility that there are people whose tendency to act justly is attributable entirely to compassion, *as long as* it is not claimed that the compassion at work is of such a degree that it prevents those possessing it from doing more than justice requires. Where compassion *alone* is the source of moral conduct—this is how Schopenhauer understands voluntary justice as well as benevolence—there can be no hard-and-fast line between "injuring no one" (Schopenhauer's principle of justice) and "helping everyone as much as one can" (Schopenhauer's principle of benevolence).[17] For when compassion alone is the motive, the only relevant factor is the well-being (especially the lack of suffering) of others, and therefore what compassion enjoins or prompts is simply the adoption of sufficient means to that end, such that any distinction concerning means (that is, between our refraining from causing suffering and our actively seeking to alleviate it) is at best a matter of secondary significance. It is only when we are preoccupied with the question (irrelevant from the point of view of compassion alone) of who is the cause of another's suffering, with "keeping [ourselves] free from the self-reproach of being the cause of another's suffering"—in other words, with our moral responsibility and the peace of our conscience, and thus, in the final analysis, *with ourselves*—that we will be prepared not to cause suffering (in accordance with the principle of justice) but, where we ourselves are not causally responsible, will not be motivated to seek actively to alleviate it (in accordance with the principle of benevolence). Although there may be good political or even moral grounds for drawing a distinction between justice and benevolence, *compassion by itself is no re-*

16. The problems we encounter in Schopenhauer's moral-psychological account of justice and benevolence in terms of two degrees of compassion are confirmed, indeed magnified, in his metaphysical account of ethics. I have omitted discussion of this so as not to diffuse the focus of this chapter. Nevertheless, Schopenhauer's metaphysical account of ethics does bear on some of the issues treated in this chapter, if only tangentially. For further discussion, see the second half of my "Schopenhauer on Voluntary Justice," *History of Philosophy Quarterly* 15 (1998): 227–244, of which an earlier version of this chapter makes up the first half.

17. See Schopenhauer, *On the Basis of Morality*, p. 69.

specter of such a distinction. As far as individual motivation is concerned, whether one draws such a distinction is a test of whether one is *entirely* motivated by compassion. Voluntary justice, based as it is on this distinction, is not entirely motivated by compassion in at least this sense: that its propensity to stop short of benevolence is due not to compassion but rather to the failure of one's compassion to completely "[counteract] egoistic . . . motives."[18]

The upshot of this is that the idea of voluntary justice loses the very basis of its distinctness. To see why, it is worth reminding ourselves that voluntary justice is meant to be distinct both from justice less strictly conceived (that is, the performance of just actions from motives that may involve some degree of egoism) and from the higher virtue of benevolence. It is supposedly distinct from justice less strictly conceived in that it is motivated entirely by compassion, whereas justice in a less strict sense may flow from prudence or at best from a mixture of compassion and prudence. It is supposedly distinct from benevolence in that, though entirely motivated by compassion, it is nevertheless so motivated to a lesser degree than is the case with benevolence. Now, if compassion itself does not admit of division into neat degrees that happen to correspond to justice and benevolence, it is clear that one of these two distinctions—either the distinction between voluntary justice and justice less strictly conceived, or the distinction between voluntary justice and benevolence—has to be abandoned. If, on the one hand, we want to maintain, with Schopenhauer, that compassion alone is the motive of voluntary justice, we will have to give up the distinction between voluntary justice and benevolence, since compassion by itself knows no boundary between them. If, on the other hand, we want to retain some distinction between voluntary justice and benevolence, we will have to give up trying to define both in terms of compassion (alone), again because compassion by itself does not draw a line between justice and benevolence. Once we give up doing that, however, we will be left with no grounds for distinguishing between voluntary justice and justice in a less strict sense. Recall that what separates voluntary justice from nonvoluntary justice, for Schopenhauer, is the purity of compassion; and so in the absence of such purity, voluntary justice can no longer be sharply distinguished from nonvoluntary justice, and we are left instead with a broader and less strict concept of justice that is no longer definable in terms of a single motive such as compassion.

18. Ibid., pp. 150, 148.

No matter which of the two distinctions is given up, there can be no such thing as a distinct concept of voluntary justice characterized by a purely other-regarding motive such as compassion. Justice is either more than voluntary justice or less than voluntary justice. When, on the one hand, it is motivated by compassion alone, justice reaches beyond voluntary justice and merges with benevolence. If, on the other hand, it is not motivated by compassion alone, justice falls short of voluntary justice (by Schopenhauer's own standards). It is only in the latter case that justice is a *distinct* virtue or disposition, and therefore, to account for justice as a distinct virtue or disposition, we have to identify motives other than, or at least in addition to, compassion in particular and other-regarding motives in general.[19]

19. Schopenhauer himself offers hints in this direction; see, for example, ibid., p. 143, and *World*, p. 371.

5

The Moral Reach of Rational Egoism

If my aim in the last chapter was to rule out a certain motive (voluntary justice) as conceptually above justice, my objective in this chapter is to rule out another motive (rational egoism) as conceptually below justice. I will try to determine whether the rational component of rational egoism, as distinct from rationality as such, is sufficient to generate a disposition toward justice.[1] I argue that rational egoism is a contingent combination of given (and hence fluctuating) self-interests and instrumental rationality, and that therefore it is impossible to construct a general, a priori model of rational egoism whose recommendations *regarding the rational egoist's own conduct* accord with principles of justice. I go on to show, however, that the rational egoist, qua *rational* egoist, is in principle capable of recommending social norms that transcend his own egoistic motives, even though, qua rational *egoist,* he may seek to free-ride with regard to these very norms. The rational egoist is thus in the paradoxical position of being able to invent a socially useful morality that he is personally unwilling to follow from his self-interested point of view. Since rational egoism is, in this sense, *motivationally* incompatible with the moral point of view of justice, I finally argue, with particular reference to Hume, that rational egoism can be accommodated within a conception of justice only by limiting its role, more strictly than Hume seems to do, to the initial establishment of just institutions. Only in this way, I intend to show, can we avoid landing ourselves with the false problem of how to bridge the logically unbridgeable *motivational* gap between rational egoism and justice.

1. My concern is thus different from that of those who debate the advantages (rationality) or disadvantages (irrationality) of altruistic and self-interested behavior, for example, Robert H. Frank, *Passions within Reason* (New York: W. W. Norton, 1988).

Justice and the Insufficiency of Rational Egoism

There are two different ways in which one can be said to be reluctant to practice justice—or to practice justice with reluctance. In the first type of case, one may have a genuine desire to practice justice, to do so *as much as* possible, and yet still feel a certain reluctance on account of having to part with whatever self-interest, particularly if it is considerable, one must give up in order to be just. What is important about this kind of reluctance is that it does not translate into the desire to practice justice as little as possible. This is because the reluctance is a function not of a principled egoism but only of a residual egoism on the part of those who genuinely try to overcome their egoism for the sake of justice and yet who may not entirely succeed either in performing the actions required by justice or in performing them always with the right attitude. It is this desire and effort to overcome one's egoism in order to be just to others that makes the attitude in question what it is, namely, a reluctant *virtue,* a virtue despite its reluctance.[2]

The case is totally different with someone who is unwilling to practice justice *in principle.* The principle is usually some form of *rational egoism,* where "egoism" denotes the nature and range of the ends pursued and "rational" indicates the manner in which the ends are to be pursued. We may thus for convenience speak of rational egoism as consisting of a teleological component (ends), which is egoistic, and a rational component (means). Rationality is sometimes defined as the use of efficient means for the pursuit of a given end, whatever the end may be.[3] While this is obviously too narrow an understanding of rationality as a whole, it serves well as a characterization of instrumental rationality, of which self-interested rationality (or rational egoism) is a species. What makes rational egoism a species of instrumental rationality is that in it the range of ends is not only given but also restricted to a particular set of ends, namely, the set of self-interested ends. It is true by definition that instrumental rationality as such is marked by the givenness of the ends pursued, whether a given end is

2. On the idea of justice as a reluctant virtue, see, for example, J. R. Lucas, *On Justice* (Oxford: Clarendon Press, 1980), pp. 3–4; and of course David Hume's description of justice as a cautious and jealous virtue, in *An Enquiry Concerning the Principles of Morals,* ed. J. B. Schneewind (Indianapolis: Hackett, 1983), p. 21.

3. See, for instance, John C. Harsanyi, *Rational Behavior and Bargaining Equilibrium in Games and Social Situations* (Cambridge: Cambridge University Press, 1977), p. 8. Harsanyi describes this as a useful commonsense concept of rationality.

self-regarding or other-regarding. But in rational egoism the restriction of given ends to self-interested ones leads to a further, important sense in which the ends pursued are *necessarily* given and hence the rationality involved is *necessarily* instrumental.

The ends that make up the teleological component of rational egoism are given, and necessarily so, in the sense that the self-interested character of one's ends is not open to question by the rational component of rational egoism. In other words, the rational component of rational egoism does not raise the question whether one *ought* to be self-interested, or whether it is *right* to be self-interested. Raising this kind of question would presuppose a point of view outside of egoism itself. It is in this sense, too, that the rational component of rational egoism necessarily pertains to means but not ends. It is of course possible for a rational egoist to call into question one or more of the specific ends that happen to make up the content of her egoism. But as long as one remains a rational *egoist,* such questioning can take place only within a framework of more general ends, themselves necessarily both given and self-regarding.

Thus, *the instrumental character of rational egoism's rational component goes hand in hand with the givenness of its teleological component.* These two features constitute the limits within which, and only within which, the rational component of rational egoism can make a rational egoist superior to an irrational or nonrational one. Given these limits, we cannot know a priori, simply by analyzing the logical properties of rationality, what kind of behavior rational egoism will recommend. The instrumental character of rational egoism's rational component makes that component itself incapable of recommending any course of action in the absence of information regarding the ends that make up rational egoism's teleological component.

The teleological component of rational egoism, in turn, is always already given, not only in the logical sense just described but also in a further, empirical sense, namely, that one's self-interests, along with one's understanding thereof, are always constituted in specific cultural and historical circumstances. The rational egoist may be able to question whether it is in his self-interest to pursue a subset of the self-interests he has formed in those empirical circumstances, but he can do so only on the basis of other, (for the time being) unquestioned self-interests also formed in such circumstances. And there is no telling in advance which of his given interests a rational egoist will question and which other given interests he will use as a basis for such questioning. The empirical givenness of interests is true, of course, of all interests, including other-regarding ones. But moral reasoning, though itself without an Archimedean point outside of interests, is an attempt to challenge this givenness, whereas rational egoism, with its necessarily instrumental character, is not. It is the rational egoist's unchallenging acceptance of the empirical givenness of (at least some of) his self-interests, over and above the logical givenness of his self-interests, that makes rational egoism a contingent combination of *self-regarding* ends, unknowable in advance, and *rational* means.

This fact has important implications for the relationship between rational egoism and justice. Since rational egoism is a contingent combination of self-regarding ends and rational means, it is contingent whether any particular such combination will recommend a course of action that coincides with what justice, with its appeal to partly *other-regarding* considerations, enjoins. It is thus impossible to construct a general, a priori model of rational egoism whose recommendations will accord with principles of justice, although it may be possible to construct a particular such model by introducing specific empirical assumptions regarding the teleological component of rational egoism and the circumstances in which rational egoism operates. Even if one succeeds in constructing a model of the latter kind, such a model cannot fit all rational egoists but only a subset of rational egoists of whom the specific empirical assumptions happen to hold.[4] In general, rational egoism cannot be counted on to lead to just behavior, and it does so, if at all, only through coincidence.

There are two ways in which the potential empirical coincidence between the recommendations of rational egoism and of justice can fail to occur. In the first place, the given ends that happen to make up the teleological component of rational egoism may be such that the most efficient means of pursuing them does not consist in a course of action that is in keeping with the requirements of justice. In the second place, there may simply not be enough instrumental rationality at work (for a particular person in a particular case) to produce a coincidence of justice and rational egoism, if we suppose that the given ends themselves do not necessarily rule out such coincidence. Clearly, only the first type of case proves the

4. Epicureanism would seem to come closest to this model of rational egoism. Given the Epicurean egoist's preferences for long-term pleasures over short-term ones, and "higher" pleasures over "lower" ones, he seems to have as good a chance as any rational egoist of developing a disposition toward justice. But it cannot be assumed that the Epicurean egoist's preferences, however "intrinsically" rational they may seem, can be generalized to cover all rational egoists.

logical insufficiency of rational egoism to recommend, on a more regular and predictable basis than mere coincidence, courses of action that are in keeping with the requirements of justice. If one were to consider rational egoism logically sufficient in this sense, one would have to treat the second type of case as representing the only way in which rational egoism can fail to recommend just behavior on a regular basis. What I hope to have shown is that the first type of case is also possible. It is this type of case that rules out *in principle* any similarity between the recommendations of rational egoism and of justice that is more than mere coincidence.

There is thus no instrumentally rational alternative to the normative route to justice. Although we cannot categorically rule out the possibility of coincidence between rational egoism and justice (given the empirical and contingent character of the teleological component of rational egoism), we should nonetheless be able to say, on the kinds of grounds I have given, that there is always the higher probability of a gap between the recommendations of rational egoism and of justice. No amount of *instrumental* rationality can serve to bridge this gap unless it is placed at the service of ends that rise above egoism, in which case the rationality in question is no longer part of rational *egoism*. To the extent, then, that we take the instrumentally rational route to justice, we will have a *principled* reluctance to practice justice, that is, a reluctance to practice justice beyond the extent required for the instrumentally rational pursuit of self-interest even if that extent falls short of justice. The reluctance is "principled" in the sense that if and when the rational egoist fails to practice justice, she, unlike the just person who may also from time to time fail to be just, does so not in spite of her intention but because of it. This is what happens whenever a complete coincidence between the recommendations of rational egoism and of justice does not materialize. We do not know on purely logical grounds how likely the recommendations of rational egoism are to coincide with those of justice. But we do know on logical grounds *the separateness of those recommendations;* if they turn out to be the same, it must be a matter of sheer coincidence.

Given this separateness, it will be perfectly sensible for a rational egoist to ask himself, "Why be moral?" or "Why be just?" and equally sensible (and not unlikely) to conclude, applying instrumental rationality to the pursuit of his given interests, that there is no reason to be moral or just—strictly speaking, to present the appearance of being such—all the time. For a rational egoist will be moral or just only to the extent, or with the frequency, dictated by the instrumentally rational pursuit of self-interest, and it is entirely possible that the extent or frequency in question will not happen to be "all the time." In other words, if one does not act morally for moral reasons, as distinct from self-interested ones, the chances are that one will act morally, if at all, only part of the time. But justice that is practiced with such logical and empirical uncertainty ceases to be justice, because justice, as a property of social institutions, must have a binding or obligatory character that does not fluctuate with self-interest, and, as a personal disposition, must consist in a motivation or a range of motivations that acknowledges and reflects this binding character. There is thus a built-in gap between justice and rational egoism, between the binding character of justice and the inability of rational egoism to create the right kind of motivation for it. The gap is not merely the obvious one between justice and egoism but the much more interesting one between justice and *rational* egoism.

The Paradox of Rational Egoism

What I hope to have shown so far is that rational egoism cannot be relied on to recommend *to the rational egoist herself* courses of action that accord with justice. In other words, the rational egoist has no principled reasons, as opposed to merely contingent ones, to be just on a regular basis. This does not mean, however, that rational egoism brings us no closer to justice than simple egoism does. Rational egoism, though incapable of generating a stable disposition toward justice, is nevertheless quite capable of producing a desire for the establishment of just institutions. For such a desire can be the entirely self-interested desire to benefit from such institutions rather than to contribute to them—in other words, the desire for others rather than oneself to be just. On the one hand, being rational, the rational egoist perceives both the benefits and costs of justice, and she perceives the latter as vastly outweighed by the former. On the other hand, being a rational *egoist,* she wants as much as possible to enjoy the benefits and avoid the costs, in the knowledge that what costs she succeeds in avoiding will be borne by others.

Even this self-interested, because one-sided, desire only for the benefits of justice and hence only for others to be just is a move in the direction of justice. The rational egoist, unlike an irrational or nonrational one, should have no difficulty seeing the point of justice. As long as one is rational, being self-interested does not prevent one from understanding that justice is necessary for the mutual satisfaction of self-interests and that justice is possible only if people are generally willing to sacrifice part of their self-interest. The self-interested point of view is thus quite sufficient for apprehending the benefits and costs of justice, however insufficient it is for producing the willingness to bear the costs. There is nothing about justice one can *see* from the moral point of view which one cannot *see* from the purely self-interested point of view.[5] Indeed, it is only because of this that the self-interested point of view of justice is still *a* point of view of justice rather than a contradiction in terms.

In this light, the gap between rational egoism and justice—or between the self-interested and the moral points of view of justice—does not seem *entirely* unbridgeable. Because the rational egoist sees the point of justice, he must also be able to see the point of the enforcement of justice. *In an impersonal sense,* the rational egoist, generalizing from his own desire to free-ride, and in the absence of the improbable knowledge that potential free-riders like himself are too few to undermine the working of just institutions, should be the first to recommend the enforcement of justice. Since under the rule of law such enforcement is supposed to be uniform and impersonal, the rational egoist's recommendation has to extend to himself. Therefore, *in a personal sense,* the rational egoist, eager as he is to avoid the costs of justice while enjoying its benefits, has no principled argument against the enforcement of justice even against himself. This cognitive achievement of rational egoism is well summed up by Schopenhauer when he remarks that "this egoism well understands itself, proceeds methodically, and goes from the one-sided to the universal point of view, and thus by summation is the common egoism of all." The outcome of this rational procedure is the recommendation that "the common egoism of all" be enforced by a common agency for all, namely, the state, which is "set up on the correct assumption that pure morality, i.e., right conduct from moral grounds, is not to be expected; otherwise it itself would be superfluous."[6] Thus, although rational egoism does not directly or by itself produce conformity to norms of justice, it is nevertheless equipped with enough self-understanding to establish an agency that will be able to produce such conformity.

The paradox of the rational egoist is that, being a rational *egoist,* he does

5. It is in something like this sense that Hume finds self-interest a sufficient (original) motive for the establishment of justice. See David Hume, *A Treatise of Human Nature,* ed. L. A. Selby-Bigge, 2nd ed., ed. P. H. Nidditch (Oxford: Clarendon Press, 1978), p. 499.

6. Arthur Schopenhauer, *The World as Will and Representation,* trans. E. F. J. Payne, vol. 1 (New York: Dover, 1969), p. 345.

not have a stable disposition toward justice, while, being a *rational* egoist, he must desire the establishment of an enforcement agency to counteract precisely the lack of that disposition. From the point of view of the rational egoist, then, the enforcement agency is both against himself and for himself, and simultaneously so. It is only through this paradox—through the invention of a double-edged agency for and against each rational egoist—that rational egoism is able to complete itself, to have the purposes of each rational egoist served by "the common [rational] egoism of all" rather than defeated by the isolated, hence no longer completely rational, rational egoism of each. In this paradox lies the significance, and the considerable (what one might call quasi-moral) achievement, of the rational component of rational egoism. The rational egoist's paradoxical situation takes him a long way toward justice—both in his capacity as a potential legislator and in his capacity as a member of society subject to such legislation. As the former, he is not in principle incapable of drawing up laws that benefit everyone, not just himself. As the latter, he can be a wholehearted supporter of such laws and at least a comprehending recipient of penalties should he be caught free-riding. Indeed, it is in the rational egoist that the enforcement of justice finds its most fitting object, since the just person needs no enforcement against him while an irrational or nonrational egoist is unable even to identify with the purpose of the law.

The gap between rational egoism and justice can be closed further still. For it will be quite rational for an egoist to extrapolate from the need for the social enforcement of justice to the desirability of the *social* inculcation of morality (as distinct from the rational egoist's own personal cultivation of morality). After all, the social inculcation of morality, where successful, promotes justice by making its enforcement, and the material and psychological costs of such enforcement, unnecessary in the first place. The rational egoist is quite capable, in Nietzsche's words, of "recommend[ing] altruism *for the sake of its utility*."[7] Although this altruism is recommended

7. Friedrich Nietzsche, *The Gay Science*, trans. Walter Kaufmann (New York: Random House, 1974), 21. Nietzsche captures particularly well the egoism that is implied by the preaching of morality. "A man's virtues are called *good*," according to Nietzsche, "depending on their probable consequences not for him but for us and society: the praise of virtues has always been far from 'selfless,' far from 'unegoistic' . . . The 'neighbor' praises selflessness *because it brings him advantages*. If the neighbor himself were 'selfless' in his thinking, he would repudiate this diminution of strength, this mutilation for *his* benefit; he would work against the development of such inclinations, and above all he would manifest his selflessness by *not* calling it *good!* . . . [T]he *motives* of this morality stand opposed to its *principle*. What this morality considers its proof is refuted by its criterion of what is moral. In order not to

from the self-interested point of view, its benefits extend, by virtue of its impersonal character, beyond the rational egoist to members of society in general. By the same token, the rational egoist has no principled reason to exempt himself from the *costs* of such altruism, having at least to present the appearance of following its precepts. Just as in the case of law, so in the case of morality, the rational egoist, qua *rational* egoist, is perfectly capable of recommending social norms that transcend his egoistic motives, even as he seeks to free-ride with regard to both law and morality. We may thus speak of the (hypothetical) invention of a publicly useful morality from the self-interested point of view.

It is only in this paradoxical fashion that the rational egoist can approach justice. Recommending justice and in so doing subjecting himself to its force, the rational egoist nevertheless has no intention of personally practicing it except when doing so is expedient or unavoidable. What underlies this paradox is the fact that the rational egoist's deliberations *about* morality—that is, about its utility—are completely devoid of moral (that is, other-regarding) considerations. Because of his inability to introduce such considerations (for the ability to do so goes beyond rational egoism), the rational egoist can bridge the gap between rational egoism and justice only in terms of his recommendations but not in terms of his own conduct and motivation. As far as the latter is concerned, the gap between rational egoism and justice is logically unbridgeable. I have already tried to show why this is the case. To see a further sense in which this is the case, it is instructive to reflect on a famous passage in Hume's *Treatise*.

Hume on Two Stages of Justice

Hume writes: "*Self-interest* is the original Motive to the *Establishment* of Justice: but a Sympathy with *public* Interest is the Source of the *moral* Approbation, which attends that Virtue. This latter Principle of Sympathy is too weak to controul our Passions; but has sufficient Force to influence our Taste, and give us the Sentiments of Approbation or Blame."[8] This

---

contravene its own morality, the demand 'You shall renounce yourself and sacrifice yourself' could be laid down only by those who thus renounced their own advantage and perhaps brought about their own destruction through the demanded sacrifice of individuals. But as soon as the neighbor (or society) recommends altruism *for the sake of its utility*, it applies the contradictory principle. 'You shall seek your advantage even at the expense of everything else'—and thus one preaches, in the same breath, a 'Thou shalt' and 'Thou shalt not.'"

8. Hume, *Treatise*, p. 670. This is an alternative version to the one on pp. 499–500.

picture of justice is more complicated than the one I have sketched so far. On the one hand, Hume seems to be saying (to put it partly in the terms I am using) that self-interest, obviously of the rational sort, is sufficient to allow one to imagine the benefits of just institutions and is hence a sufficient motive for the establishment of such institutions. This seems a very similar point to the one I have made about how far rational egoism can take us in the direction of justice. On the other hand, Hume is no longer speaking of rational egoism when he goes on to say that "sympathy with public interest" is what causes people *to value* justice and thereby turns justice into a *moral* virtue. Interestingly, Hume seems to be saying these two things about the *same* community of (in this regard) like-minded persons and by implication about each individual member of that community. The question thus arises as to how these things can be true of the same community or of the same individual if the first is meant to apply to rational egoists and the second clearly is not.

The best way of escaping this apparent contradiction, in my view, is to give Hume's passage what may be called a *diachronic* reading. In such a reading, we treat the self-regarding origin of justice and the subsequent other-regarding approbation of justice as two phases in the evolution of justice: people will come to approach justice in the spirit of the second phase only after the first phase has been accomplished and then, as Nietzsche would say, "forgotten."[9] This kind of reading finds support in an important passage (among others) in which Hume says that once the rules of justice are established and found to be in the public interest, "the sense of morality in the observance of these rules follows *naturally*, and of itself."[10] Such a reading accords, moreover, with Hume's conception of the subjective circumstances of justice. Given that sympathy with the public interest or the interest of others is already in short supply in the circumstances of justice—indeed, it is this very shortage that in large part makes justice necessary in the first place—it cannot be invoked as a motive that will help make justice possible. It thus makes perfect sense for Hume to distinguish the sympathy-engendered, moral approbation of justice from the original, self-interested motive of justice and to exclude sympathy from being a major motive in the original establishment of justice. Yet, Hume suggests, it is quite possible for sympathy to play a significant role at a later stage in the

9. See Friedrich Nietzsche, *Human, All Too Human*, trans. R. J. Hollingdale, 2 vols. in 1 (Cambridge: Cambridge University Press, 1986), 1:92.

10. Hume, *Treatise*, p. 533.

development of the motives of justice. He is thus raising the possibility of a developmental dimension to the sentiment of justice. I shall explore this dimension in detail in later chapters, in connection with a similar insight found in Nietzsche and Rawls.

If we bracket, for now, the developmental dimension of justice and focus instead on its culmination in the (current) moral approbation of justice, we will be offering a *synchronic* reading of Hume's passage. In this synchronic reading, justice is valued *from the moral point of view,* that is, through sympathy with the public interest. But such a point of view is sufficient, cautions Hume, only to produce a way of apprehending justice and feeling about justice—as something of moral value—but not to bring about action in keeping with it. As Hume put it (in the passage cited at the beginning of this section), the "Principle of Sympathy is too weak to controul our Passions; but has sufficient Force to influence our Taste, and give us the Sentiments of Approbation or Blame." This seems to leave room, within the synchronic account, for the *continuing* role of self-interest as the motive of justice, that is, as the *current* motive of justice.

Such a synchronic reading is not incompatible with Hume's conception of the subjective circumstances of justice, since Hume invokes sympathy, in this synchronic account, not as a sufficient motive of justice but only as the cause of the moral approval of justice. According to this reading, even *after* justice is instituted, the "original Motive to the *Establishment* of Justice" remains responsible for the acts of justice that a moral agent or a moral community is capable of performing. In other words, the point of view from which justice is *practiced* remains self-interested, just as the point of view from which justice was originally instituted was self-interested. Yet the same moral agents who are capable of practicing justice only from the self-interested point of view are quite capable of *apprehending* justice from the moral point of view—through "Sympathy with *public* Interest"—and it is from the latter point of view that they attach moral value to justice.

In his second *Enquiry,* Hume takes the further step of treating sympathy—now renamed the "sentiment of humanity," a phrase without the original term's psychological baggage—as a major *motive* of justice and not merely, as in the *Treatise,* as a point of view from which justice is apprehended and approved. This seems a perfectly logical step to take, inasmuch as the moral approbation of justice already implies the desire to be just for moral reasons, even if, given the subjective circumstances of justice, this desire may not always be strong enough to counteract other desires that happen to stand in the way of just conduct. Hume takes this step in the *Enquiry,* however, without modifying his original idea, first developed in the *Treatise,* of what constitutes the motive for the establishment of justice. The result is the accentuation of a problem that already exists in that famous passage in the *Treatise,* namely, the gap between (what appear to be) two incompatible sets of motives that are simultaneously in play.

It seems to be this understanding of justice that draws Alasdair MacIntyre's criticism (in the context of his account of the difficulties besetting an emotivist theory of morality). According to MacIntyre, commenting on the second *Enquiry,* "Hume's invocation of sympathy is an invention intended to bridge the gap between any set of reasons which could support unconditional adherence to general and unconditional rules and any set of reasons for action or judgment which could derive from our particular, fluctuating, circumstance-governed desires, emotions and interests . . . But the gap is logically unbridgable [sic], and 'sympathy' as used by Hume . . . is the name of a philosophical fiction."[11] Put another way, the gap is between justice as the principled adherence to unconditional norms and rational egoism as a contingent combination of given ends and rational means that bears only an expedient relationship to any set of such norms. When MacIntyre describes this gap as *logically* unbridgeable, he means, presumably, that it is logically impossible for the same person to be a rational egoist *and* a just person—that it is logically impossible for a rational egoist, short of giving up rational egoism, *also* to acquire the motivations or reasons for action characteristic of a just person. The rational egoist could of course act *as if* he possessed such motivations, but that would be due to the threat of legal sanctions rather than sympathy.

It is presumably in this sense that MacIntyre calls Hume's concept of sympathy a philosophical fiction. Not that sympathy (in Hume's sense) does not exist, but it cannot possibly do the job it is supposed to do, that is, to bridge the gap between two incompatible sets of motivations or reasons for action. Indeed, we can go further and argue that the invocation of sympathy to bridge this gap changes the very nature of the gap itself and is inconsistent with there being such a gap at all. If an agent for whom the gap is supposed to exist can be moved by sympathy to attach moral value

11. Alasdair MacIntyre, *After Virtue,* 2nd ed. (Notre Dame, Ind.: University of Notre Dame Press, 1984), p. 49; see also pp. 229–230. Needless to say, by the time Hume wrote the second *Enquiry,* he had dropped the term, perhaps even the concept, of sympathy, in favor of the less problematic sentiment of "humanity" (*Enquiry,* p. 43n). But the validity or otherwise of MacIntyre's criticism is not affected by this change.

to justice and consequently to acquire the desire to be just for moral reasons, then he is simply no longer a rational egoist but a just person. And if he is no longer a rational egoist, there is, for him, no gap to bridge between his reasons for action and the rational egoist's; just as, conversely, there is, for the rational egoist, no gap to bridge between her reasons for action and the just person's. Thus, to invoke sympathy to bridge such a gap is in effect to deny that *this* kind of gap exists at all. This is not to say that a just person cannot experience a gap between his different reasons for action, but since he cannot simultaneously be a rational egoist and a just person, the gap must be of a different kind.

This calls for a major revision of the synchronic account of justice. As soon as we bring the moral approbation of justice into the picture, as Hume does, we must accept that selfishness exists no longer as a full-fledged desire, in the form of rational egoism, but only as an impediment, in the form of what Hume calls the "passions," to the desire to be just. For the moral approbation of justice entails the desire to be just for moral reasons (that is, out of sympathy with the public interest), and if one desires, with whatever degree of practical efficacy, to be just for moral reasons, then one is no longer a rational egoist. Even when an agent who approves of justice nevertheless omits from time to time to act in accordance with justice, the omission has the character, psychologically and otherwise, of failure to be just rather than success in being egoistic. If we are to describe this omission in terms of a gap, it will no longer be the gap between the self-regarding motive of justice and the other-regarding approbation of justice but, *within* the latter, between one's sincerely held values and one's ability always to act accordingly. Unlike the rational egoist, an agent who has come to apprehend and value justice from the moral point of view no longer acts from "the original [self-regarding] Motive to the *Establishment* of Justice," although self-interest may still from time to time prevent him from living up to the moral point of view. At this stage, *rational* egoism is no longer in play, but only a kind of *residual* egoism that one intends, but still sometimes fails, to overcome for the sake of justice. Thus, for those who have, as it were, reached the second stage of justice, the synchronic picture of justice consists not in the simultaneous presence of the two stages that make up the diachronic picture, but in the second stage alone.[12] It is only by seeing the just person in this way, and especially by

12. A similar understanding of the possibility of change in the motives of justice (if not of the actual motives characteristic of the second stage) can be found in Nietzsche, *Human,* 1:92. I discuss this idea of Nietzsche's in Chapter 9.

treating the egoism still present in the just person no longer as *rational* egoism, that we can avoid what MacIntyre calls the logically unbridgeable gap—what I have tried to show to be a logically impossible gap—which MacIntyre criticizes Hume for trying in vain to bridge.

The most important upshot of the present discussion, then, is that justice requires motivational capacities that are not available from rational egoism. Since rational egoism's (instrumentally) rational component cannot preempt its teleological component to produce a disposition in keeping with the binding or obligatory nature of justice, justice stands in need of motives other than those of rational egoism. Such motives typically come under the rubrics of impartiality and (fair) reciprocity. Impartiality and reciprocity, as we shall see, differ from rational egoism in adopting to a greater or lesser degree the moral point of view. It is only by virtue of their share of the moral point of view that impartiality and reciprocity can in principle be motivationally sufficient for the purpose of justice. If a point of view is *entirely* other-regarding, however, justice ceases to be a virtue distinct from benevolence. For, as I tried to show in the last chapter, only a self-interested point of view has reason to insist on a hard-and-fast line between justice and benevolence. If justice is to maintain its integrity and distinctness, neither merging with benevolence nor sinking into rational egoism, it must involve some combination of other-regarding and self-regarding points of view. It is this combination that makes the concept of justice *both conceptually distinct and motivationally sufficient.* The various ways in which the two points of view are combined and balanced yield different accounts of justice, such as in terms of impartiality and reciprocity. I now turn to exploring such combinations, beginning, in the next chapter, with impartiality.

6

Impartiality and Justification

I may have left the impression in the preceding chapters, just as I may still do in the succeeding ones, that I regard justice as a disposition which, though sufficiently other-regarding to count as a virtue, is more self-regarding than other-regarding. In fact, I do not hold such a view, not least because what is important for understanding the disposition toward justice is neither its self-regarding aspect on its own nor its other-regarding aspect on its own, but how the two aspects combine to produce the distinct virtue of justice, in which neither egoism nor altruism retains its separate presence. All the same, it seems to me that the self-regarding aspect of justice tends to be underplayed and its many complexities insufficiently appreciated. Thus, the way in which the disposition toward justice is understood, and the possibility and the limits of justice are assessed, tends to be shaped more by a sense of how justice is different from egoism than by an appreciation of how it is different from altruism. For this reason, beginning with the next chapter, I will devote more attention to the self-regarding aspect of justice, insofar as it is distinct from its other-regarding aspect, and always, of course, as it interacts with the latter.

In the meantime, however, it is essential to take proper account of the other-regarding aspect of justice, not only for the sake of a more balanced overall account but also in its own right. I want both to see how difficult it is to live up to the other-regarding aspect of justice and to show what it takes to achieve it, and hence what it is that is achieved.

To that end, I devote this chapter to an examination of the concept of impartiality. While I consider justice as impartiality an attractive ideal, I find problematic the way in which it tends to be developed in terms of some idea of justification. In my view, this understanding of justice as impartiality rests on a mistaken moral psychology, one that falls short of the ideal of impartiality itself. My aim in this chapter is threefold. First, I intend to bring out certain systemic tensions between the normative ideal of impartial justifiability and the empirical practice of justification. I aim to show, further, that a conception of justice as impartiality in which the ethical focus is on justifying one's actions (even in a fully conscientious manner) is too self-centered to produce impartially valid norms. Finally, I provide a rough sketch of an alternative, other-centered moral psychology for justice as impartiality, one whose requirement for individuals is close to altruism even as the social ideal of impartiality retains its intermediate position between altruism and egoism.

Impartial Justification versus Impartial Motivation

Impartiality is conceived in certain influential accounts of justice in terms of some idea of justification—whether the abstract justifiability of norms or the actual practice of justification on which such justifiability may depend.[1] Understanding impartiality in this way immediately raises the question whether and if so how justifiability should be linked with the actual process of justification. Indeed, this question poses a dilemma, and the na-

1. On the face of it, Jürgen Habermas and Thomas Scanlon are among the most powerful proponents of this view. In taking issue with aspects of this view in what follows, however, I do not direct my criticisms at their accounts, for two main reasons. First, Habermas and Scanlon in different ways unequivocally build the very motive of impartiality, not just the use of formally impartial arguments (a distinction I draw in the next section) into the idea of justification itself. For this reason, they are not open to some of the major criticisms I make of the conception of impartiality in terms of justification, although precisely for this reason Habermas faces problems of a different kind, which I discussed in Chapter 3. For my purposes, there is no need to determine whether Scanlon faces the same problems (such problems are not insurmountable anyway, as noted in Chapter 3). Second, in the case of Scanlon in particular, the subject matter is not justice but a morality of right and wrong as precisely circumscribed by "what we owe to each other." See Thomas Scanlon, *What We Owe to Each Other* (Cambridge, Mass.: Harvard University Press, 1998), esp. chap. 4, sec. 8. Morality so conceived is broader than justice; it may even be said in some sense to cut across the distinction between justice and benevolence, if only by virtue of the fact that the morality of what we owe to one another "involves not just being moved to avoid certain actions 'because they would be wrong,' but also being moved by more concrete [and positive] considerations such as 'she's counting on me' or 'he needs my help'" (pp. 155–156). Given this conception of his subject matter, Scanlon's emphasis on the central importance of reasons and justifications does not, or at least need not, suffer from the excessive preoccupation with oneself that is characteristic of some conceptions of *justice* as impartiality—the kind of preoccupation with which I take issue toward the end of this chapter. In a similar fashion, Habermas's assignment of a crucial role to justification is balanced by his strong espousal of the value of solidarity. See my discussion of Habermas's account of subject-centered justice in Chapter 3.

ture of this dilemma is very clearly revealed in Brian Barry's account of impartiality, an account that by virtue of its clarity and boldness repays extended critical scrutiny.[2] On the one hand, Barry insists that for a legal or moral norm to be worthy of adoption, it "should be both defensible and *actually defended* by engaging—not perfunctorily but seriously—with the arguments put forward by objectors."[3] It is arguably to Barry's credit that he tries to avoid a quasi-metaphysical, operationally inaccessible sense of justifiability but instead treats justifiability as intrinsically linked to the actual activity of justification. Moreover, he conceives the activity of justification not in the hypothetical fashion characteristic of, say, Rawls's original position but in a largely empirical manner.[4] These features constitute a possible strength in Barry's position, and yet they also make his position harder to defend in other ways. In particular, when impartiality is linked to the actual activity of justification, a large burden falls on proving the very strong *empirical* claim that the desire for impartiality "has force with almost all of us to some degree"; as we shall see presently, the degree in question must be sufficient, or be such as can be made sufficient, for the purposes assigned to it by justice as impartiality.[5] Barry is not unaware of

2. For his account of impartiality in terms of justification, see Brian Barry, *Theories of Justice* (Berkeley: University of California Press, 1989), and *Justice as Impartiality* (Oxford: Clarendon Press, 1995). In *Justice,* Barry makes explicit a point left implicit in *Theories,* by drawing a distinction between first-order and second-order impartiality: "What the theory of justice as impartiality calls for are principles and rules that are capable of forming the basis of free agreement among people seeking agreement on reasonable terms. If we call impartiality in this context second-order impartiality, we can contrast it with first-order impartiality, which is a requirement of impartial behaviour incorporated into a precept. Roughly speaking, behaving impartially here means not being motivated by private considerations" (p. 11). Barry makes it very clear that it is second-order impartiality that properly characterizes a theory of justice as impartiality. In fact, "justice as impartiality does not require, and is indeed inconsistent with, a rule of universal first-order impartiality" (p. 213; see also p. 245). Barry's question, then, is, What does it take to achieve second-order impartiality? I agree that this is the right question to pose. I will argue, however, that the achievement of second-order impartiality takes more than Barry supposes, and that some degree of first-order impartiality may be necessary for second-order impartiality. I make this argument without using the terms "first-order" and "second-order impartiality," however.

3. Barry, *Justice,* p. 103, emphasis added.

4. See ibid., chap. 3.

5. Ibid., p. 10. More specifically, we can identify at least three distinct though related claims that Barry makes for impartiality as a motive of justice. To use the formulations in Barry, *Theories,* these claims are the following: First, impartiality is an *independent* motive, one that is "not reducible to even a sophisticated and indirect pursuit of self-interest" (p. 7), nor to pure altruism, for that matter. Second, impartiality is a *sufficient* motive for acting

such problems, for he is careful to say that "the motive is the desire to act justly: to wish to conduct oneself in ways that are *capable of* being defended impartially."[6] With this kind of formulation, he is clearly resisting any (straightforward) reduction of impartial justifiability to the activity of impartial justification.

Barry's ambivalence here reflects a deep tension between the pragmatic-empirical and the ethical-conceptual aspects of impartiality, between impartiality as rooted in the actual practice of justification and impartiality as virtually synonymous with what is right independent of the empirical and necessarily flawed process of justification. Impartiality in the first sense is empirically accessible but is for that very reason open to various abuses that can occur in any actual practice of justification.[7] To such abuses impartiality in the second sense is immune, but only at the cost of putting impartiality beyond empirical reach and turning it into an ineffectual ideal. There is another problem with the latter approach, for how can even the most conscientious among us be sure of having reached the goal of impartiality thus conceived, especially given our general tendency (which I will discuss later) to consider ourselves impartial when we are actually still partial to our own interests? For these reasons, the complete bypassing of actual justification would hardly be a desirable option. I will return to this option later in this chapter, discussing its pros and cons, respectively, in the last two sections. But first I want to examine what is arguably the more plausible option overall, namely, an account in which impartial justifiability is defined in terms of the actual practice of impartial justification.

By impartial justification I mean justification that is carried out through the use of arguments which take an impartial form—"without appealing to personal advantage,"[8] as Barry puts it. When impartial justifiability is understood in terms of impartial justification, the burden of impartiality falls largely on the use of such arguments. We might indeed say that im-

---

justly, in the sense that "it can be in itself a good reason for doing it" (p. 363). And third, impartiality is a *natural* motive that "develops under the normal conditions of human life" (p. 364) such that "human beings are and always have been moved by considerations of justice as impartiality" (p. 363). These distinct claims are summed up in the statement that "the desire to be able to justify our conduct in an impartial way is an *original* principle in human nature" (p. 364, emphasis added).

6. Ibid., p. 363, emphasis added.

7. Barry is by no means unaware of such risks. See, for instance, his account of the "need for skepticism" in *Justice,* pp. 168–173.

8. Barry, *Theories,* p. 361.

partiality is in the first instance a property of the arguments used for the purposes of justification.

We must be careful not to say, however, that the use of impartial arguments by itself constitutes impartiality. Procedurally impartial justification can produce results worthy of being considered impartially justifiable only if the use of impartial arguments is motivated in turn by the conscientious desire to achieve such results. Otherwise, there is no telling whether formally impartial arguments have not been abused—used for (unspoken) purposes other than to arrive at impartial results. Under this uncertainty, each instance of (apparently) successful justification has, strictly speaking, only an empirical rather than a moral status, even if that status is granted practical—say, legal—force. The use of impartial arguments is a necessary but not a sufficient condition of impartial justifiability. For that to be a sufficient condition, it has to be the case that participants in a justificatory process are willing to use impartial arguments *because and only because* they are motivated by the conscientious desire to find impartially justifiable grounds for their actions. Thus, using impartial arguments and having impartial motives are two sides of the same coin, and it is their being two sides of the same coin that constitutes justice as impartiality.

Something like this, in my view, is what we *must* mean if we define impartial justifiability in terms of impartial justification. Whenever we give the results of impartial argumentation the moral status of impartial justifiability, not just the empirical (if practically important) status of having actually been successfully justified to the relevant parties, we must be taken to assume an equation between using impartial arguments and having impartial motives. The problem is that we seldom can safely make this assumption: using impartial arguments simply does not reliably go together with having impartial motives in undertaking to justify one's actions. Barry's *empirical* claim that the desire for impartiality "has force with almost all of us to some degree" is clearly false if the degree in question is considered to be anywhere near sufficient for us to take using impartial arguments as even prima facie evidence of having impartial motives. But this is precisely the claim that has to be true if the activity of impartial justification is to yield something we can call impartiality without meaning by this merely that it has been arrived at through an actual process of justification in which only formally impartial arguments have been used.

Consider, for example, Barry's suggestion that "the motivation for being just is the desire to act in ways that can be defended . . . without appealing to personal advantage."[9] The crucial idea here is the injunction against invoking self-interest to justify a course of action. This injunction is undoubtedly important, but to treat it as a guarantee of impartiality would be to forget that one can seek personal advantage without *appealing to* personal advantage. Indeed, for someone in pursuit of self-interest, it is not only possible but most of the time necessary not to appeal to self-interest. It is a fact of life, whose causes I will consider shortly, that self-interest, openly expressed as such, is generally not allowed to serve as an argument in the resolution of conflict of interests. Given this constraint, even the justification of a proposed course of action motivated entirely by self-interest has to rely on what purport to be impartial arguments. This is evident in deliberations in the public sphere, where the arguments invoked often appear to be impartial but where consensus is seldom reached largely because the unspoken aim of each side is to justify a course of action that is motivated at least in part by (masked) self-interest.[10] In such situations, the willingness to justify a course of action "without appealing to personal advantage" says more about the public constraints on argumentation than about the private motives for undertaking such argumentation in the first place. It is one thing to use impartial arguments for the justification of a course of action, and quite something else to be motivated in so doing by concern with impartiality. It is one thing not (to be allowed) to appeal to personal advantage for the purpose of justification and something entirely different not to be motivated by personal advantage.

This is not to deny the value of impartial justification. It is not for nothing that in the public sphere one has to justify one's action *to others*.[11] We can imagine certain courses of self-interested action—such as those blatantly harmful to others—which it would be extremely difficult to persuade others to accept on anything remotely resembling impartial grounds. The very fact that one has to defend one's action to others, even when such defense does not spring from impartial motives, will afford oth-

9. Ibid.

10. See Stuart Hampshire, *Justice Is Conflict* (Princeton: Princeton University Press, 2000), pp. 90–91.

11. Habermas situates this essentially modern phenomenon in the larger context of "the rationalization of society." He devotes both volumes of *The Theory of Communicative Action* to this broad theme. For a glimpse of his account of the need for justification, see, for example, Jürgen Habermas, *The Theory of Communicative Action*, vol. 1, *Reason and the Rationalization of Society*, trans. Thomas McCarthy (Boston: Beacon Press, 1984), pp. 43–74.

ers the opportunity of raising objections and sometimes even exercising the right of veto. Under the best of circumstances, the willingness to defend one's action to others may show a genuine respect for their interests and perspectives. But then genuine respect for others already lifts us from the empirical level of impartial arguments to the moral level of impartial motives.

In the absence of such impartial motives, however, the desire to *defend to others* is simply the desire to *defend oneself*—that is, to defend one's self-interest—and so the willingness to justify one's action to others need be no more than the willingness to respond to objections from others. If such willingness contains an element of respect for others, it does so only in the sense of considering their objections worth answering—and this in no small measure because in the public sphere, objections from others have to be answered anyway, whether one likes it or not. Not surprisingly, justification is often a weapon of self-defense, impartial arguments serving merely as its socially permitted ammunition. One has to defend *to others* because it is a socially imposed necessity, but *what* one defends remains one's own interest.

When this is the case, the only thing that the institution of impartial justification can accomplish is to disallow the use of overtly self-serving arguments for the promotion of self-interest. To the extent that this contributes to the cause of justice, it does so not by improving motivation but by improving the repertoire of arguments allowed for the defense of self-interest. But the institutionalization of impartial argumentation is itself a fragile achievement. For as long as impartial motives are lacking, impartial arguments are merely rhetorical devices—the facade behind which self-interest clashes against self-interest. Even the veto power that sometimes resides in the institution of impartial justification is constantly in danger of being neutralized through the use of what Habermas calls systematically distorted communication.[12] And so whenever supposedly impartial arguments are used in the absence of genuinely impartial motives, they depend for their service to justice on the perpetual vigilance of all against the potential sophistry of each.[13]

It would therefore be unduly optimistic to treat a system of impartial

12. See, for example, Jürgen Habermas, *Moral Consciousness and Communicative Action*, trans. Christian Lenhardt and Shierry Weber Nicholsen (Cambridge, Mass.: MIT Press, 1990), p. 188.

13. One should also not underestimate problems presented by the socially and culturally specific nature of justification. What one finds justifiable, even upon serious reflection, is deeply influenced by the prevailing mores, institutions, and so on of one's community. Even

justification as if it could leave behind the circumstances of justice that made it necessary in the first place. When Barry says, "That justice comes into play where there is a conflict does not tell us anything about the way in which it should operate when it does come into play,"[14] he is in effect saying that the circumstances of justice should not determine the kind of arguments we use in justifying our actions to one another. Although self-interest is part of the motivation for establishing a system of justice/justification, the argument goes, such a system, once established, should nevertheless permit only impartial arguments. This is entirely correct. But there is no reason to believe that the institution of impartial justification can thus neutralize the self-interest that was part of the original motivation of justice. The circumstances of justice, seemingly silent in impartial arguments, speak loudly through the self-interested uses to which such arguments are often put.

Barry on the Empirical Circumstances of Impartiality

How likely impartial arguments are to be used from self-interested motives might be inferred from those empirical circumstances that make the employment of impartial arguments necessary and possible in the first place. It is thus helpful to determine exactly what these circumstances promote and to see whether they promote anything beyond the mere employment of impartial arguments.

The Necessity of Impartiality

To this end, Barry's account of the empirical circumstances of impartiality promises to be a highly instructive one, in that he makes the strong claim that "the desire to be able to justify our conduct in an impartial way is . . . one that develops *under the normal conditions of human life*."[15] In examining this claim, we should bear in mind something I said earlier, namely, that any concept of impartiality that relies on the empirical process of jus-

slavery, for example, could appear justifiable to many people in a slave society. Justification presupposes a background of norms from which it is extremely difficult to distance oneself, especially in a wholesale fashion. The same problems apply to conscience, at least up to a point. Genuinely impartial justification, which transcends not only self-interest but also parochial community or national values, is an extremely tall order.

14. Barry, *Theories,* p. 155.

15. Ibid., p. 364, emphasis added.

tification and gives the results of such justification the moral status of impartiality depends on this claim being true. This also explains why Barry makes a serious attempt to prove this claim.[16]

Elaborating on "the normal conditions of human life," Barry suggests that the desire to be able to justify one's conduct is "more likely to come to the fore in conditions of approximately equal power than in conditions of radical inequality."[17] Equality of power is important, Barry explains, because it creates mutual dependence: "The experience of dependence on others is an important predisposing factor [in acquiring moral motivation]. There is nothing like constantly finding oneself in situations where one has to *gain the cooperation of others in order to achieve one's own ends* for encouraging one to cultivate the habit of looking at things from the other person's point of view and asking oneself what kind of conduct the other might reasonably find acceptable."[18] This is clearly true, but there can be different reasons for seeing things from other people's perspective and asking oneself what kind of conduct they may reasonably consider acceptable. Not all such reasons show a concern with impartiality, still less an altruistic concern for others. Some of these reasons, indeed those mentioned by Barry himself, have to do with the recognition of others not as persons worthy of equal respect and consideration but as competitors of equal power. Not surprisingly, Barry makes a "proposition of speculative moral psychology," namely, that "equality of power, or at least a not too extreme inequality of power, is what is conducive to the formation and elicitation of moral motivation."[19] This is again true, up to a point, but it is not clear that Barry is correct to attach the epithet "moral" to the motivation thereby formed or elicited.

Where one's aim is to "gain the cooperation of others in order to achieve one's own ends" under conditions of roughly equal power, we have reason to suspect that the habit of impartiality bespeaks a practical strategy rather than a moral concern—a concession in the face of the power of others to obstruct one's own ends rather than a willingness to help them further their ends. What is missing here is any desire to treat others as ends in themselves. The desire, at least the predominant desire, is rather, as Barry says very explicitly, "to achieve one's own ends." It is only

16. Although most of what Barry has to say on this issue is found in *Theories,* the issue itself is equally relevant to Barry's project in *Justice.*

17. Barry, *Theories,* pp. 289–290.

18. Ibid., p. 289, emphasis added.

19. Ibid., pp. 289–290.

because the pursuit of one's own ends is constrained by conditions of roughly equal power that one *has to* learn to observe the needs and perspectives of others. "The experience of dependence on others," rather than serving, as Barry believes, as "an important predisposing factor" in acquiring the capacity for impartiality, simply leaves one with no choice. Insofar as such empirical conditions are conducive to impartiality, this is so not in the sense that they give rise to the desire for *justifiability* but in the sense that they make *justification* necessary. And it is the necessity of justification rather than the desire for justifiability that leads to what Barry calls the habit of impartial reasoning. In the end, what circumstances of roughly equal power promote is not impartiality in a moral sense but rather the sober realization that, like it or not, one has to acknowledge, and sometimes even help further, others' self-interest in order to promote one's own. This realization in turn produces a certain objectivity of observation, a momentary suspension of one's own interest and perspective. If we are to call this habit of mind impartiality, it is a merely *cognitive* impartiality devoid of moral concern, a discovery procedure aimed strategically at "gain[ing] the cooperation of others" and ultimately at "achiev[ing] one's own ends." While the cooperative instincts thereby acquired have undeniable practical value, there is no reason to attribute further, moral value to what one is otherwise already strongly motivated to do by self-interest—what one has no choice but to do, given the desire to satisfy self-interest under objective constraints.

Barry himself insists, rightly, that "there has to be some reason for behaving justly that is not reducible to even a sophisticated and indirect pursuit of self-interest."[20] What he apparently fails to see is that any such reason, if it is not to be reducible to egoism, must not depend on conditions of equal power. *Impartiality, as distinct from prudence, obtains precisely because, or to the extent that, it is not contingent upon, even in the sense of being facilitated by, relations of power.*[21] The very fact that a habit of mind is facilitated—brought to the fore, as Barry puts it—by conditions of equal *power* shows that it is not a genuine concern with impartiality. To the extent that one allows such conditions to be relevant, one shows respect for others' power rather than for their humanity, and this kind of respect in turn betrays egoism concerning ends combined with prudence concerning

20. Ibid., p. 7.

21. This is one of the things emphasized by Habermas through the concept of communicative action as opposed to strategic action. See, for example, Habermas, *Theory,* pp. 285–287, and *Moral Consciousness,* p. 58.

means. And so we end up with nothing but "a sophisticated and indirect pursuit of self-interest."

This is not to rule out the possibility that even situations characterized by the need to "gain the cooperation of others in order to achieve one's own ends" under conditions of equal power can *over time* somehow lead to moral insight, to the emergence of genuine respect for others as ends in themselves. The crucial qualification here is "over time," for what conditions of equal power help to bring about *directly* or *immediately* is not genuine considerateness or genuine impartiality. In this connection, Nietzsche speaks of a *gradual* transition from the opportunistic origins of justice to the disinterested desire for justice, and he explains this transition in terms of the "forgetting" of those origins and the social inculcation of justice as an intrinsic virtue.[22] Whether or not his account entirely succeeds, Nietzsche is surely right to recognize a gap, at once temporal and logical, between the circumstances of justice and the development of justice into a moral virtue, between what makes justice necessary in the first place and what will later help make it possible. It is an open question whether, and how, this gap can be bridged. But there is little doubt that when one knows—to be more precise, when one has the knowledge forced upon one by conditions of equal power—that other people have needs and perspectives of their own, it does not *automatically* follow that one will take these needs and perspectives into consideration for others' sake instead of manipulating them to advance one's own interest or at best accepting them as mere facts of life. Indeed, from the point of view of someone who sets out in pursuit of self-interest, it seems a short and logical step from being forced by conditions of equal power into an acknowledgment of others' interests and perspectives to treating these interests and perspectives as nothing more than a constraint on the pursuit of one's own interests.

Barry needs to show how such a move can be blocked, how cognitive knowledge can lead instead to moral insight—and do so directly. His failure to show this leaves one unconvinced when he insists that he is not "reinstating the 'circumstances of justice' through the back door." To be sure, he is "not saying that the *reason* for acting morally is that, under conditions of approximately equal power, it is necessary for the pursuit of one's own advantage to cooperate with others on terms that can be mutually accepted as reasonable"; rather, "the motive for acting morally remains . . . the desire to be able to justify our conduct." Nevertheless, when

22. See Friedrich Nietzsche, *Human, All Too Human,* trans. R. J. Hollingdale, 2 vols. in 1 (Cambridge: Cambridge University Press, 1986), 1:92.

Barry immediately goes on to say that the "point is simply that the desire is more likely to come to the fore in conditions of approximately equal power than in conditions of radical inequality,"[23] he is clearly affirming the connection between *empirical* conditions of roughly equal power and the *moral* desire to act justly. In the passage as a whole, then, Barry must be taken to claim that *conditions of roughly equal power promote a disposition or motive (that is, impartiality) which is nevertheless radically discontinuous from such conditions.*

This paradoxical claim hinges on Barry's confidence in the efficacy of justification when the parties are restricted to the use of impartial arguments. He seems to believe that such a restriction by itself constitutes a decisive break with the empirical circumstances of justice.[24] But as we saw earlier, it is always possible to circumvent this restriction by putting impartial arguments to uses that are themselves self-interested. Clearly, this restriction can ensure the discontinuity from the empirical circumstances of justice only of the impartial arguments themselves, but not of the motives for using such arguments. Yet the motives matter greatly, as we have seen, and Barry fails to show how *they* are discontinuous from the circumstances of justice. Unless that can be shown, the discontinuity of impartial arguments from the circumstances of justice is only superficial, for the use of impartial arguments in and of itself merely reflects a constraint on the pursuit of self-interest imposed by conditions of roughly equal power. That this is the case is confirmed in the daily use, sometimes subtle, sometimes not so subtle, of formally impartial arguments by all manner of people to promote causes that are themselves motivated by anything but an impartial regard for the general good.

The Accident of Impartiality

I do not mean to suggest that self-interest always has to intervene. But we must be careful to distinguish the overcoming of self-interest in favor of impartiality from the mere suspension of self-interest by circumstances. I pointed out earlier that a realistic approach to conditions of roughly equal power can help produce a certain strategic objectivity, a temporary suspension of one's own interest and perspective. Such suspension of self-interest, in the type of case discussed earlier, occurs *by design* for the promotion of self-interest. But it can also occur *by default* in those situations in which

23. Barry, *Theories,* pp. 289–290.

24. See, for example, ibid., p. 155.

one's interests happen not to be at stake or, as Hume observes, are suspended by institutional constraints.[25] In this type of case, the suspension of self-interest, though without any ulterior motive behind it, is similarly contingent and temporary, and similarly compatible with egoism and prudence. This is because the suspension of self-interest by default comes about not through the *overcoming* of self-interest, as in the case of genuine impartiality, but through the *contingent* irrelevance or absence of self-interest. The resulting appearance of impartiality is not an accomplishment but an accident.

Barry, however, seems quite prepared to base justice on the accident of impartiality. If, as he suggests, "the sense of justice often has more free play at the stage when the forms of institutions are being decided on," this is only because self-interest is more likely to be suspended, in the sense of not being *immediately* affected, at this stage. Thus what Barry calls the sense of justice is largely a function of the temporal and psychological distance between the setting up of just institutions and their impact on self-interest. This is confirmed in his acknowledgment that the sense of justice comes under greater strain "at the stage when people are deciding whether or not to comply with the demands that institutions make on them."[26] In other, plainer words, justice is more easily preached than practiced, and this because self-interest is not immediately affected by, and hence is more easily suspended during, mere deliberations about justice.

This need not be a cause for worry, according to Barry. For "all that is often necessary is that those whose own interests are not directly affected should support the course of impartial justice." It does not greatly matter if "people who are prepared, say, to vote for a fair system for assessing contributions to some collective project may not be sufficiently motivated to pay their contributions voluntarily." The solution, Barry suggests, "is, obviously, to vote also for a system of sanctions to ensure compliance."[27] Things are generally more complicated than this: for one thing, many people can be quite farsighted with regard to their self-interest, and for another, even in the absence of foresight, ideological beliefs can intervene on behalf of future self-interest. In real life, situations seldom arise in which, to borrow Hume's words, "*nothing* gives [people] any particular byass."[28]

25. See David Hume, *A Treatise of Human Nature,* ed. L. A. Selby-Bigge, 2nd ed., ed. P. H. Nidditch (Oxford: Clarendon Press, 1978), p. 537.

26. Barry, *Theories,* p. 366.

27. Ibid.

28. David Hume, *An Enquiry Concerning the Principles of Morals,* ed. J. B. Schneewind (Indianapolis: Hackett, 1983), p. 49.

Even if Barry's proposal were practicable, one could still ask whether impartiality, in any strict sense of the term, figures at all in his scheme of things. The way Barry introduces sanctions at the second stage casts, retrospectively, a rather negative light on the supposed impartiality that marks the first stage of deliberations about justice. Since the sanctions introduced at the second stage are made necessary by the known reluctance to practice justice on the part of the deliberating subjects themselves, the impartiality that is operative at the first stage turns out to be little more than *impartiality by default.* The possibility of impartiality, Barry in effect says, varies with the temporal and psychological proximity of self-interest, and accordingly, the tendency toward injustice caused by the immediacy of self-interest can be countered only with weapons, among them legal sanctions, that are forged when self-interest happens to be less immediate. In this way Barry puts impartiality—an impartiality of sorts—within the reach of all who find themselves in this morally fortunate happenstance. Yet by the same token, he divests impartiality of difficulty and effort, and hence of moral value.

Justification and Conscience

One factor that can go some way toward preventing the abuse of impartial arguments is one's own role as interlocutor in the process of justification.[29] It is extremely important, as Barry points out, that one's conduct be "defended *to oneself,*"[30] not just to others. Defending one's actions to oneself has the effect of directing the activity of justification inward, and this can make the defense of one's conduct either easier or more difficult. On the one hand, one is no longer directly answerable to objections from others, so that one is free to be swayed by self-interest and to rationalize one's conduct accordingly. But on the other hand, the fact that the audience for justification is none other than oneself presents the possibility that the activity of justification may shift truly inward—to the tribunal of one's conscience. To the extent that this happens, impartial justification ceases to be an instrument of self-defense and becomes instead a weapon of self-critique. For conscience can erect a barrier, not insurmountable to be sure but still substantial, between self-interest and its justification with impartial arguments. That justification has to satisfy one's conscience counter-

29. For an illuminating discussion of issues closely related to this one, see Hannah Arendt, "Thinking and Moral Considerations," *Social Research* 38 (1971): 417–446.

30. Barry, *Theories,* p. 361, emphasis added.

acts the potentially opportunistic and ideological character of justification that is aimed solely at silencing the objections of others. Even when one has succeeded in justifying one's conduct to others, one may yet fail to do so to oneself.

Yet even the concern to justify one's conduct to oneself in the best sense—that is, before one's conscience—is in an important sense a concern *with oneself*.[31] When I am trying to determine for myself whether my conduct is justified, what is uppermost in my mind is not *directly* whether my conduct is beneficial or harmful to others, but rather whether it is justified. The desire to justify myself to myself is ultimately the desire to be able to live with myself and, better still, to feel (morally) good about myself; and this desire in turn can all too easily express itself as the desire to be at peace with some external authority (say, my community) that dwells in my conscience. In its concern with oneself, conscience is not *intensionally* identical with the desire not to harm others. Indeed, conscience, including its effects, is not even *extensionally* identical with the desire not to harm others. For it is by no means impossible for ordinarily conscientious people to be able to live with actions that in some way harm others, as long as such actions are not prohibited by law. This is not to downplay the importance of conscience; but if conscience is *all* I have, then as long as I can live with what I do, it matters little whether what I do is of benefit or harm to others. Conscience, concerned first and foremost with one's own peace of mind and only then with the well-being of others, if at all, cannot be relied on to deliver impartiality, if by impartiality we mean equal concern for oneself and for others.

All the same, there is one sense in which justifying one's conduct to oneself marks an advance over justifying it to others. Justifying one's conduct to others, unless accompanied by impartial motives, is at best only instrumental in promoting justice, while justifying it to oneself, that is to one's conscience, is a moral act in itself, despite its self-centeredness. Put another way, if the concern to justify one's conduct to others, in the absence of impartial motives, is a concern with the appearance of justice, the concern to justify it to oneself—to make sure that one is just—is a concern with justice itself. What is at issue is no longer the justification of one's conduct but its justifiability, and one must turn to one's conscience to determine the latter. For conscience, however self-centered, is the only repository of impartial motives as opposed to mere impartial arguments, and

31. As I discuss this feature of conscience in detail in Chapter 11, a few observations may suffice for now.

impartial motives, as we have seen, are to justifiability what impartial arguments are to justification.

Yet if justifying one's conduct to oneself shows a concern with justifiability, it nevertheless cannot but retain some of its empirical character as an act of justification. For this reason, justification, even to oneself, is always at one remove from justifiability. And as justifying one's conduct to others can easily turn into an act of deception, so justifying it to oneself can easily become an act of self-deception.[32] The fact that conscience can be unknowingly self-serving is a function not of insincerity—for self-deception properly so called is unconscious—but of an *intrinsic* gap between aiming at impartiality and achieving it, as we shall see in the next section.

Toward an Other-Centered Concept of Impartiality

I have argued that an understanding of impartiality in terms of impartial justification is inadequate even when justification is addressed both to others and to oneself. Such an understanding is inadequate in an even more important sense, I shall argue further, because the very desire to act in impartially justifiable ways, even at its most sincere, is too self-centered to achieve the goal of impartiality. In this sense, yet to be elaborated, we may describe an understanding of impartiality in terms of impartial justification as a *self-centered* concept of impartiality. I do not mean to suggest, of course, that the desire to justify one's conduct to others or to oneself is selfish. Nevertheless, such a desire, even when (as in the case of conscientious justification) not selfish in any ordinary sense, is still overly concerned with not being wrong oneself rather than with others' not being harmed. Thus my point is that this concept of impartiality places too much weight on justification, and the idea of justification in turn places too much weight on one's concern with being right. One of the problems with justification to others, as we have seen, is that such justification is often pursued opportunistically rather than conscientiously, which is why justification to oneself can serve as a useful corrective. What I intend to show is that even when one's concern to defend one's actions, to others or to oneself, is fully conscientious, such a concern is still too self-centered to achieve impartiality. This criticism is meant to apply not only to the empirical flaws of justification but also to the (psycho)logical flaws of the very search for justifiability.

A suitable starting point is the idea that impartiality occupies something

32. See Habermas, *Moral Consciousness*, p. 188, on what he calls "intrapsychic disturbance of communication."

of an intermediate position. For what impartiality is not, if not what impartiality is, can be captured, in a rough-and-ready fashion, by saying that it occupies an intermediate position between altruism and egoism, between the active point of view of justice and the passive point of view;[33] that is to say, it is neither altruism pure and simple nor egoism pure and simple. Any viable concept of impartiality, as Barry rightly suggests, must preserve its distinctness, and as a first approximation, this distinctness can be preserved through a simultaneous distancing from altruism on the one hand and from egoism on the other.[34] It may be tempting to see the resulting distinctness of impartiality in terms of the combination of altruism and egoism, of the active and the passive points of view. This view of impartiality, which we may call the *combinational* view, implies that both altruism and egoism retain their original character when they make up the combination called impartiality. It is as if there is a division of labor between altruism and egoism, with altruism being concerned with justice to others (not to cause harm) and egoism with justice to oneself (not to suffer harm). This picture does seem to jibe, up to a point, with what we know of how people lead their moral lives. The problem with this view of impartiality is that it turns impartiality into the site of a conflict of motives, between the concern for others and the concern for oneself. If such a conflict of motives is to be held in a sufficiently steady balance to count as impartiality, there has to be a third factor besides altruism and egoism to serve as the reason for favoring one kind of balance rather than another. The most promising candidate for this third factor is some concept of equality, say, equal concern or equal respect. Once a third concept such as equality is introduced, however, we can dispense with the polar concepts of altruism and egoism. The resulting view of impartiality is what we may call the *unitary* view, in which impartiality, instead of being both altruistic and egoistic, is neither.[35] On this view, when one acts impartially, one is made to do so not by two conflicting motives that happen to be in a state of balance, but by a single motive, say, equal concern.

33. See Chapter 4 on the active and passive points of view of justice.

34. See Barry, *Theories,* p. 372.

35. This is the kind of view that Barry seems to hold. To say that impartiality is neither pure altruism nor pure egoism does not preclude saying that it is, in some distinctive combination, both altruism and egoism. But to say the latter is to suggest a sense in which impartiality is not an original motive but a motive derived from other, more basic motives. For Barry, however, "the desire to be able to justify our conduct in an impartial way is an *original* principle in human nature" (ibid., p. 364, emphasis added). This implies that when Barry calls impartiality an intermediate position between altruism and egoism, he does so in a neither-nor sense, not in a both-and sense.

Clearly, when we understand impartiality as equal concern, we are still placing impartiality somewhere between altruism and egoism. As Barry reminds us, impartiality is "delicately poised between two poles, and . . . its integrity depends on maintaining an intermediate position. If it is pulled too far in either direction it turns into something else."[36] This need not mean, however, that impartiality is at an *equal* distance from the two poles and that therefore the danger of impartiality "turn[ing] into something else" is the *same* with respect to both poles. On the contrary, there is a sense in which impartiality as equal concern is closer to altruism than to egoism, and it may therefore be called an *other-centered* concept of impartiality.

For this concept of impartiality, with its focus on concern rather than justification, requires for its implementation an effort to go beyond impartiality in the direction of altruism. Impartiality—or the need for impartiality—presupposes an existing, natural partiality to oneself, which it is the function of the cultivation of impartiality to counteract. The imperative of impartiality is not addressed to those who are already equally concerned with others as with themselves. In this sense, impartiality is not a natural or spontaneous and hence unconscious virtue. It is rather the conscious negation of a natural partiality toward oneself. For this reason, the achievement of impartiality requires self-criticism and self-overcoming. Here lies the altruistic tenor of impartiality: the virtue of impartiality represents a striving to be altruistic against the background of egoism. Given one's natural partiality to oneself, to be impartial is already to be partial to others. Given the natural imbalance between concern for oneself and concern for others, to be able to correct that imbalance is already to show more concern for others than for oneself. Thus, although the goal to be reached is one of *equal* concern, the willingness to reach it represents a victory of altruism over egoism.

Just as there is a natural imbalance between concern for oneself and concern for others, so there is a natural gap between trying to be impartial and becoming impartial. This is because one's natural partiality to oneself can easily cause one to locate impartiality at a point closer to one's own interest than to the interest of others. Thus, the effort at impartiality has a natural tendency to fall short of its goal: one will not succeed in becoming impartial if one tries merely to be impartial.[37] It is rather only when one tries to be partial to others that one may be able to overcome the natural

36. Ibid., p. 372.

37. It is for a similar reason that Lawrence Becker finds generosity to be important in reciprocal exchanges. See Lawrence C. Becker, *Reciprocity* (New York: Routledge & Kegan Paul, 1986), p. 154.

partiality to oneself and attain impartiality. This means that in order to attain impartiality, one has to be more concerned with looking after others' interests than with making sure that one is not pursuing one's own interests in the wrong way. These two concerns do not coincide intensionally or even extensionally. Objectively considered, impartiality is between egoism and altruism, but subjectively considered, impartiality is virtually identical with altruism.

This is why the desire to act in ways that can be justified to others and to ourselves, even assuming such a desire to be entirely conscientious, is still not other-regarding enough to counteract the natural partiality toward ourselves and help us reach the goal of impartiality. It is true that the conscientious effort to justify our actions is an attempt to overcome our self-interestedness, but such an effort is inadequate for the purpose of impartiality, given our natural partiality toward ourselves. One important consequence of this natural partiality is that we cannot help adopting a partial point of view in determining what is impartial, and therefore, as I said before, we tend to locate impartiality at a point closer to our own interest than to the interest of others. This is an important reason why people with conflicting interests can conscientiously seek an impartial solution yet fail to find one that *both* sides agree is impartial. When our desire in trying to be impartial is to justify ourselves (however conscientiously) rather than to be directly concerned for others, it is all too easy to be blind to our partiality toward ourselves in judging what is impartial. The moral, then, is that because most of us are naturally more given to egoism than to altruism, self-overcoming on behalf of others, rather than self-justification to others (however conscientious), is the only bridge to impartiality.[38] Indeed, this is the other-regarding aspect of justice as such.[39]

38. It seems that to the extent that altruism thus helps one achieve impartiality, it will also prevent one from *claiming to be* impartial. Insofar as one practices impartiality spontaneously, as few actually do, one is not conscious of being impartial—either in one's effort or in one's success. When, however, one is conscious of being impartial, that consciousness often leads to self-righteousness, or at least betrays the fear of being called partial. It seems to be often in such states of mind that one makes claims to impartiality.

39. Nevertheless, the requisite motivational capacities must not be presumed to exist from the start in the original subjective circumstances of justice but can become available only through the creation of more favorable subjective circumstances as a result of successful socialization. See Chapter 3 on Habermas and the subjective circumstances of justice.

7

A Progress of Reciprocity

The self-regarding and other-regarding aspects of justice converge in the concept of reciprocity, whose precise nature is the subject of this chapter. We are now in a position to pick up where we left off in Chapter 1, having seen in the intervening chapters what the disposition toward justice, including its reciprocal element, is not. It is as well to recall the formulation of reciprocity with which Chapter 1 ended, namely, reciprocity under reasonable norms. By this I meant conditional compliance with broadly reasonable norms, where the concept of the reasonable is to be taken in a fairly elastic sense. What this formulation enables us to do, we may recall, is to identify a minimally normative concept of reciprocity that constitutes part of the disposition toward justice as such, as distinct from the different kinds of full-fledged normative content that can be superimposed on it by rival substantive conceptions of justice. This in turn allows us to focus on the minimally normative concept of reciprocity, since our concern here is not with the normative question of the validity of norms but with the explanatory question of the disposition to conform to them (as long as they are broadly reasonable). To examine this minimally normative concept of reciprocity is, as I tried to show in Chapter 1, to study two things at the same time. For in binding ourselves to a shared norm, we also form a reciprocal or conditional relationship with one another, a relationship that falls under such rubrics as mutual advantage and mutual respect. It is the nature of this reciprocal relationship between agents (what we may call the affective as opposed to the normative aspect of reciprocity), and by implication the nature of their commitment to norms, that I investigate in this chapter.[1]

1. It is worth emphasizing that when I discuss mutual advantage, I am not treating it as a full-fledged normative theory of justice, as Rawls does, for example, in contrasting mutual

In particular, I explore what may be called a developmental conception of reciprocity, one in which the conscious motive of reciprocity progresses from mutual advantage to mutual good will under institutionally secured conditions. In working out this conception of reciprocity, I draw quite heavily on Allan Gibbard and John Rawls, as their writings exemplify in highly instructive ways both the explanatory power and some of the pitfalls of such a conception. Gibbard and Rawls, in my view, are essentially right to understand reciprocity as having its motivational roots in the seeking of advantage and subsequently developing beyond these roots into a moral sense of fairness, while still being dependent on a predictable background of mutual advantage. By taking this background for granted from the outset, however, they produce a model of reciprocity that applies more to spontaneous exchanges between acquaintances under implicit rules of fair play than to society-wide cooperation between strangers under explicit rules of justice. The latter situation, I argue, is characterized in the first instance precisely by the absence of that background, and the sense of justice that is socially promoted as a solution to this absence has a very different character from that of a spontaneous sense of fair play. I therefore propose substantial modifications to Gibbard's and Rawls's account of reciprocity and put forward a different account of the sense of justice. In particular, I try to bring out the conditionality of the progress from mutual advantage to mutual good will and show that the sense of justice is not merely a product of this progress but one of its essential conditions.

Reciprocity as Mutual Good Will

A two-step reduction is often at work in accounts of justice: the disposition to be just is reduced to some notion of reciprocity, which in turn is re-

---

advantage ("understood as everyone's being advantaged with respect to each person's present or expected future situation as things are") with impartiality on the one hand and reciprocity on the other. See John Rawls, *Political Liberalism* (New York: Columbia University Press, 1993), pp. 16–17. Rather, having defined reciprocity as a minimally normative concept, I am treating mutual advantage as one kind of reciprocal relationship so defined, to be contrasted with another, say, mutual good will. It will be particularly important to keep this in mind when I apply the term "mutual advantage" so understood to Rawls, who for the most part uses the term in the other, fully substantive sense. Rawls does, though, occasionally use the term "reciprocal advantage" (see, for example, John Rawls, *A Theory of Justice,* rev. ed. [Cambridge, Mass.: Harvard University Press, 1999], p. 155) in a sense close to that in which I use the term "mutual advantage."

duced to enlightened egoism.[2] The first reduction is unavoidable, its precise significance depending on how reciprocity is construed. The second reduction, however, while seemingly also unavoidable, presents a serious problem for any account of the disposition toward justice and may usefully serve as our starting point.

To reduce reciprocity to enlightened egoism is to construe reciprocity in a specific sense, that is, in terms of mutual advantage (understood here as including mutual restraint), where advantage is to be taken in the straightforward sense of tangible self-interests. Help is mutually rendered, or self-restraint mutually exercised, in order that those involved get what they want or avoid what they do not want. Such reciprocity is something one practices not because one wants to but because one has to—and this in order best to satisfy one's self-interest. Here reciprocity is merely a means, something that does not follow from the nature of one's ends but is dictated by empirical constraints not of one's own choosing, that is, conditions of roughly equal power. Each of those involved is pursuing an end that is not itself reciprocal but only contingently dependent on reciprocity by virtue of specific empirical conditions. So understood, reciprocity is a combination of egoism and realism: egoism at the level of ends and realism at the level of means, and hence enlightened egoism.

What we have here is a straightforward case of *reciprocity as mutual advantage*. But if there were nothing more to reciprocity than mutual advantage, reciprocity would be indistinguishable from rational egoism or prudence. And since justice is not reducible to rational egoism (as I tried to show in Chapter 5), it would follow that reciprocity thus understood would fall short of justice—indeed that justice as reciprocity would be a contradiction in terms. To be a coherent concept, therefore, justice as reciprocity must be distinguishable from rational egoism, just as, at the other

2. Nietzsche, for example, makes the first reduction when he claims that "the characteristic of *exchange* is the original characteristic of justice," and in the same aphorism he goes on to make the second reduction when he further points out that "justice goes back naturally to the viewpoint of an enlightened self-preservation, thus to . . . egoism." Friedrich Nietzsche, *Human, All Too Human,* trans. R. J. Hollingdale, 2 vols. in 1 (Cambridge: Cambridge University Press, 1986), 1:92. To cite another example, Schopenhauer too reduces reciprocity to egoism when he says of Kant's categorical imperative (accurately or not): "Thus it is expressed here . . . that moral obligation rests absolutely and entirely on assumed *reciprocity.* Consequently, it is utterly egoistic and obtains its interpretation from egoism. Under the condition of *reciprocity,* egoism cunningly acquiesces in a compromise." Arthur Schopenhauer, *On the Basis of Morality,* trans. E. F. J. Payne (Indianapolis: Bobbs-Merrill, 1965), p. 91.

end, it must be distinguishable from the nonreciprocal virtue of benevolence.[3] This means that a way must be found of conceiving reciprocity in terms other than those of mutual advantage. It is obvious that *mutual* advantage entails reciprocity, so the question is whether reciprocity has to entail mutual *advantage*.

Let us picture, then, albeit with a measure of naïve optimism to begin with, a kind of justice as reciprocity in which the reciprocity is a matter, say, of mutual affection, mutual attachment, mutual respect, or mutual good will. Friendship, for example, unlike love, is necessarily reciprocal, with good feelings from one person being the precondition of similar feelings from the other and vice versa. Yet it does not seem correct to think of such reciprocity in terms of mutual *advantage,* at least not in the same sense in which we speak of the exchange of services or favors. Nor does it seem accurate to regard the expectation to have one's friendly feelings reciprocated as an egoistic motive, at least not on a par with the desire to have one's service or favor returned in kind. This is because friendship, unlike relationships based on mutual advantage, is an end in itself. So too is the reciprocity that goes together with friendship, for the kind of reciprocity in question is constitutive of friendship, not merely instrumental to it.

Justice, to be sure, serves for the most part to regulate the relationship between strangers rather than friends, and arguably it is needed only to the extent that friendship or some other close bond is lacking. Nevertheless, the kind of reciprocity characteristic of friendship can be present, if to a smaller degree, also in relationships of lesser intensity or duration that are based on mutual good will. Think of those cases, mentioned by Gibbard, in which "I might be decent to him because he has been decent to me. I might prefer treating another well who has treated me well, even if he has no further power to affect me."[4] The motivation here is *intrinsically reciprocal,* as Gibbard puts it, whereas a mere interest in mutual advantage is *instrumentally reciprocal.*

The stipulation "even if he has no further power to affect me" is crucial here, in that it highlights the absence of considerations of advantage behind my willingness to reciprocate. In the absence of such considerations, what prompts me to reciprocate is a sense of fairness that is called into play by the fact that "he has been decent to me." That my motive is fairness

3. On benevolence as a nonreciprocal virtue, see Chapter 1.

4. Allan Gibbard, "Constructing Justice," *Philosophy and Public Affairs* 20 (1991): 264–279; quotation from p. 266.

rather than advantage is manifest in the fact that I am reciprocating with a view to the past ("he *has been* decent to me") rather than to the future ("he has no further power to affect me").[5] It is only when I am acting in response to what someone did for me in the past rather than in anticipation of what someone might do for me in the future that I may be said to be truly reciprocating.[6] This temporal requirement of reciprocity is most unequivocally fulfilled when "I . . . prefer treating another well who has treated me well . . . *even if he has no further power to affect me*"[7]—that is, even if I have nothing further to gain from reciprocating and can get away with not reciprocating. It is presumably this retrospective feature of reciprocity that makes it possible for Gibbard to say that "motivations of reciprocity are not purely egoistic . . . [M]otives of fair reciprocity cannot be reduced to motives of prudence. Justice as Fair Reciprocity is not a version of Justice as Mutual Advantage."[8]

The retrospective character of reciprocity is so important because it implies a change in the *substance* of what I do when reciprocating. It is true that the past action with regard to which I am reciprocating may well be one describable in terms of advantage. For this reason, it may appear that even if I am reciprocating with an eye only to the past, I may still be *returning advantage with advantage,* and thus the two actions taken together seem to constitute a case of reciprocity as mutual advantage. This cannot be the whole story, however. The fact that someone has treated me

5. There is of course a future-oriented aspect to my action even when I am reciprocating, but that aspect, aimed purely at someone else's future good, has nothing reciprocal about it.

6. Lawrence C. Becker, in *Reciprocity* (New York: Routledge & Kegan Paul, 1986), seems to be making a similar point in terms of the distinction between what he calls a recipient's virtue and a giver's virtue. Thus, "reciprocity is a *recipient's* virtue. It is the way people ought to be disposed to *respond* to others. It says nothing about how people ought to behave, or feel, when they *give* a gift" (p. 93). It is in something like this spirit that J. R. Lucas, in *On Justice* (Oxford: Clarendon Press, 1980), p. 186, takes Rawls to task, remarking that "Rawls's recommendation of a maximin strategy [in *A Theory of Justice*] . . . has little to do with justice. It is prospective, not retrospective." In this connection, it is also worth mentioning Kant's concept of the duty of gratitude as "not a merely *prudential* maxim of encouraging the other to show me further beneficence by acknowledging my obligation to him for a favor he has done *(gratiarum actio est ad plus dandum invitatio),* for I would then be using my acknowledgment merely as a means to my further purposes." Immanuel Kant, *The Metaphysics of Morals,* trans. Mary Gregor (Cambridge: Cambridge University Press, 1991), pp. 248–249, "The Doctrine of Virtue," sec. 32.

7. Gibbard, "Constructing Justice," p. 266, emphasis added.

8. Ibid., p. 267. Becker also points out, though only in passing, that "the disposition to reciprocate is essentially retrospective" (*Reciprocity,* p. 116).

well may mean that he or she has acted to my advantage. But to the extent that I am reciprocating my benefactor retrospectively, I am not reciprocating *for the sake of advantage.* And when I am reciprocating and yet doing so not for the sake of advantage, I am not perceiving the action with regard to which I am reciprocating in terms of advantage *alone,* and, for this reason, I am not reciprocating with regard to advantage alone. Rather, I see in my benefactor's past action, over and above its value as advantage, an expression of good will. It is this good will that I am reciprocating, above all, when I reciprocate with a view entirely to the past, and I am reciprocating it *with* good will. What we have here is *reciprocity as mutual good will.*[9]

"Intrinsic" seems another apt term for this kind of reciprocity, for returning someone's good will is not a mere means but an end in itself.[10] To regard the return of good will as an end in itself is to treat those whose good will is returned as ends in themselves. We no longer view them, as we would in the case of reciprocity as mutual advantage, as holders of power equal to ours and hence potential foes to be reckoned with, but rather as beings worthy of respect or good will regardless of whether they have any power to affect us materially. It is in their capacity as the latter that we return their good will with good will. And we choose to do so because we have a certain conception of ourselves and of others rather than because we are constrained by conditions (of roughly equal power) that are not of our own choosing. Of course, this kind of intrinsic reciprocity need not exclude the mutual satisfaction of material interests. The important thing is that reciprocity is not practiced *in order to* satisfy such interests. Rather, the spirit of reciprocity makes it a matter of course that the interests of all involved will be satisfied, to an extent depending on the nature and depth of the reciprocal relationship. In an atmosphere of intrinsic mutual good will, mutual advantage is not what people seek, and yet interests that would otherwise have to be satisfied by actions calculated for mutual advantage are taken care of by actions performed from spontaneous good will.

Once we distinguish between mutual good will and mutual advantage,

9. This concept should be distinguished from what Kurt Baier calls "Limited Conditional Good Will." Baier's concept seems to capture something intermediate between what I have called reciprocity as mutual advantage and reciprocity as mutual good will. See Kurt Baier, *The Rational and the Moral Order* (Chicago: Open Court, 1995), esp. pp. 187–188.

10. Becker makes the point that "reciprocal exchanges (of good for good) are typically a potent source of pleasure *in themselves*" (*Reciprocity,* p. 89, emphasis added).

we are in a position to argue that only reciprocity as mutual good will, or intrinsic reciprocity, manifests the genuine instinct of justice: it alone is the kind of reciprocity to which justice can fittingly be reduced. Such reciprocity is still conditional, to be sure, as reciprocity in any sense whatsoever has to be, but it goes beyond the mere seeking of advantage.[11] In perceiving others' actions as an expression of good will and responding likewise with good will, one is moved by the desire, if at all consciously reciprocal, not to let others down, not to hurt their feelings. Even though this desire is conditional on the manifestation of the same desire on the part of others, it nevertheless remains the desire to do justice to others, that is, to be just.

Conditions of Reciprocity

The picture I have sketched of reciprocity as mutual good will features a kind of *conscious* motivation that lifts us above the mere seeking of mutual advantage. There is another side to reciprocity that is less conscious and less visible and yet no less crucial. If what raises intrinsic reciprocity above mere mutual advantage and makes it no less than justice is that the reciprocity involved is intrinsic, what makes it *no more than* justice is its reciprocity, intrinsic though it is. After all, intrinsic reciprocity, while distinct from mere mutual advantage, does not have the unconditional quality that marks the higher, more altruistic virtue of benevolence (or that sometimes marks the more intense emotion of love). It is my (implicit) demand for reciprocity that makes my good will toward others a matter of justice rather than unconditional love or benevolence. While the just person rises above mere self-interest in possessing intrinsic good will, he stops short of benevolence inasmuch as this good will depends on the good will of others. In this way, the good will that characterizes justice is both intrinsic and conditional—intrinsic in the sense of going beyond considerations of mere advantage, but conditional in the sense of being dependent on manifestations of good will on the part of others.

Both intrinsic and conditional? This is indeed what distinguishes justice from prudence or mere mutual advantage on the one hand and from benevolence on the other. Yet this is also something that makes the desire to be just seem puzzling at first sight. It is not obvious how, in the desire to

11. See Becker's discussion of the role of generosity in reciprocal relationships (*Reciprocity*, p. 154). It is important that generosity be taken not only in a quantitative but also, more crucially, in a qualitative sense, that is, as abundant good *will* or generosity of *spirit*.

be just, one can rise above considerations of mere advantage and yet still insist on reciprocity, unless the desire to be just is in some sense *indirectly or unconsciously* dependent on considerations of advantage after all—unless, that is, reciprocity as mutual good will is somehow traceable to reciprocity as mutual advantage. This is exactly how Gibbard explains mutual good will, even the apparent unconditionality of benevolence.[12] Gibbard, we may recall, is responsible for the idea of intrinsic reciprocity. But such intrinsic reciprocity, according to him, is only apparent, because the retrospectiveness of reciprocity is only apparent. Perhaps the most telling case is that of gratitude, which, in contrast to flattery or bribery, seems a perfect example of purely retrospective reciprocity. As Gibbard sees it, though, this is only apparent. In terms of its evolutionary function, he argues, if not in terms of conscious intention, gratitude is future-oriented, in that it

12. This account appears in Allan Gibbard, *Wise Choices, Apt Feelings* (Oxford: Clarendon Press, 1990). It may seem that Gibbard's treatment of reciprocity in this book is at odds with his later characterization of "intrinsic reciprocity" in his review article "Constructing Justice," which I discussed earlier. I would suggest, however, that there is an underlying continuity between the two accounts. Although in his review article Gibbard emphasizes the independence of intrinsic reciprocity from mutual advantage, he is nevertheless prepared, though not without misgivings, to entertain the idea that those incapable (for lack of ability, not willingness) of contributing to society have no claim to justice *on grounds of reciprocity*. What Gibbard proposes to mitigate this unpalatable consequence is that "fair reciprocity is not everything" (p. 272), meaning by this that the interests of those incapable of contributing have to be accommodated in accordance with considerations outside of justice (as reciprocity). This proposal is not implausible. But it implies that the primary *substance* of reciprocity, as Gibbard conceives of it, is not good will but power, in the sense of being able *materially* to affect others through help or harm. Such a conception treats people not as bearers of good will regardless of whether they have any power materially to affect others, but as holders of the power to help or harm and hence potential benefit-creators to share with and potential troublemakers to reckon with. One of the clearest formulations of such a conception is by David Gauthier, *Morals by Agreement* (Oxford: Clarendon Press, 1986), e.g., pp. 114–116. This is why reciprocity has no room for those who are incapable of materially contributing to society. To thus exclude from the distribution of material benefits those incapable of contributing to their social production is to espouse a particular conception of justice as reciprocity in which the only reasons for justice are reasons of mutual advantage. It turns out that Gibbard's intrinsic reciprocity is not so intrinsic after all. We might suggest, then, that one way of depriving reciprocity of its independence from mutual advantage is not to insist on what the retrospective character of reciprocity implies about the substance of reciprocity, that is, good will. This is the case with Gibbard, "Constructing Justice." A more direct way of depriving reciprocity of its independence from mutual advantage is, of course, not to insist on the retrospectiveness of reciprocity itself. This is true of Gibbard's evolutionary account of reciprocity in *Wise Choices.*

reacts to the past in order to serve the future. The same is true, less surprisingly, of fair dealing and retaliation. "Many of our chief moral sentiments," says Gibbard, "are reciprocal overtly: a sense of fair dealing, feelings of gratitude, urges to retaliate. No surprise here for Darwinians: A sense of fair dealing prompts one to cooperate, and that elicits cooperation from others. Gratitude prompts the kinds of actions that will draw more favors. Retaliation deters."[13]

Once reciprocity is made out to be prospective rather than retrospective, it naturally takes on the character of exchange, or mutual advantage. For exchange is by nature future-oriented; it is interested in the past only in relation to the future, that is, only with a view to assessing the ability and reliability of those with whom one is about to enter into an exchange. Not surprisingly, Gibbard, having found sentiments of reciprocity to be future-oriented, immediately goes on to say, openly invoking the idea of exchange, that "these sentiments *pay,* on the whole—or at least they pay in the central case, in an ongoing interaction between oneself and someone else."[14] The telling (albeit dead) metaphor "pay" is echoed by yet another metaphor of exchange, as Gibbard tells us, expounding on the function of a sense of justice, "reciprocity needs *terms of trade.* Judgments of fairness may work to set the terms and to stabilize them."[15] And he is careful to point out that "social practices of course are not always the outcomes of overt bargaining" and yet "they *share a structure with bargaining.*"[16] Such a structure can be found, according to him, even in the apparently unconditional, that is, nonreciprocal, virtue of benevolence. Even here, "we develop unconditional scruples, perhaps, in response to cues that playing fair is a good bet." That this is the case seems to be shown by the fact that "friends evoke benevolent feelings and actions far more than strangers or acquaintances."[17] To the extent that this is so, even benevolence may be said to share a structure with reciprocity.

What nevertheless sets benevolence apart from reciprocity—what makes benevolence unconditional, if only apparently—is that benevolence contains no *conscious* expectation of return. Despite his proposition that "unconditional benevolence . . . might be evoked by special cues" which "sug-

13. Gibbard, *Wise Choices,* p. 261.

14. Ibid., emphasis added. From this it is but a short step to viewing reciprocity no longer in terms of "sentiments" but as a "marvelous strategy" called "tit-for-tat" (ibid.).

15. Ibid., emphasis added; see also p. 262.

16. Ibid., p. 262, emphasis added.

17. Ibid., pp. 258, 259.

gest, in effect, that the prospects of return are good," Gibbard is careful to say, in the same breath, that unconditional benevolence is "benevolence without *thought* of return."[18] In other words, benevolence is marked by a separation, as it were, between its conscious intention and its unconscious motivation. Unconsciously, it responds to cues suggesting the likelihood of return, but consciously, it performs good deeds as if for their own sake. Such a separation is also part of Gibbard's concept of intrinsic reciprocity. To say that "I might prefer treating another well who has treated me well, even if he has no further power to affect me,"[19] is to say that I am willing to reciprocate "without thought of return." Thus, the proviso "without thought of return" supplies the key to intrinsic or purely retrospective reciprocity. It is the absence of *conscious* expectation of return that preserves the temporal integrity of reciprocity by fixing its attention firmly on the past. What, then, accounts for the absence of conscious expectation of return?

The answer, though not made explicit by Gibbard, seems to be that there are situations in which no thought of return is necessary. These are situations in which it can generally be taken for granted that actions will be answered in kind. If this is the case, the pure retrospectiveness of reciprocity is an illusion regarding the character of one's motives, an illusion made possible by a particularly fortunate state of affairs. If it can be brought about that people routinely and reliably perform acts of reciprocation, it is not hard to imagine the *demand for* reciprocation (the thought of return) receding gradually from consciousness. When this happens, all that my consciousness registers of reciprocity is its retrospective dimension, the desire to return good will with good will. Its prospective dimension, rou-

18. Ibid., p. 259, emphasis added. This idea is also expressed or hinted at in the following: "Many familiar kinds [of benevolence] seem more or less to track the likely returns. People may act *with no thought of return,* but their benevolent impulses can be stilled by indications that no return is in the offing. There is no great evolutionary mystery why we might be like that" (ibid., emphasis added). "Clearly *we do feel benevolent at times, often without thought of return.* Still, a cool observer might conclude that our benevolent feelings come when cues suggest they will pay, and we act on these feelings when cues suggest the actions will pay. Genuine charity is a puzzle" (ibid., p. 260, emphasis added). "Moral sentiments from gratitude to fairness to rancor each move us, one way or other, to give good for good and ill for ill. We support schemes for common advantage, each trading support for a share in the benefits. Call these motivations of fidelity; they work against the impulse to cheat" (ibid., p. 264). "Reciprocity needs terms of trade . . . Standards of justice select one scheme, and thus shape and regulate motivations of fidelity" (ibid.).

19. Gibbard, "Constructing Justice," p. 266.

tinely taken care of in a stable environment of mutual advantage and hence routinely below the threshold of conscious motivation, comes to the fore only when it can no longer be taken for granted. This is why "people may act with no thought of return, but their benevolent impulses can be stilled by indications that no return is in the offing."[20] The implication here is that it is only when mutual advantage is assured that one's conscious motive in acts of reciprocation can *afford* to rise above it. If this is the case, the progress from reciprocity as mutual advantage to reciprocity as mutual good will is but a function of achieving conditions under which no thought of advantage is necessary. Intrinsic reciprocity is not so much an individual achievement as the product of a successful social practice.

This, it seems, is the central insight of Gibbard's evolutionary account of intrinsic reciprocity. It captures well the kind of exchange that typically takes place within a limited circle of acquaintances. Indeed, as Pierre Bourdieu shows with the example of gift exchange, the absence of conscious expectation of return on the part of both parties to an exchange is a necessary condition of the success of such an exchange and constitutes its very "meaning." What makes the spontaneity of such an exchange possible, however, is precisely its opposite, namely, a background of predictability (of return), and the *implicit* knowledge thereof, against which people can afford to act in apparent disregard of the possibility of return and thus appear (even to themselves) to be acting out of spontaneous generosity or intrinsic good will. Since this appearance constitutes the "meaning" of such exchanges, any conscious expectation of return is not just unnecessary but positively disruptive.[21]

Such a background of predictability does not exist, however, to anything like the same degree in the case of strangers, whose reciprocal relationship with one another has to rest on impersonal norms shared on a society-wide level. Given the sheer scale on which such reciprocation has to take place, there is no comparable predictability of mutual advantage to make conscious expectation of advantage unnecessary. And given the nature of the relationship between reciprocating strangers, the scheme of cooperation involved does not have, in the first instance, the kind of meaning that is based on the appearance of spontaneity and intrinsic good will. This kind of meaning becomes possible between strangers cooperating on a so-

20. Gibbard, *Wise Choices*, p. 259.

21. See Pierre Bourdieu, *The Logic of Practice*, trans. Richard Nice (Stanford: Stanford University Press, 1990), chap. 6.

ciety-wide level only if, or to the extent that, society manages to establish the same degree of underlying predictability that characterizes the seemingly spontaneous reciprocal relationships of the narrower and more intimate kind. Something like this seems to be what Rawls envisages for a well-ordered society.

The Importance of Reciprocity in Rawls

A well-ordered society rests, according to Rawls, on the formation of individual moral character in accordance with three psychological laws. Each of these laws charts a stage in the development of a person's sense of justice, beginning with love of parents, followed by ties of friendship and trust outside the family, and culminating in a principled attachment to social institutions that constitutes the sense of justice. The important thing about these laws is that they all rely on presuppositions regarding not the (innate) dispositions of individuals but the character of relevant institutions.

The first law, which concerns the development of a child's love for his parents and family institutions, bases that development on the presupposition "that family institutions express their love by caring for his good." Love of parents is followed, at the next stage, by the development of ties of trust and friendship in a social setting, and this can happen, according to the second law, only "given that a person's capacity for fellow feeling has been realized by acquiring attachments in accordance with the first law, and given that a social arrangement is just and publicly known by all to be just." Finally, at the third stage, a person develops a sense of justice through acquiring a certain understanding of and attachment to his society's institutions, but not before yet further presuppositions, as set forth in the third law, are fulfilled, namely, that "a person's capacity for fellow feeling has been realized by his forming attachments in accordance with the first two laws" and that "a society's institutions are just and are publicly known by all to be just."[22]

What stands out in these three laws is the priority of the justness of institutions. What is less conspicuous, in Rawls's brief formulation of the three laws, is that the concept of justice invoked in them is one based psychologically on the idea of reciprocity. This idea is made explicit when Rawls later elaborates on the three laws. It then becomes clear that the priority of in-

22. Rawls, *Theory*, p. 429.

stitutional justice is a function of the idea of reciprocity, as he understands it. According to Rawls, the sense of justice "*arise[s] from* the manifest intention of other persons to act for our good. Because we recognize that they wish us well, we care for their well-being *in return*. Thus we acquire attachments to persons and institutions according to how we perceive our good to be affected by them. The basic idea is one of reciprocity, a tendency to answer in kind."[23] In this light, when Rawls says (in an earlier passage) that "the most striking feature of these laws (or tendencies) is that their formulation refers to an institutional setting as being just, and in the last two, as being publicly known to be such,"[24] this cannot simply mean that the principles designed to regulate social cooperation are just and publicly known to be such, regardless of whether and to what extent these principles are actually followed. To be sure, that these principles are considered just may, in an ideal situation, be a necessary condition of their being acted upon by members of society. But it is their being acted upon, and being acted upon because they are considered just, that constitutes the sufficient condition for an institutional setting to count as just in the sense in which Rawls takes such a setting to be a prerequisite for the development of a sense of justice by individuals. Since, according to Rawls, a capacity for a sense of justice is "built up by responses *in kind*," the condition that the institutional setting be just and publicly known to be such must mean that members of society are actually following those principles of justice—responding in kind—and are publicly known to be doing so.[25]

Thus we need, in retrospect, to attach much greater importance to an aspect of the second law that is not explicitly treated as one of the relevant presuppositions but which is nonetheless an equally crucial precondition. The two explicitly stated presuppositions, we may recall, are that "a person's capacity for fellow feeling has been realized by acquiring attachments in accordance with the first law" and that "a social arrangement is just and publicly known by all to be just." Under these preconditions, according to Rawls, a person is able to develop trust and good will toward others, but,

23. Ibid., p. 433, emphasis added.

24. Ibid., p. 430.

25. Ibid., p. 433, emphasis added. In this regard, Rawls's line of reasoning is very similar to that of Jürgen Habermas as found, for example, in "Law and Morality," in *The Tanner Lectures on Human Values*, vol. 8, ed. Sterling M. McMurrin (Salt Lake City: University of Utah Press, 1988), pp. 217–279 (see esp. p. 245); and *Justification and Application: Remarks on Discourse Ethics*, trans. Ciaran P. Cronin (Cambridge, Mass.: MIT Press, 1993), p. 155. This and related points are discussed in Chapter 1.

as Rawls later makes clear, this can take place only if those around him "with evident intention *comply with* their duties and obligations, and *live up to* the ideals of their station."[26] Now, either we have to treat this as a further precondition, or else we have to interpret the precondition that "a social arrangement is just and publicly known by all to be just" as meaning more than it explicitly says, that is, as meaning, in addition, that people actually follow the principles of justice and are publicly known to be doing so in a social arrangement that is just and publicly known to be just. The same is true of the third law. There a person is able to acquire an attachment to just social arrangements not only on the basis of the explicitly stated presuppositions but also because "he recognizes that he and those for whom he cares *are*"—not merely would be or might be—"the beneficiaries of these arrangements."[27]

The upshot of all this is that Rawls's idea of the priority of a just social setting is of a piece with his concept of reciprocity. And this in turn, I would suggest, is so because the concept of reciprocity in question is at least in part one of mutual advantage. On the face of it, Rawls's concept of reciprocity appears broad enough to encompass what I distinguished earlier as mutual advantage and mutual good will. But matters look different if we ask whether Rawls's concept of reciprocity is retrospective or prospective. Although none of his remarks on reciprocity constitutes a direct answer to this question, it is significant that he, like Gibbard, sees reciprocity as having an evolutionary function:

> Surely a rational person is not indifferent to things that significantly affect his good; and supposing that he develops some attitude toward them, he acquires either a new attachment or a new aversion. If we answered love with hate, or came to dislike those who acted fairly toward us, or were averse to activities that furthered our good, a community would soon dissolve. Beings with a different psychology either have never existed or must soon have disappeared in the course of evolution. A capacity for a sense of justice built up by responses in kind would appear to be a condition of human sociability.[28]

This seems a plausible account of reciprocity, but the account, couched as it is in evolutionary terms, also implies a particular concept of reciproc-

26. Rawls, *Theory,* p. 429, emphasis added.

27. Ibid., p. 430, emphasis added.

28. Ibid., p. 433.

ity. The very fact that Rawls sees reciprocity as serving an evolutionary function shows that the reciprocity in question is prospective rather than purely retrospective, for it is hard to see purely retrospective reciprocity as having any function, evolutionary or otherwise. And, as we saw in my discussion of Gibbard, to the extent that reciprocity is prospective, it is characterized by mutual advantage. Therefore, one cannot avoid construing Rawls's concept of reciprocity in terms of mutual advantage—or what Rawls himself calls "reciprocal advantage."[29]

From Mutual Advantage to Mutual Good Will

If Rawls's concept of reciprocity contains an element of mutual advantage, it does not by any means exclude mutual good will. As a matter of fact, his concept of reciprocity has a developmental dimension, a built-in dynamic that leads from mutual advantage to mutual good will. To say, as I did earlier, that Rawls's concept of reciprocity is essentially one of mutual advantage is to insist that mutual good will cannot serve as an initial assumption that is required for the establishment of a just society. This is quite compatible with holding that once a just society is set in motion by other factors, it will be capable of generating mutual good will over and above the conscious motive of mutual advantage. Thus, Rawls has no difficulty believing that "identification with the good of others . . . might be quite strong," and yet for him this is something to be expected only "in a social system regulated by justice as fairness," that is, only in a social system where mutual advantage is assured.[30] Indeed, once a just social system is established, it will in due course bring about "*transformations* of our pattern of final ends" until our ends come to be informed by good will toward others. This comes about "from our recognizing the manner in which institutions and the actions of others affect our good."[31] In this way, mutual good will does figure in Rawls's concept of reciprocity, but the important thing is that it does so not as an initial assumption but only as an

29. Ibid., p. 155. On the face of it, Rawls is discussing this idea in the context of the original position, but the fact that he regards it as a "more realistic idea of designing the social order" (than the utilitarian alternative) makes clear that the motive involved is also a feature of the real world. It is perhaps not accidental that the expression (and concept) "reciprocal advantage" is one that is used by David Hume in *A Treatise of Human Nature,* ed. L. A. Selby-Bigge, 2nd ed., ed. P. H. Nidditch (Oxford: Clarendon Press, 1978), p. 519.

30. Rawls, *Theory,* p. 438.

31. Ibid., p. 432, emphasis added.

end product of justice—not as an input, if you will, but as an output of a just society.[32] In other words, mutual advantage is the basis of mutual good will, and mutual good will the result of mutual advantage, and the progression from the one to the other may be appropriately described, in the words of Hume, as a "progress of the sentiments."[33]

That this is the case is also shown by changes in the concept of reciprocity as we move from the Rawlsian original position, where hypothetical agents deliberate about principles that are to regulate a well-ordered society, to the well-ordered society itself. For the most part, Rawls does not directly invoke the idea of reciprocity in his discussion of the original position. But clearly some notion of reciprocity is involved here, inasmuch as the original position presupposes as a background the circumstances of justice as Hume understands them. Given this understanding of the circumstances of justice, the only notion of reciprocity that is compatible with or inferable from it, *at the outset,* is one of mutual advantage. In other words, mutual advantage rather than mutual good will is the only motive that can realistically be counted on for the purpose of setting a well-ordered society in motion. As Rawls remarks, contrasting his position with utilitarianism, and here with unambiguous reference to the real world rather than to the hypothetical original position, "altruistic inclinations no doubt exist. Yet they are likely to be less strong than those brought about by the three psychological laws formulated as reciprocity principles; and a marked capacity for sympathetic identification seems relatively rare. Therefore these feelings provide less support for the basic structure of society."[34]

It is only *within* a well-ordered society, and as a result of it (because mutual advantage is assured), that reciprocity can predictably and substantially take on the further dimension of mutual good will. Once a well-ordered society is firmly established, a situation may arise in which mutual advantage is so assured that people come to take it for granted and thus

32. The logic at work here is not unlike that expressed by Jon Elster and Karl Ove Moene in the introduction to their edited volume *Alternatives to Capitalism* (Cambridge: Cambridge University Press, 1989), p. 5. According to them, "we may hope that trust will come about as a by-product of a good economic system (and thus make the system even better), but one would be putting the cart before the horse were one to bank on trust, solidarity and altruism as the preconditions for reform."

33. Hume, *Treatise,* p. 500.

34. Rawls, *Theory,* p. 438. The same cautionary note is sounded in Rawls, *Political Liberalism,* p. 87.

forget that mutual good will has its basis in mutual advantage. As they thus lose conscious awareness of the role of mutual advantage in producing mutual good will, so they may even lose conscious awareness of the reciprocal nature of good will itself and come to believe that they are imbued with innate, unconditional good will toward others, who happen, independently or nonreciprocally, also to have the same good will toward them. Some such scenario would seem to fit well with Rawls's evolutionary account of reciprocity, as it would Gibbard's. In this regard, Rawls's well-ordered society looks remarkably like Bourdieu's gift exchange community writ large. In an environment where reciprocity (of advantage and of good will) is a fact of life, or to the extent that it is, consciousness of it has no role to play. Rather, it is more conducive to the continuation of such reciprocity that people, while noticing the mutuality of good will, come no longer to regard the mutuality as an integral part of good will but to believe instead that mutual good will is but the result of the unconditional good will each feels toward all.

There is thus a sense in which Rawls places at the end of a process (of the development of a just society) what utilitarianism places at the beginning. In this initial position, sympathy (one need not be too precise about the meaning of the term "sympathy" in this context) serves for utilitarianism as a necessary assumption for the construction of a just society. This is where, in Rawls's view, utilitarianism goes wrong. Instead of waiting for sympathy, or good will, to emerge from a just society that is itself based on lesser, more common motives, utilitarianism, according to Rawls, makes the mistake of "appealing *straightway* to the capacity for sympathy as a *foundation* of just conduct *in the absence of reciprocity*." In so doing, utilitarianism depends for the motivating of just conduct on "weaker and less common inclinations" than the desire for mutual advantage.[35] Rawls is clearly right here, and he must also be right to treat (mutual) good will as a product rather than, as in utilitarianism, an origin of a just society. If Rawls is right, then, and utilitarianism wrong about the place of sympathy in relation to justice, certain profound implications follow for our understanding of the nature and possibility of justice.

There is, as Rawls observes, an important reason why utilitarianism treats sympathy as a foundation of justice, namely: "Those who do not benefit from the better situation of others must identify with the greater sum (average) of satisfaction else they will not desire to follow the utility

35. Rawls, *Theory*, p. 438, emphasis added.

criterion."[36] Psychologically, *sympathy is for utilitarianism a source of the unconditional element in justice.* It is what helps make the social goal of the greatest overall sum of happiness unconditional for each individual regardless of his or her share of that sum.[37] Rawls is critical of this role of sympathy, disagreeing with utilitarianism not only over whether sympathy *can* serve as a foundation of just conduct, as we have seen, but also as to whether sympathy *should* serve as such a foundation, given utilitarianism's reasons for appealing to sympathy.

On both of these grounds, the first empirical, the second normative, Rawls rejects sympathy as a foundation of justice. In so doing, he takes the momentous step of *divesting justice of the unconditional element that comes from sympathy,* and this irrespective of the uses to which such an unconditional element may be put. Commenting on John Stuart Mill's idea of justice in terms of the balance of self-interest and regard for the interest of others, Rawls argues that "the contract doctrine achieves the same result, but it does so not by an ad hoc weighing of two competing tendencies, but by a theoretical construction which leads to the appropriate reciprocity principles as a conclusion."[38] It is of crucial importance that the "two competing tendencies"—sympathy and self-interest—do not have equal roles to play in Rawls's theoretical construction. What happens instead, as we have seen, is that one of the two tendencies, sympathy, is discounted from the motivational picture in Rawls's theory, so that the desire for reciprocal advantage becomes the sole motivational foundation of justice. As a result, justice no longer has what Rawls calls a "double origin" consisting of sympathy and self-interest, as it clearly does for Mill, but only a single origin in the shape of mutual advantage.

Mutual Advantage and the Conditionality of Justice

So we are back with the notion of reciprocity as mutual advantage, *to begin with.* The more advanced kind of reciprocity, reciprocity as mutual good will, has to await the full realization of a well-ordered society. Until then, the desire to reciprocate is *overtly* prospective. And when such overtly prospective reciprocity serves as the sole motivational *starting point* of justice, the sense of justice itself is *overtly* conditional, each person's willingness to

36. Ibid.; see also p. 155.

37. Sympathy can of course also be invoked in utilitarianism in favor of the worse off in cases of diminishing marginal utility.

38. Rawls, *Theory,* p. 440.

be just dependent on his or her being benefited by a similar willingness on the part of all. The willingness to form such a conditional relationship of mutual benefit and restraint is taken by Rawls to belong to "reasonable moral psychology," as he calls it. "Persons are reasonable in one basic aspect," says Rawls, "when, among equals say, they are ready to propose principles and standards as fair terms of cooperation and to abide by them willingly, *given the assurance that others will likewise do so.*" It is essential that not only "everyone accepts," but also everyone "*knows that everyone else accepts,* the very same principles of justice."[39] This is indeed a reasonable moral psychology, one that captures particularly well the spirit of justice. What is reasonable about it is at once the willingness to reciprocate and the demand for reciprocation from others. If the willingness to reciprocate raises the disposition toward justice above rational egoism,[40] the demand for reciprocation from others places this disposition below unconditional benevolence. As a result, justice, including the virtue thereof, occupies an intermediate position that is both normatively defensible and motivationally realistic.

This reasonable moral psychology entails, however, that a sense of justice consists in the desire to follow a hypothetical imperative rather than a categorical one. In other words, it is an *integral* part of a sense of justice to attach conditions, overtly and consciously to begin with, to fulfilling the requirements of justice.[41] This fact lies at the heart of a sense of justice, and it is a serious omission on Rawls's part not to follow through the implications of this fact for how the sense of justice should be understood. I will point out some of these implications toward the end of this chapter, but first it is necessary to show why certain complications Rawls has introduced in *Political Liberalism* do not change the conditional character of the sense of justice.

It may appear that Rawls succeeds in turning the hypothetical imperative of justice into a categorical one when he distinguishes "conception-dependent desires," among them the "ideal of citizenship as characterized in justice as fairness," from "object-dependent desires."[42] Owing to their

39. Rawls, *Political Liberalism,* pp. 86, 49, 35, emphasis added.

40. A discussion of the gap between rational egoism and the requirements of justice can be found in Chapter 5.

41. For more extensive discussion on this point, see Chapter 1.

42. Rawls, *Political Liberalism,* pp. 82–84. This seems in part a response to the kind of criticism made, for example, by Michael J. Sandel, *Liberalism and the Limits of Justice* (Cambridge: Cambridge University Press, 1982), p. 165.

conception-dependent or principle-dependent desires, reasonable persons, Rawls tells us, though "not moved by the general good as such," nevertheless "desire *for its own sake* a social world in which they, as free and equal, can cooperate with others on terms all can accept."[43] This seems a far cry from Hume's account of the motive of justice, as Hume operates with object-dependent desires alone. There is no doubt that Rawls's account of desires as encompassing not only object-dependent desires but also principle-dependent and conception-dependent ones is richer and more plausible, and capable of accounting for behavior that is hard to explain in terms of object-dependent desires alone. But he does not address *the relationship* between these different types of desire in the moral psychology of individuals and society—the kind of question that would immediately arise from, say, a Humean, Marxian, or Nietzschean perspective. It is revealing, in this connection, that although Rawls rejects (or at least radically expands) Hume's account of motivation by introducing principle-dependent and conception-dependent desires,[44] he has not abandoned Hume's conception of the objective circumstances of justice as arising from scarcity of resources.[45] Clearly, so long as the objective circumstances of justice are conceived in this way, the central problematic of justice will remain the conflict between object-dependent desires. To be sure, such conflict, as I tried to show in Chapter 2, typically takes the form of competing conceptions of the good, encompassing as they do both principle-dependent and conception-dependent desires. Yet it is arguable that principle-dependent and conception-dependent desires seldom if ever completely subordinate object-dependent desires, assimilating them without residue and placing them entirely at the service of higher ends. This is not to deny that once principle-dependent and conception-dependent desires are effectively formed, they give shape and meaning to object-dependent desires, which is why even conflicts directly involving object-dependent desires tend to take the form of competing conceptions of the good. But the important point here is that as long as the pursuit of object-dependent desires is not *entirely* subordinated to the pursuit of principle-dependent or conception-dependent desires, the introduction of conception-dependent desires by itself cannot make the requirement of

43. Rawls, *Political Liberalism,* p. 50.

44. See ibid., p. 84.

45. Rawls explicitly subscribes to such a conception in *Theory,* pp. 109–110.

justice a categorical imperative, or the disposition toward justice an unconditional virtue.

Thus, despite Rawls's introduction of conception-dependent desires, the imperative of justice remains a hypothetical imperative. It can have the appearance of not being hypothetical only to the extent that the hypothetical condition is fulfilled. But what does it take to fulfill the hypothetical condition in the first place? How can everyone be assured that others will do their part in a society-wide scheme of cooperation? Does the sense of justice simply depend on that assurance, or does it (also) contribute to it, and in either case, how? What do answers to these questions tell us about the nature of the sense of justice even when, under ideal conditions, the sense of justice is relieved of the "strain of commitment" and acquires the appearance of unconditionality? And what do they tell us about the possibility and limits of justice, both as a virtue of individuals and as a property of institutions? These questions—and one can think of others—are largely deflected by Rawls's exclusive concern with what he calls "strict compliance theory,"[46] characterized by the assumption that people "generally comply with society's basic institutions, which they regard as just."[47] This is an assumption that I think we should not make if our aim is to understand the psychology of justice. For this assumption passes over huge differences between the spontaneous, self-enforcing reciprocity that is constitutive of exchanges between acquaintances and the consciously contrived reciprocity that marks cooperation between strangers on a society-wide scale. Because of such differences, the predictability of compliance characteristic of the former cannot be taken for granted for the latter. Indeed, the very absence of predictability is precisely what makes the sense of justice necessary among strangers in the first place, and thus the sense of justice must have a very different character from the sense of fair play among acquaintances that implicitly relies on a background of predictability.

We have seen earlier that in Bourdieu's model of personal exchange within a confined social space, a seemingly spontaneous mutual good will is the subjective correlate of objectively predictable reciprocal relationships and in turn constitutes the meaning of those relationships. Up to a point, this could also serve as a model of the society-wide practice of justice, but it cannot do so *to begin with*. For the very absence of predictability in society-wide cooperation is a problem that has to be overcome before this

46. Ibid., p. 8.
47. Rawls, *Political Liberalism*, p. 35.

model can apply. Until then, a sense of justice, instead of having a background of predictable mutual advantage to rely on, must serve as one of the solutions to the very absence of that background. Indeed, given the nature and scope of society-wide cooperation, it is possible that a sense of justice will *always* have to serve this remedial function to some degree, not least by inculcating the separation of morality from advantage. These circumstances are constitutive of the sense of justice.

There is thus a serious flaw in any account of the sense of justice that assumes general compliance with the rules of society-wide cooperation. Such general compliance may exist—indeed, has to exist—if a society that is stable for the right reasons is to be possible, but its existence is something that has to be explained rather than assumed when we are trying to construct an account of the sense of justice. A sense of justice, instead of being explained against the background of general compliance, may well have to go into the explanation of how that very background can come about in the first place. To be sure, it may be useful to assume general compliance or at least reasonably favorable circumstances in constructing a purely *normative* theory of justice (or one kind of such theory), but to make this assumption is precisely *not* to explain how general compliance or reasonably favorable circumstances can come about. The task of *explanation*—of the possible (but by no means guaranteed) emergence of reasonably favorable circumstances and of the role of the sense of justice in this process and the nature of the sense of justice as affected by this process—must therefore begin by not making this assumption. This suggests a rather different way of approaching the sense of justice, one which foregrounds the hypothetical character of the sense of justice and investigates the means whereby the hypothetical condition is fulfilled artificially (rather than spontaneously, as in the case of reciprocal relationships between acquaintances) and the sense of justice is made to appear unconditional. Only in this way, in my view, can we get to the heart of the sense of justice.

8

Two Paths to Unconditional Justice

In reflecting on the conditionality of justice, it is crucial to distinguish between the motivation of justice on the one hand and the practice and institutional dimension of justice on the other. As I tried to show toward the end of the last chapter, justice has a conditional character as far as its motivation is concerned, in that a just person undertakes to follow certain norms only provided that others do the same. Such a reciprocal *commitment* to justice marks a break with rational egoism, as we saw in Chapter 5, and yet the *reciprocal* nature of the commitment still gives the norms of justice the status of conditional imperatives. No system of justice, however, can rest securely on a general understanding of the norms of justice as conditional imperatives. One of the main aims of a system of justice is to create predictability and trust and thereby to counteract the otherwise naturally contagious tendency of injustice,[1] and this aim dictates that every individual has to practice justice unconditionally in relation to every other individual.

Thus the motivational conditionality of justice comes into conflict with the fact that the practice and the system of justice have to be unconditional, at least in those areas that are precisely demarcated by law. The system of justice exists to offset the conditionality of the motivation of justice, to take contingency and uncertainty out of the human willingness and ability to treat one another justly. Indeed, the more conditional the motivation of justice is, the harder the system of justice must work to en-

1. As Hume puts it: "You are, therefore, naturally carried to commit acts of injustice as well as me. Your example both pushes me forward in this way by imitation, and also affords me a new reason for any breach of equity, by shewing me, that I should be the cully of my integrity, if I alone shou'd impose on myself a severe restraint amidst the licentiousness of others." David Hume, *A Treatise of Human Nature,* ed. L. A. Selby-Bigge, 2nd ed., ed. P. H. Nidditch (Oxford: Clarendon Press, 1978), p. 535.

sure that justice is *practiced* unconditionally. Ultimately, society's problem is how to make the practice of justice unconditional in the face of the motivational conditionality of justice.

In this chapter I discuss two ways in which society deals with this problem. In the first place, society monopolizes the right to punish breaches of reciprocity and in so doing makes itself the sole locus of the conditionality of justice. It is to the extent that society thus preserves the reciprocity of justice that individuals who are motivated by mutual advantage can afford to accept the legal requirement to practice justice unconditionally. In the second place, given that the extent in question can never be complete, society has an interest in turning the legal requirement into a moral obligation and thereby injecting an element of unconditionality into the very motivation of justice. I argue that such unconditionality of motivation is most likely to emerge in a theistic context, if anywhere. I try to show, however, that what a theistic context makes possible is only an illusion of unconditionality, conducive though such an illusion may sometimes be to the unconditional practice of justice.

The Locus of Reciprocity

The practical and institutional unconditionality of justice has to be created out of the motivational conditionality of justice. Even as society seeks to overcome the motivational conditionality of justice, it must accommodate and coax it. For justice can be institutionally unconditional only in a way that nevertheless accords with the motivational conditionality of justice. The motivational conditionality of justice, not least the natural desire for revenge that is part of it, must be pacified if it is not to make impossible the unconditional practice of justice.

The compromise solution that typically emerges from this contradiction is that the state makes itself the sole locus of the conditionality (that is, the reciprocity) of justice, thereby protecting each individual from breaches of reciprocity by all other individuals. In exchange for such protection, individuals have to follow the imperatives of justice as if the duty to do so were unconditional and nonreciprocal. In this way, the reciprocity of justice between individuals translates into a reciprocal relationship each individual has with the state, as best captured in the notion of a social contract.[2] A so-

2. Hobbes immediately comes to mind as a pioneer of this general way of thinking. See Thomas Hobbes, *Leviathan,* ed. C. B. Macpherson (Harmondsworth: Penguin, 1968), e.g., chaps. 14, 15.

cial contract marks the transfer of reciprocity from the realm of individual relationships to the realm of the relationship between individuals and the state. Only the state is entitled to act on the premise that justice is reciprocal and conditional. And it follows that only the state has the right to punish breaches of reciprocity. As Hegel puts it, in a context quite relevant to our own, "Instead of the injured party, the injured *universal* now comes on the scene."[3] Individuals, deprived of the power and, ideally, the incentive to react to such breaches, have to practice justice unconditionally, leaving it entirely to the state to ensure that other people do the same.[4]

There is a corresponding change in the locus of reciprocity within individual psychology. When we speak of reciprocity, we refer in the first instance to a relationship between individuals or to a disposition whose exercise depends on the relationship between individuals. This may be expressed by means of the following formula: I will (have the incentive to) do certain things, beneficial or harmful, to others if others do the same to me. Once the right of direct or naked reciprocity is taken away from them by the state, individuals are made to see reciprocity essentially as a relationship with society. This relationship is captured by a new formula: I will (have the incentive to) do certain things if I have determined that on balance (and by some benchmark that I deem appropriate) I am a beneficiary of the society which enjoins me to do these things.[5] Since my desire to be just is conditional, my willingness to follow society's norms of justice depends on the results of such determination. Other things being equal, the more I see myself as benefiting from society, the more I am prepared to follow its norms.[6] It may of course be a necessary condition for my being such a beneficiary that most people follow the norms of justice most of the

3. G. W. F. Hegel, *Hegel's Philosophy of Right,* trans. T. M. Knox (London: Oxford University Press, 1967), para. 220 (p. 141).

4. It is only in this sense that what Judith N. Shklar (*The Faces of Injustice* [New Haven: Yale University Press, 1990], p. 93) says of revenge is true, namely, that it is "the very opposite of justice, in every respect, and inherently incompatible with it." See also Immanuel Kant, *The Metaphysics of Morals,* trans. Mary Gregor (Cambridge: Cambridge University Press, 1991), p. 252.

5. Gibbard captures the spirit of this kind of exchange very aptly: "Justice is fairness in exchange, but *on a grand scale:* it is fairness in the terms governing a society-wide system of reciprocity . . . The citizen of a well-ordered society is motivated to return benefits fairly, and *this general motivation becomes a motivation to conform to the rules of a social structure that he considers fair.*" Allan Gibbard, "Constructing Justice," *Philosophy and Public Affairs* 20 (1991): 264–279; quotation from p. 266, emphasis added.

6. See Arthur Schopenhauer, *On the Basis of Morality,* trans. E. F. J. Payne (Indianapolis: Bobbs-Merrill, 1965), p. 124.

time. But it is beyond my legal power, of which I have none, to see to it that other people do so, and it is beyond my cognitive power to ascertain whether, and how often, they do so. These powers rest with the state, and thus my relationship with other individuals is mediated through my relationship with the state. It is the state's responsibility to ensure that everybody benefits from everybody else's following the same norms of justice. Accordingly, individuals ascertain whether the state has fulfilled its part of the contract by determining whether on balance they are more beneficiaries of the state's enforcement of justice than victims of breaches of justice that go undetected or unpunished. Assuming that the social structure is accepted as more or less just, an individual will lose the incentive to practice justice unconditionally, not when he considers (isolated) *individuals* to have failed to reciprocate, but only when he considers the *state* to have failed (in a significant way) in its responsibility to enforce the norms of justice.

So it turns out that the unconditional practice of justice is only apparently unconditional, for it is conditional upon the state's preservation of the reciprocity of justice and thereby of the advantages of justice for each individual. Our willingness to practice justice, no longer *directly* dependent on reciprocation from other individuals, has come to depend on our sense of whether the state has succeeded in maintaining *its* reciprocity with us. To the extent that the state succeeds in enforcing the basic framework of reciprocity, observance of the requirements of justice can come reasonably to be seen as unconditional by all individuals, but only because all can rely on others to comply, in the face of such state supervision, with the norms of justice. Indeed, if the extent in question is substantial and durable, individuals may come to take the actual achievement of mutual advantage so much for granted that they will lose conscious awareness of the reciprocal and conditional nature of justice. It is only in such favorable circumstances that justice can take on the appearance of being unconditional. Short of this, the state's preservation of the reciprocity of justice requires above all the institution of punishment.

Reciprocity and Punishment

Punishment is not extraneous to justice, not something brought in from outside of justice to bridge gaps in the ongoing chain of reciprocity. As institutionalized retaliation, it follows naturally from the reciprocal character of justice. Since my willingness to be just is based on reciprocity, I feel both disadvantaged and betrayed when others fail to be just to me as I have been just to them. This sense of double loss, involving interest and respect, cries out for retaliation against the offender, retaliation that society exacts on my behalf in the form of punishment. Socially administered retaliation, ostensibly meant to cause pain or loss of freedom, is at bottom aimed at restoring the reciprocity of justice.[7] What is at stake is not only my material interest or even integrity of life and limb but also my fundamental equality with others, which an offender's breach of reciprocity, if not responded to in kind, would have undermined.[8] We might say that punishment is a kind of negative reciprocation, society's response to failure of reciprocation on the part of individuals. When society punishes an individual for failure of reciprocation, it follows precisely the principle of reciprocity and does so with the support of the law, although the injured individual could follow the same principle only against the law.[9] This intrinsic link between justice and violence cannot be removed without removing the reciprocal foundation of justice itself. The only thing that can be done is to socialize or institutionalize it, to substitute for the individual violence of retaliation the collective violence of legal punishment.

Punishment represents the transfer of the locus of justice, and with it the locus of violence, from the realm of direct relationship between individuals to the realm of relationship between individuals and the state.[10]

7. Something like this is presumably (part of) the rationale for Becker's idea that "we ought to be disposed to *make* reciprocation a requirement," that is, "to be disposed to ascribe blame to people who do not reciprocate, or to coerce them into reciprocating, or to punish them or to extract compensation from them for their failure to reciprocate." See Lawrence C. Becker, *Reciprocity* (London: Routledge & Kegan Paul, 1986), p. 130. It is in this light that Becker's insistence that "evil received should not be returned with evil" (p. 94) should be understood. By definition, punishing someone for failure of reciprocation does not count as returning evil with evil.

8. It is, I think, in something like this sense that Hegel says, "Crime is to be annulled, not because it is the producing of an evil, but because it is an infringement of the right as right" (*Philosophy*, para. 99, p. 70). For a discussion of Hegel's idea of annulment, see David E. Cooper, "Hegel's Theory of Punishment," in *Hegel's Political Philosophy: Problems and Perspectives*, ed. Z. A. Pelczynski (Cambridge: Cambridge University Press, 1971), pp. 151–167, esp. pp. 159, 163–165.

9. For discussions of Kant's theory of punishment as based on the principle of reciprocity, see Hans Saner, *Kant's Political Thought*, trans. E. B. Ashton (Chicago: University of Chicago Press, 1973), p. 32; and Jeffrie G. Murphy, *Kant: The Philosophy of Right* (New York: Macmillan, 1970), pp. 141–142.

10. Such a transfer, of course, is usually taken to cause some improvement of the motive involved, that is, from the emotional to the moral or rational. See, for example, Susan Meld Shell, *The Rights of Reason: A Study of Kant's Philosophy and Politics* (Toronto: University of Toronto Press, 1980), p. 162.

The lawbreaker, as Nietzsche puts it, is "a breaker of his contract and his word *with the whole*."[11] Just as a breach of reciprocity is against the whole, in the shape of the state, so it is punishable only by the whole, even though its concrete impact is on individuals. What the state does, in taking it upon itself to punish breaches of reciprocity, is to make it illegitimate for *individuals* to treat justice as conditional. This is what is meant by the injunction that prohibits individuals from taking the law into their own hands. Justice remains conditional, but this applies only to the relationship between individuals and the state, for the state metes out benefit and punishment to individuals in a way that is conditional upon whether they follow society's norms of justice. In this sense, justice involves conditional actions by the state. But precisely for this reason, justice requires unconditional actions of individuals. The state acknowledges and safeguards the conditionality of justice by punishing breaches of reciprocity, and as long as the state succeeds in this responsibility, it is entitled to demand the unconditional performance of just actions by individuals.

Even as punishment of offenders helps make the practice of justice unconditional for everyone else, it still answers to the motivational conditionality of justice. For it is only by preserving the reciprocity of justice, in the relationship between each individual and the state, that punishment makes it psychologically acceptable for individuals to practice justice as a set of unconditional imperatives governing the relationship between individuals. Punishment exists to create fear in those who may be tempted to commit breaches of reciprocity and at the same time to give a certain satisfaction to those who have no such desire and yet who, being human, also have no desire to practice justice unilaterally. For such reciprocity-abiding citizens, punishment of reciprocity-breakers serves to ease the pain of resentment and, even more important, to prevent such resentment from turning into resentment against the state itself. Through punishment the state exacts "a kind of repayment for the advantages the criminal has enjoyed hitherto,"[12] and in so doing provides psychological relief for those who practice justice unconditionally but whose motivation remains conditional. As long as the unconditional practice of justice rests upon reciprocity as its motivational foundation, punishment is an indispensable means of mediating between them and ensuring the former despite the latter. The

11. Friedrich Nietzsche, *On the Genealogy of Morals* (together with *Ecce Homo*), trans. Walter Kaufmann and R. J. Hollingdale, (New York: Random House, 1967), II, 9.

12. Ibid., II, 13.

meaning of punishment boils down to this: the state takes the conditionality of justice—and the harshness and brutality that go with it—upon itself so that individuals are both legally compelled and psychologically motivated to practice justice *as if* unconditionally.

The Transfiguration of Justice

The state takes it upon itself to satisfy the reciprocity condition of justice, as we have seen, when it monopolizes the power of punishment. But no state can be entirely successful in that gigantic enterprise. The resort to punishment is a measure not only of the state's power (even here punishment can easily be perceived as too little and it is almost always too late) but also of its failure, and thus even with the mediation of punishment, the unconditional practice of justice is constantly strained by the conditionality of its motivation. Ideally, this strain is removed, and justice made to appear unconditional, when the reciprocity condition is met by most of the people most of the time. If this happens, the motivational conditionality of justice will be more or less lost from consciousness, and the illusion of unconditionality will *naturally* arise. For this to happen, however, the state must first *artificially* create the illusion that justice is motivationally unconditional in order that individuals will be prepared to practice justice even when the reciprocity condition is not adequately satisfied to begin with.

The more the state itself fails to satisfy the reciprocity condition and dissipate consciousness of the motivational conditionality of justice, the more it will find it expedient to seek to transform that motive itself and make it unconditional. In other words, to the extent that the state fails in its responsibility to underwrite the conditionality of justice, individuals must be encouraged to make up for it by their virtue, by their willingness to practice justice for its own sake and with no reference even to possible reciprocity. To this end, the state needs an ideology of the unconditionality of justice, whose function it is to cause the forgetting of the rationale for and the conditionality of justice *before* the conditions of such forgetfulness are satisfied.[13] Thus, the inculcation of an unconditional motive of justice marks a significant shift of responsibility from the state to the individual in

13. Where breaches of reciprocity are *not* subject to legal punishment (that is, are not matters of justice in the legal sense), reciprocity, or tit for tat, is within the power and discretion of individuals. But even here it may be in the interest of social stability and cooperative ef-

the fight to make justice unconditional. Where such inculcation is successful, the unconditional practice of justice will occur, no longer in spite of a motivational conditionality but because of the unconditionality of the motivation itself.

Recall that one important factor that makes the motivation of justice conditional is the (in part) instrumental character of justice, that is, justice as a means to the mutual satisfaction of self-interest under conditions of roughly equal power. Since this is the case, making the motivation of justice unconditional requires somehow distancing justice from self-interest, even from the reciprocal satisfaction of self-interest. This almost amounts to keeping the idea of justice but doing away with the motive that led to its invention in the first place. To the extent that such a radical separation of justice from its original motive is achieved, no matter how it is achieved (more of this later), justice will become an end in itself, a duty to be practiced for its own sake. To practice justice for its own sake is to practice it unconditionally, that is, with no concern for reciprocity and hence independently of conditions other people may or may not satisfy.[14] Other people being just—or a sufficient number of other people being just for a sufficient amount of the time—is a necessary condition for my desire to be just only to the extent that I treat justice as a means and I want to benefit from being just. Once I am determined to practice justice regardless of whether I benefit from so doing (even though I may still prefer to benefit from so doing if possible), I will, by the same token, practice justice regardless of whether other people do the same. That is to say, I will practice justice for its own sake, unconditionally.[15]

---

ficiency to make the practice of norm-following as unconditional as possible. In this case, because compliance with norms is not made unconditional by law, it can be made unconditional only by making the motivation of norm-following itself unconditional.

14. "Unconditionally" need not mean "absolutely" here. For justice to be practiced unconditionally, as an intrinsic (rather than instrumental) value, is just for it to have value that is not a function of its ability to contribute to realizing another value and hence is independent of conditions set by the latter value. An intrinsic value admits in principle to being more or less than, or equal to, some other value, although being an intrinsic value itself, it does not stand in an instrumental relation to the latter value. In this sense an intrinsic value need not have "absolute" (as opposed to "relative") value or be an absolute value. When I speak of justice being (treated as) an intrinsic value, I leave open the question whether it is also (treated as) an absolute value. To practice justice from an (apparently) unconditional or intrinsic motive is, strictly speaking, to practice justice independently of conditions of *reciprocity,* not necessarily independently of *all* conceivable conditions, for the latter would presuppose justice being an absolute value.

15. Compare my account of the conditional versus unconditional aspects of the disposition toward justice with Bernard Williams's account of the instrumental versus intrinsic val-

To practice justice for its own sake and unconditionally? This sounds almost like a contradiction in terms. For practicing justice for its own sake is tantamount to denying that which makes justice necessary in the first place, namely, the desire to satisfy self-interest under conditions of roughly equal power. Thus, to practice justice for its own sake is to practice it outside of the very context of justice. Since this is the only human context of justice, trying to go outside of it means *inventing* for justice a context that has to be in some sense suprahuman, that is, transcendental or otherworldly. Only some kind of transcendental context can provide the "mode of subjection" *(mode d'assujettissement),* to use Michel Foucault's very apt expression, whereby people are "invited or incited to recognize" an unconditional obligation.[16] What a transcendental context supplies is the conceptual possibility of an unconditional or, as Richard Niebuhr calls it, an absolute relationship that is not available in the human context of jus-

---

ues of truth in *Truth and Truthfulness* (Princeton: Princeton University Press, 2002). According to Williams, "no society can get by . . . with a purely instrumental conception of the values of truth" (p. 59). The same, I have argued, is true of justice, for not dissimilar reasons. Williams also writes, "One important way of securing [the disposition toward trustworthiness] is that the parties come to think that trustworthy behaviour, such as keeping one's word, has an *intrinsic value,* that it is a good thing (many other things being equal) to act as a trustworthy person acts, just because that is the kind of action it is" (p. 90). This, I have tried to show, is also more or less true of the disposition toward justice, although the social cultivation of the intrinsic virtue of justice is a very tall order. Williams goes on to suggest that "it is in fact a *sufficient* condition for something (for instance, trustworthiness) to have an intrinsic value that, first, it is necessary (or nearly necessary) for basic human purposes and needs that human beings should treat it as an intrinsic good; and, second, they can coherently treat it as an intrinsic good. This means that it is stable under reflection" (p. 92, emphasis added). This, as I see it, clearly does not apply to the case of justice. For, as I have tried to show and will show further, people's being able to treat justice as an intrinsic or unconditional virtue depends largely on their interests' being reliably and predictably served by the instrumental function of justice (see Chapter 7) and by the state's enforcement of a basic framework of reciprocity (discussed earlier in this chapter). If this is the case, the intrinsic virtue of justice, and the whole understanding of justice in such terms, may not be stable under reflection, but only under the assumption (itself not always empirically true) that the condition of reciprocity is amply satisfied. In the end, justice is not as intrinsic a virtue as it may appear to be, although, equally, justice could not sustain itself if it were totally devoid of the intrinsic or unconditional value society is capable of creating for it. Whether the same holds of the intrinsic value of truth is a somewhat separate matter.

16. Michel Foucault, "On the Genealogy of Ethics: An Overview of Work in Progress," in *The Foucault Reader,* ed. Paul Rabinow (New York: Pantheon Books, 1984), pp. 340–372; quotation from p. 353. For elaboration of the idea of "mode of subjection" and the framework of which it is a part, see Michel Foucault, *The History of Sexuality,* vol. 2, *The Use of Pleasure,* trans. Robert Hurley (New York: Vintage Books, 1990), pp. 26–28.

tice.[17] Once I form such an unconditional relationship with some god or godlike figure (the actual identity of such a figure does not matter), it renders unconditional my relationship with fellow human beings, which in the human context of justice can only be conditional. And in so doing, it imparts unconditionality to my motive of justice, whose conditionality would be unavoidable in the purely human circumstances of justice. This may be called the transcendental transformation—or transfiguration—of justice. The nature of such transfiguration is well captured by Niebuhr: "If I consider my neighbor only in his value-relations to myself there is no room for justice . . . but only for the reciprocity of eye for eye and helping hand for helping hand. But if I consider him in his value-relations to all his neighbors and also in his value-relation to God, then there is room not only for relative justice but for the formation and reformation of relative judgments by reference to the absolute relation."[18] In this transcendental context, I no longer recognize the original motive of justice (that is, the mutual satisfaction of self-interest under conditions of roughly equal power) but only what is supposed to be the original source of the imperative of justice, namely, God. It is from my relationship with this source that my *current* motive of justice derives, and this transcendentally derived motive is unconditional because my relationship with its source is unconditional. By virtue of this transcendental relationship I am capable of comprehending what would be incomprehensible in the purely human context of justice, namely (in Kantian terminology), that justice is not a hypothetical but a categorical imperative. And once I comprehend the nature of justice in this way, I will desire to be just even in the absence of reciprocation from others.

It is understandable, in this light, why Kant's attempt to establish duty for its own sake cannot succeed without drawing upon hidden (or not so hidden) theistic premises, or, put another way, why Kant fails to show how it is possible to provide a nontheistic foundation for the *unconditionality* of duty—and this despite his explicit claim to the contrary.[19] In this con-

17. My concern throughout, I should emphasize, is with moral psychology, not with theology in its own right. For this reason, I draw on what I regard as *psychologically* illuminating interpretations of Christianity, regardless of whether they are "standard" *theological* interpretations. In most cases they happen not to be.

18. Richard Niebuhr, *Christ and Culture* (New York: Harper and Row, 1951), p. 240.

19. See, for instance, Immanuel Kant, *Critique of Practical Reason*, in *Critique of Practical Reason and Other Writings in Moral Philosophy*, trans. and ed. Lewis White Beck (Chicago: University of Chicago Press, 1949), p. 229, where Kant writes: "It is also not to be

nection, Schopenhauer shrewdly observes that the concept of duty, "together with its near relatives, such as those of *law, command, obligation,* and so on, taken in this unconditional sense, has its origin in theological morals."[20] I take Schopenhauer to mean not that such unconditional concepts happen to have originated in a theistic context, but that they necessarily depend on the invention of such a context for their appeal and even their comprehensibility. The lesson of Kant's enterprise is that a theistic context is the only kind of context in which an unconditional relationship is possible, and hence the only kind of context in which the motive of justice can be made unconditional. Unlike Kant, we may not find it necessary or even desirable to make the motive of justice unconditional, but those who do cannot escape the necessity of going outside the human context of justice. Paul Tillich is not making exaggerated claims for the role of religion in morality when he locates the unconditional character of the moral imperative in its religious dimension.[21] Nor is Montesquieu entirely off the mark when he claims that "religion, even a false one, is the best warrant men can have of the integrity of men,"[22] inasmuch as "the integrity of men" depends on the possession of unconditional motives, which in turn are made possible by religion alone.

---

understood that the assumption of the existence of God is necessary as a ground of all obligation in general (for this rests, as has been fully shown, solely on the autonomy of reason itself)." He does concede, however, that "in order to bring either an as yet uneducated or a degraded mind into the path of the morally good, some preparatory guidance is needed to attract it by a view to its own advantage or to frighten it by fear of harm" (p. 250). Now, everybody is "uneducated" at some stage in his or her life, and what better way to attract or frighten everybody than through the concept of God. But even after the uneducated becomes educated, and the degraded upright, by acquiring "the pure moral motive," Kant still cannot help describing their progress as "richly compensated" for the "sacrifice" they have made, that is, in a language that smacks of reward.

20. Schopenhauer, *On the Basis of Morality,* p. 54. See also G. E. M. Anscombe, "Modern Moral Philosophy," *Philosophy* 33 (1958): 1–19, esp. pp. 6, 8, 19.

21. See Paul Tillich, *Morality and Beyond* (New York: Harper and Row, 1963), p. 22: "The religious dimension of the moral imperative is its unconditional character."

22. Montesquieu, *The Spirit of the Laws,* trans. and ed. Anne Cohler, Basia Miller, and Harold Stone (Cambridge: Cambridge University Press, 1989), p. 465. Freud writes, however, pointing to the other side of the same coin, "It is no secret that the priests could only keep the masses submissive to religion by making . . . large concessions . . . to the instinctual nature of man," and, more important, "in every age immorality has found no less support in religion than morality has." Sigmund Freud, *The Future of an Illusion,* trans. and ed. James Strachey (New York: W. W. Norton, 1961), p. 48.

The Illusion of Unconditionality

Upon closer scrutiny, it will turn out that a disposition toward justice sustained by a theistic outlook is far from being as unconditional as it appears. My relationship with God, supposing I believe in God, may be unconditional in one sense, but it is quite conditional in another. It is unconditional only insofar as I take God to be infinitely powerful. In one fundamental respect, however, God's power is not *qualitatively* different from the power of ordinary mortals or of the state, for God's power, as conceived in theism itself, includes the all too familiar power to reward and punish. Accordingly, my relationship with God is conditional in the sense that I submit to God on condition that (I believe that) God wields the power to reward and punish. It is unconditional, if at all, only in the sense that (I believe that) this condition is, as it were, unconditionally, that is, unquestionably, fulfilled, which is to say that I see no room for doubting that God holds the power to reward and punish and that such power is infinite. If the conditionality of my relationship with God is a function of (what I take to be) the *nature* of God's power, the unconditionality of that relationship is a function of (what I take to be) the *infinitude* of that power.

The infinitude of God's power is in turn a function of the "postponement" of final reward and punishment to an afterlife, whereby God's power is immune from disproof by empirical reality. I noted earlier that my relationship with God is conditional in the sense that I am motivated by the prospect of God's reward and punishment. Since such reward and punishment come only in the afterlife, my relationship with God becomes unconditional *for this "earthly" life*. The conditional aspect of my relationship with God, however, is thus rendered unconditional only superficially and for practical purposes. For any relationship based on reward or punishment, no matter how remote or indirect, is a form of exchange, and therefore my relationship with God, based as it is on reward and punishment, is a form of exchange. The idea of an afterlife merely provides a special locus for my exchange with God; it does not change the fact that my relationship with God is one of exchange.

It follows that my relationship with God, though it is inherently unconditional in one sense and practically unconditional in another, does not make my *motive* of justice unconditional, since I am still swayed by considerations of reward and punishment. In other words, my belief in God can help make only my *practice* of justice unconditional, and if it does so more effectively than the secular state can, this is so only because I believe God's power to be greater than the earthly power to reward and punish wielded by the secular state. To be sure, this belief may be sufficient to cause me to practice justice unconditionally for the duration of my ("earthly") life, since I shall never be able to test the conditional aspect of my relationship with God as long as I believe in the afterlife. Nevertheless, although the imperative of justice may thus have the *effect* of an unconditional imperative, it remains a conditional imperative *in spirit,* that is, as far as the motive of compliance is concerned.

When justice is moved from its human to an apparently transcendental context, the underlying exchange relationship accompanies it, with only its objects and timing changed. What we find in otherworldly religion is not the elimination of exchange but the replacement of one kind of exchange with another, say, the replacement of worldly pleasure and pain with eternal happiness and damnation. Moreover, it is always tempting to smuggle earthly reward into the heavenly bargain.[23] And with the introduction of earthly reward, the relationship with God is liable to become almost as conditional as that with earthly authorities.[24] In the end, theistic illusions of various kinds do not generate *real* unconditionality but merely change the terms of trade: Be just in this world in a way that might *seem* to be unconditional, if this world were the only one, and in the next world reciprocity will be reestablished.

Not surprisingly, attempts have often been made to purge the relationship with God of hedonism. All such attempts rest on the assumption that

23. "But seek ye first the kingdom of God, and this righteousness; and all these things shall be added unto you" (Matt. 6:33). Nietzsche comments, "All these things: namely, food, clothing, all the necessities of life." Friedrich Nietzsche, *The Antichrist,* in *The Portable Nietzsche,* ed. and trans. Walter Kaufmann (New York: Viking Press, 1954), 45.

24. Nietzsche, once again, is perhaps the most perceptive in this regard. "Alas, that is my sorrow: they have lied reward and punishment into the foundation of things, and now also into the foundations of your souls, you who are virtuous," writes Nietzsche in *Thus Spoke Zarathustra* (in *Portable Nietzsche,* pp. 205–206). In biblical sayings such as "For if ye love them which love you, what reward have ye? do not even the publicans the same? And if ye salute your brethren only, what do ye more *than others?* do not even the publicans so?" (Matt. 5:46–47), Nietzsche sees "the principle of 'Christian love': in the end it wants to be *paid* well" (*Antichrist,* 45). And commenting on the saying "Whosoever will come after me, let him deny himself, and take up his cross, and follow me. *For.* . ." (Mark 8:34), Nietzsche writes, "Christian morality is refuted by its *For's:* its 'reasons' refute—thus is it Christian" (*Antichrist,* 45). (The quotations from the Bible are given in the form, including emphasis, in which they are cited by Nietzsche.)

what makes an exchange an exchange is its hedonistic element. On this assumption, it is possible to turn the exchange with God into something other than exchange by removing the hedonistic element from it. Tillich, for example, very much in a Kantian spirit, regards the conditionality of an imperative as a function of a hedonistic telos, in which "no unconditional imperative is at work, but merely the very much conditioned advice to calculate well what amount of pain must be suffered in order to attain to the greatest amount of pleasure."[25] It thus seems to follow that the absence of hedonism is both a necessary and a sufficient condition for having an unconditional relationship with God and thereby subscribing to unconditional imperatives, including the imperative of justice.

This line of reasoning is pushed to the limit by Søren Kierkegaard, and it is instructive to see whether it can lead to a moral psychology that is entirely free of conditionality. For Kierkegaard, hedonism (or eudaemonism) and exchange are one and the same, since both seek the certainty or high probability of reward. When such certainty is offered by the church in return for belief in God, it immediately turns Christianity into "an intellectual transaction, a profitable stock-exchange speculation." Thus, he considers genuine religiosity possible only when "actual time separates the good and the reward . . . so much, so eternally, that sagacity cannot join them again, and the eudaemonist declines with thanks." Indeed, the reward must be so objectively uncertain that one has to believe it "against the understanding." Such objective uncertainty, or "infinite abstraction," makes the ethical possible, and when carried to the extreme of absurdity, opens the way to the religious. Religious faith consists in the strongest possible subjective firmness—the "infinite passion of inwardness"—in the face of the highest possible objective uncertainty. "Therefore eternal happiness, as the absolute good, has the remarkable quality that it can be defined only by the mode in which it is acquired"—namely, an adventure marked by the greatest possible difficulty and suffering, even by lunacy.[26]

In this way, Kierkegaard goes to the limit in his attempt to purge the relationship with God of hedonism. He does not thereby succeed, however, in purging the relationship with God of conditionality. For any relationship, including the relationship with God, will retain its conditionality, its character as exchange, so long as the concept of reward plays a part in it. It

25. Tillich, *Morality,* p. 28.

26. Søren Kierkegaard, *Concluding Unscientific Postscript to Philosophical Fragments,* trans. Howard V. Hong and Edna H. Hong (Princeton: Princeton University Press, 1992), pp. 422–423, 342–343, 232–233, 611, and 426–427.

is true, in the case of Kierkegaard, that the certainty of reward is eliminated and the object of reward changed (from earthly pleasure to eternal happiness). But the concept of reward itself, and by implication that of exchange, is retained, and so the relationship with God remains conditional.[27] In the final analysis, the conditionality of a relationship is determined not by the hedonistic character of the exchange involved but by the fact of exchange itself, whatever its character. To act with a view to reward, whatever it is, and however unobtainable, is still to act with a view to self-interest. No matter how much risk one takes, with how much passion of inwardness, how much lunacy, and how much suffering (these are all Kierkegaard's expressions), if one is motivated by reward, then ultimately one is risking for self-interest. Thus, Kierkegaard, willing to go to the greatest lengths to make the reward inaccessible but unable to give up the idea of reward itself, ends up accomplishing no more than the eudaemonist he ridicules, namely, a self-deceiving movement "from eudaemonism to the ethical within eudaemonism," or "a fleeting resemblance to the ethical."[28] With his exchange of virtue for eternal happiness, Kierkegaard's true believer turns out to be a hedonist in ascetic disguise—or, in the words of Nietzsche, a "Christian, who is, in fact, only a kind of Epicurean, and, with his 'faith makes blessed,' follows the principle of hedonism as far as possible."[29]

In laying bare the logic of Kierkegaard's failure, I am not suggesting that Kierkegaard, or anyone else for that matter, should have gone further along that path. In theory, the only way to separate virtue from reward and hence from self-interest is not to introduce objective uncertainty or even absurdity, as Kierkegaard does, but to do away with the concept of reward altogether, so that there will be nothing to separate virtue from. It is not clear, however, that this is humanly possible in practice. Even if it is possible (say, in the form of unconditional benevolence), it must remain a mystery, something that is difficult enough to comprehend, let alone to motivate those not already inexplicably endowed with this virtue to acquire it. Kierkegaard's failure is thus a poignant demonstration of the impossibility of *motivated* unconditionality of virtue.

Different moralities, then, as long as they are motivated by considerations of reward and punishment, however indirectly or obliquely, are but

27. See ibid., pp. 149, 183.

28. Ibid., pp. 422–423 and 426n, respectively.

29. Nietzsche, *Nietzsche Contra Wagner,* in *Portable Nietzsche,* p. 670.

different forms or sites of exchange. One such motivated morality cannot be morally superior to another, since all alike are motivated by considerations of reward and punishment. They differ only in their appraisal of what counts as the most rewarding exchange and in the manner in which the motive of exchange is disguised. But if one such motivated morality, that is, one form of exchange, cannot be morally superior to any other, it can nevertheless be more effective in inducing the semblance of unconditional motives. The most effective morality—the most secure locus of exchange—is, for obvious reasons, one in which reward and punishment are delayed to the afterlife. The greater the distance that an exchange places between virtue and reward, the more effectively it will produce the seemingly unconditional exercise of virtue. Yet at the same time, what lends the appearance of unconditionality to an exchange is precisely what will make that exchange difficult to comprehend and accept. In the limiting case, such as that imagined by Kierkegaard, the distance between virtue and reward can be so huge that the exchange, though in principle still an exchange, ceases to make practical sense. This is the great practical dilemma of theistic exchange: An exchange that cannot fail (in this life) is also an exchange that one has the least (worldly) incentive to enter into.

Small wonder that only extraordinary circumstances of (worldly) deprivation lend plausibility to this kind of exchange, as they once did. Such circumstances no longer obtain to anything like the same degree in the modern world of relative comfort and prosperity. For the modern world, "'God' is far too extreme a hypothesis" (as Nietzsche puts it),[30] and it has come to seem increasingly implausible to postpone reward and punishment to an afterlife. The only way left of motivating people to act morally is by reference to some kind of exchange that is supposed to take place here and now—an exchange whose conditionality, whose character as exchange, is manifest in this life rather than in an alleged afterlife. There is no longer any rationale for unconditional morality, including justice.

30. Friedrich Nietzsche, *The Will to Power,* ed. Walter Kaufmann, trans. Walter Kaufmann and R. J. Hollingdale (New York: Random House, 1967), 114.

9

Forgetting and Resentment

The transfiguration of justice, as we saw in the last chapter, is the transformation of justice from a conditional motive into what appears, even to the just person himself or herself, an unconditional one. But even as the motive of justice is rendered unconditional in this significant yet qualified sense, the new motive remains recognizably the characteristic motive of justice, betraying in oblique ways, over and above its reliance on theism, discussed in the last chapter, the origins of justice in the desire for mutual advantage. This ambiguity of justice—at once (apparently) unconditional and (obliquely) conditional—invites analysis in terms of forgetting. With the idea of forgetting I intend to capture, on the one hand, the *extent* of the transfiguration of justice, that is, how much the transfiguration elevates justice above its prudential origins. On the other hand, using the idea of forgetting in the sense of the disappearance of something from consciousness but its simultaneous retention in the unconscious, I intend to point up the *limits* of the transfiguration of justice, that is, how even after its transfiguration, justice remains tied to its prudential origins. In this chapter I try to show how such limits are reflected in the moral emotion of resentment, which both expresses and conceals the conditionality of justice through an unconscious displacement of the exchange involved in justice from the plane of material interests to that of moral standing. I further argue that there is a double link between resentment and punishment, in that the affective side of resentment seeks revenge against the offender in the form of punishment, while the cognitive or impersonal side of resentment provides a justification for such revenge.

Two Ways of Forgetting the Original Motives of Justice

The need for the explanatory notion of forgetting arises from the qualitative difference between the way in which justice must originally have been set in motion and the way in which justice can be motivated once it is already in motion. This is an important insight of Nietzsche's, and I see no reason to depart in essentials from his account of the gap between the origins and the later practice of justice, nor from his extrapolation of the notion of forgetting from such a gap. Nietzsche's account of the origins of justice has a long intellectual lineage, traceable, as he himself says, to Thucydides—as well as, one might add, to Glaucon in Plato's *Republic*. For Nietzsche,

> justice (fairness) originates between parties of approximately *equal power* . . . : where there is no clearly recognizable superiority of force and a contest would result in mutual injury producing no decisive outcome the idea arises of coming to an understanding and negotiating over one another's demands: the characteristic of *exchange* is the original characteristic of justice. Each satisfies the other, inasmuch as each acquires what he values more than the other does. One gives to the other what he wants to have, to be henceforth his own, and in return receives what one oneself desires. Justice is thus requital and exchange under the presupposition of an approximately equal power position . . . Justice goes back naturally to the viewpoint of an enlightened self-preservation, thus to the egoism of the reflection: "to what end should I injure myself uselessly and perhaps even then not achieve my goal?"[1]

This is not a historical account but what Nietzsche was later to call a genealogical one, where one takes a "way of thinking and valuing," in this case justice, as given and uses the method of "backward inference" to extrapolate from it "the want behind it that prompts it."[2] In this sense, the origins of a social practice are the circumstances that made it both necessary and possible. In accounting for the origins of justice in the way he does, Nietz-

1. Friedrich Nietzsche, *Human, All Too Human,* trans. R. J. Hollingdale, 2 vols. in 1 (Cambridge: Cambridge University Press, 1986), 1:92.

2. Friedrich Nietzsche, *Nietzsche Contra Wagner,* in *The Portable Nietzsche,* ed. and trans. Walter Kaufmann (New York: Viking Press, 1954), p. 670. This is of course an oversimplified account of what Nietzsche means by genealogy. For an illuminating comprehensive account, see Raymond Geuss, "Nietzsche and Genealogy," in *Morality, Culture, and History* (Cambridge: Cambridge University Press, 1999), pp. 1–28. See also Bernard Williams, *Truth and Truthfulness* (Princeton: Princeton University Press, 2002), esp. chap. 2. As it happened, Nietzsche did not produce a fully worked-out genealogy of justice (as he did of morality), although his brief remarks on this topic (as well as his genealogy of morality) provide intriguing hints as to how he might have carried out such a project.

sche is saying, in the spirit of a genealogical backward inference or thought experiment, that these are the only (or most likely) circumstances in which justice could have been both necessary and possible. What makes justice necessary, for Nietzsche, is the kind of egoism of which Hume offers a richer account in his conception of the circumstances of justice. To this Nietzsche adds, more explicitly than Hume does in the second *Enquiry*, "the presupposition of an approximately equal power position" as a factor that makes justice not only necessary but also possible. Given these circumstances of egoism and equality of power, Nietzsche infers, the only motive for originally establishing justice is "the viewpoint of an enlightened self-preservation," and that is why "the characteristic of *exchange* is the original characteristic of justice."

The original motive of justice, however, will not necessarily be the motive of those who are subsequently induced to practice justice once justice is firmly instituted. According to Nietzsche, "especially because children have for millennia been trained to admire and imitate such actions, it has gradually come to appear that a just action is an unegoistic one: but it is on this appearance that the high value accorded it depends; and this high value is, moreover, continually increasing, as all valuations do: for something highly valued is striven for, imitated, multiplied through sacrifice, and grows as the worth of the toil and zeal expended by each individual is added to the worth of the valued thing."[3] To make the same point in the terms I am using, we might say that justice, originally understood as expressing a conditional commitment, has come to be practiced, by some if not by all, from motives that make it out to be unconditional. There thus emerges a gap between the original motive of justice and its subsequent motive.

Given this gap, we have to posit some transformation in order to explain how it is possible to move from the way justice originated to the way justice is subsequently practiced. In view of its egoistic origins, Nietzsche believes, justice can become a virtue practiced for altruistic reasons and valued in its own right only through forgetting. "Men have," says Nietzsche, "*forgotten* the original purpose of so-called just and fair actions."[4] Like the idea of the original motive of justice, the idea of forgetting is invoked here in the spirit of a genealogical backward inference. For forgetting is the *con-*

3. Nietzsche, *Human,* 1:92. A similar point is made in David Hume, *A Treatise of Human Nature,* ed. L. A. Selby-Bigge, 2nd ed., ed. P. H. Nidditch (Oxford: Clarendon Press, 1978), pp. 533–534.

4. Nietzsche, *Human,* 1:92.

dition of possibility for the fact that justice is subsequently practiced in ways that are incompatible with its origins. In making genealogical use of the idea of forgetting, Nietzsche bypasses the empirical question as to whether forgetting is ontogenetic or phylogenetic, or both. Clearly, understanding the forgetting of the origins of justice in genealogical terms already implies treating such forgetting as a phylogenetic process. The question is whether forgetting the original motive of justice is also an ontogenetic process, something that occurs in the moral development of every individual.

Here Habermas's developmental account of the sense of justice is instructive. According to him (here borrowing key concepts from Lawrence Kohlberg), "*preconventional notions of bonds and loyalties* are based either on the complementarity of command and obedience or on the symmetry of compensation. These two types of reciprocity represent the natural embryonic form of justice conceptions inherent in the structure of action as such." Habermas is referring here to what I have been calling the original motive or motives of justice. Such motives are later superseded—"forgotten"—when, first at the so-called conventional stage, "conceptions of justice [are] conceived *as* conceptions of justice" and then, at the so-called postconventional stage, "the truth about the world of preconventional conceptions [is] revealed, namely that the idea of justice can be gleaned only from the idealized form of reciprocity that underlies discourse."[5] Although Habermas seems to underestimate the difficulty of the forgetting that is necessary for moving from the preconventional through the conventional to the postconventional stage, and although his division, borrowed from Kohlberg, of moral development into these stages is open to question, he is clearly right to describe an individual's mature sense of justice as both developing out of the original roots of justice and moving away from those very roots. What we can learn from Habermas is that the kind of forgetting that Nietzsche identifies in the development of justice is a process that each and every individual has to go through. And because it is in this way also an ontogenetic process, forgetting the origins of justice is an *ongoing* phylogenetic process, a process whose significance, difficulty,

5. Jürgen Habermas, *Moral Consciousness and Communicative Action,* trans. Christian Lenhardt and Shierry Weber Nicholsen (Cambridge, Mass.: MIT Press, 1990), p. 165. Habermas remarks earlier, in a similar vein, that "golden rules and obedience to the law are ethical imperatives that merely sue, as it were, for what is already implicit in social roles and norms prior to any actual moral conflict: the complementarity of behavioral expectations and the symmetry of rights and duties" (p. 164).

and consequences are repeated for each individual and each generation. Thus, the idea of forgetting captures, not only apropos of society but apropos of each individual, the *extent* of the transfiguration of justice: through forgetting, justice comes to be practiced from (conscious) motives incompatible with its origins, that is, from motives other than the mutual satisfaction of self-interest, and hence from motives that hide from view the conditionality and reciprocity of justice.

Such forgetting occurs spontaneously—without any effort by individuals or society to produce a motive of justice different from its original one—to the extent that the mutual advantages made possible by the general practice of justice can be taken for granted. When people become accustomed to deriving reciprocal advantages from practicing justice, it may be expected that the conscious seeking of advantage will gradually disappear from their practice, even from their understanding, of justice. But forgetting in this sense does not eliminate or in any way rise above the original motive of justice. What happens is merely that the original motive, rooted in mutual advantage, is rendered redundant as a *conscious* motive by circumstances that already make mutual advantage a fact of life—something to be expected rather than to be struggled for. Predictably, such a motive will become conscious again if the advantages of justice fail regularly and seriously to materialize. What this goes to show is that the forgetting in question, though spontaneous, remains conditional.

Even such relatively superficial forgetting can take place only under exceptionally conducive circumstances, and such circumstances, before they are available to make spontaneous forgetting possible, have themselves to be brought about first through forgetting of a very deliberate sort. This is the kind of forgetting Nietzsche must have in mind when he suggests that the forgetting of the original motive of justice is achieved through the conscious effort of society to make people, especially children, acquire a motive of justice different from the original one. Such an effort amounts to the suppression, or *forced* forgetting, of the original motive of justice, in that a new motive of justice is created not to fill a vacuum left by the spontaneous disappearance of the original motive from moral consciousness but rather to dislodge and replace the original motive, which would otherwise remain conscious under existing circumstances. This is not to imply anything negative about forced forgetting, a term I use descriptively here. It is perhaps in the very nature of justice that the spontaneous forgetting of its original motive can occur, to the limited extent that it can realistically be expected to occur, only after forced forgetting (the creation of a more elevated motive of justice than the original one) has helped bring about a widespread sense of justice owing to which mutual advantage unfailingly accrues to the practice of justice.

Forced forgetting, however, even as it succeeds in removing the original motive of justice from conscious motivation, produces resentment, and resentment, as we shall see, betrays that motive, serving as a reminder that the original motive of justice is not transcended but merely suppressed.

Resentment and Exchange

Resentment marks the limit of the transfiguration of justice, and it does so because it represents the elimination of the conditionality of justice from consciousness but its simultaneous retention in the unconscious. Driven into the unconscious by forced forgetting, the conditionality of justice finds expression in a *moral* reaction to breaches of reciprocity by others—a reaction that takes the form of the emotion of resentment rather than any conscious calculation of material loss. In feeling resentment, I see myself as disapproving of another person because he has done something wrong, not simply or even primarily because he has harmed my interest. Experienced thus as a moral emotion, resentment, even as its negative affects register a sense of personal loss, nevertheless gives me a sense of *moral* superiority to the wrongdoer. This sense of moral superiority can arise only because I am willing to forgo retaliation in kind and in so doing to endure some kind of material loss. The conscious willingness is what constitutes my sense of duty, causing me to practice justice from what I take to be an unconditional motive. The very fact, however, that I consider something my duty implies a measure of unwillingness on my part to do what the duty requires. It is the function of a sense of duty to render such unwillingness ineffectual—to cultivate, as Kant puts it, a moral "respect for the law whose yoke must be borne whether liked or not." Although the yoke "imposed by reason" is what Kant calls a "mild yoke," there is still a price to be paid, of a kind that Kant does not seem to heed.[6] For when the unwillingness to obey the law (especially in the face of failure of reciprocation by others) is rendered repugnant to the moral agent, it does not simply disappear but goes instead into his or her unconscious only to reappear in

6. Immanuel Kant, *Critique of Practical Reason*, in *Critique of Practical Reason and Other Writings in Moral Philosophy*, trans. and ed. Lewis White Beck (Chicago: University of Chicago Press, 1949), p. 191.

consciousness, in a transmuted form, as resentment. The more a sense of duty renders my unwillingness unconscious, the more such unwillingness will turn into a kind of self-righteous resentment that serves to make up for my sense of material loss. For to the extent that I am no longer conscious of my unwillingness, that unwillingness ceases to be an object of self-criticism and turns instead into complacent resentment of others, to which I feel entitled because my consciousness tells me that I am unconditionally willing to be just. Such conscious willingness gives me the illusion of autonomy, while resentment betrays my heteronomous inability to give up the motive of exchange, a motive extraneous to duty, and hence my inability to perform duty for duty's sake.

Resentment bespeaks, then, an unconscious unwillingness to give up what one is consciously willing to give up. The unconscious unwillingness in turn bespeaks some sort of imposition upon a moral agent, both by society and, through the internalization of social norms, by oneself. Thus understood, resentment is a kind of moralized anger caused at once by one's sense of loss in exchange and by one's sense of being imposed upon, and yet it is a crucial feature of resentment that both of these causes are rendered more or less unconscious by the moral terms through which one's anger is channeled. Indeed, my sense of being imposed upon springs from my sense of loss in exchange: I feel imposed upon because I have to act—and feel—as if I were willing to endure a loss in exchange without retaliation, which deep down, beyond the reach of my moral consciousness, I am not. In this sense, we might think of resentment as resulting from a socially enforced impotence in the shape of the obligation to obey the law.[7]

This sense of unwilling loss in exchange is a necessary ingredient in the emotion of resentment. On the one hand, as long as it is open to me to respond to breaches of reciprocity in kind, I will have no psychological need to feel resentment. On the other hand, regardless of whether it is open to me to respond to breaches of reciprocity in kind, if I act out of benevolence and expect nothing in return, I will not be disposed either to respond in kind or to feel resentment. It is only when I am motivated by considerations of reciprocity, when nevertheless it is not open to me to respond to breaches of reciprocity in kind, and when I view my not re-

7. On the crucial connection between resentment and impotence, see Max Scheler, *Ressentiment,* new ed., trans. Lewis B. Coser and William W. Holdheim (Milwaukee: Marquette University Press, 1994), pp. 30–31, 49.

sponding in kind in terms of my sense of duty and hence my superior moral character, that I have both the occasion and the psychological need for resentment. Not surprisingly, as Rawls points out, "barring self-deception, egoists are incapable of feeling resentment."[8] This is because possessing certain *virtues*—or having certain "natural attachments" inseparable from such virtues—is a necessary condition for experiencing certain *moral* emotions. Yet not all virtues or virtue-based natural attachments create what Rawls calls the liability to resentment. We need to distinguish, as Rawls does not, the virtues with which resentment is compatible from those with which it is not. When Rawls says that "this liability is the price of love,"[9] this will be true only if the love in question is conditional. But love need not be conditional, and unconditional love will not lead to resentment even when it is unreciprocated. What is liable to cause resentment is not a virtue or a virtue-based relationship as such but the demand for reciprocity that is built into it, and this demand is not necessarily built into all virtues.

Clearly, such a demand is intrinsic to the virtue of justice and the kind of attachment corresponding to it. For this reason, Rawls is right to see the liability to resentment as inevitably fulfilled, "assuming that persons are possessed of interests and aspirations of their own, and that they are prepared in the pursuit of their own ends and ideals to press their claims on one another—that is, so long as the conditions giving rise to questions of justice obtain among them."[10] This is indeed, as Rawls claims, a normal human situation, one in which there is a normal attachment characterized by mutual trust and mutual advantage and, corresponding to that attachment, a normal moral emotion in the shape of resentment.[11] I do not want to deny this, of course, or to assert that it is at all common to find virtues and virtue-based attachments that are free of the conditionality characteristic of justice. My point is simply that the demand for reciprocity, whether or not fully conscious, is a necessary condition of resentment.

When such a demand for reciprocity is not met, a just person, by virtue

8. John Rawls, *A Theory of Justice,* rev. ed. (Cambridge, Mass.: Harvard University Press, 1999), p. 427.

9. Ibid., p. 428.

10. Ibid.

11. As Rawls puts it, "One main consequence of this doctrine is that the moral feelings are a normal feature of human life. We could not do away with them without at the same time eliminating certain natural attitudes" (ibid., p. 427). See P. F. Strawson's very similar account in *Freedom and Resentment* (London: Methuen, 1974), chap. 1.

of being a just person, will seek a psychological equivalent of reciprocity. For the sense of unwilling loss that is intrinsic to the virtue of justice makes resentment not only possible but also necessary. My sense of loss, unwillingly borne, prompts me to seek compensation. Since compensation is unavailable in a material form, that is, in the form of direct retaliation, I will have to settle for resentment as a psychological substitute. The satisfaction afforded by resentment is possible because the exchange intrinsic to justice is highly flexible in form. As Nietzsche says, "Recompense to the injured party for the harm done" can be "rendered in any form (even in that of a *compensating affect*)."[12] Let down by others in an exchange relationship but unable or unwilling to respond in kind, I can nevertheless exact a price from them—and a reward for my not responding in kind—in the form of the right to resent and feel superior. In this way, an exchange that fails to be carried out in terms of interest is completed in terms of moral standing. That resentment can thus serve as a substitute for retaliation is so because it represents not the denial of exchange, which would go against the grain of justice, but only the moralization of exchange—the carrying out of exchange in moral terms.[13]

It is by giving such oblique expression to the motivational conditionality of justice that resentment serves to reinforce the unconditional practice of justice. Thanks to resentment, the failure of others to reciprocate need no longer cause me to suspend the terms of the exchange but only to show a certain moral reaction. Such a moral reaction, even as it implies the context of exchange, serves to hide the exchange from my conscious awareness, and in so doing it serves to forestall my "egoistical repentance."[14] We might say that resentment safeguards the unconditionality of justice in ac-

12. Friedrich Nietzsche, *On the Genealogy of Morals* (together with *Ecce Homo*), trans. Walter Kaufmann and R. J. Hollingdale (New York: Random House, 1967), II, 13, emphasis added.

13. Bernard Williams urges us to resist "the idea that having a virtue or admirable disposition of character should also involve a disposition to assess others" (*Ethics and the Limits of Philosophy* [Cambridge, Mass.: Harvard University Press, 1985], p. 36), and he rightly locates such an idea in a morality centered on justice. The disposition to assess others—negatively—is an integral part of resentment, and as such it serves a necessary function in any morality in which justice, by nature a conditional virtue, has to be practiced unconditionally.

14. This term is taken from Arthur Schopenhauer, *The World as Will and Representation*, trans. E. F. J. Payne, vol. 1 (New York: Dover, 1969), where Schopenhauer writes: "Even from an ethical point of view, a deed too noble for [one's] character, which has sprung not from pure, direct impulse, but from a concept, a dogma, will lose all merit even in his own eyes through a subsequent egoistical repentance" (p. 304; see also pp. 296–297). Such "ego-

tion by expressing the conditionality of justice in affects. Resentment can perform this function only because it gives affective expression to the conditionality of justice in an unconscious fashion. Founded as it is on exchange, resentment sustains itself by being unconscious of its own foundation. The fact that moral revenge can serve as a substitute for material retaliation is predicated on my *not* seeing it that way. If I came to see that my resentment is grounded in exchange equally with the desire for material reciprocity, I would no longer be able to maintain my moral self-righteousness. Resentment must produce strong affects if it is to counteract my sense of material loss sufficiently to pacify my urge to respond in kind, and such affects depend on my obliviousness to the roots of my resentment.

To achieve this obliviousness is the function of forced forgetting. Forced forgetting simultaneously gives rise to resentment and hides its origins. As a product of forced forgetting, resentment betokens the eviction of the conditionality of justice from consciousness and yet its simultaneous retention in the unconscious. The conditionality of justice, relocated in the unconscious, now takes the form in consciousness of what passes for a purely moral reaction to breaches of reciprocity by others. The focus of resentment is not on the fact that someone guilty of a breach of reciprocity has harmed my interest but on the fact that in so doing he or she has violated a moral norm and committed a moral wrong. In resentment an exchange relationship is experienced in moral terms, and because it is so experienced, it is not consciously an exchange at all. Thus resentment can give me a feeling of moral superiority, based on the (false) idea, itself best left unconscious, that in rising above material retaliation, I have also risen above self-interest and exchange.

Resentment and Punishment

The sense of moral superiority—the self-righteous and compensatory aspect of resentment—is seldom sufficient, however, to balance the sense of loss in exchange. There is a gap between material loss and psychological

---

istical repentance" occurs when it turns out that all the "virtue" one has laboriously acquired has failed to bring any reward. One important reason why a sense of duty, apparently so deeply ingrained, can suddenly, or gradually (as the case may be), disappear is that an exchange whose character as such has been hidden through resentment comes to be revealed as naked exchange. As a result, duty is swept away by "egoistical repentance."

compensation that leaves me still with the feeling—the vengeful aspect of resentment—that justice has not been *done,* has not been carried out in *deeds.* Even as I derive what psychological compensation I can from a sense of moral superiority, I seek yet further compensation in a form as close as possible to my original impulse of retaliation. In other words, I seek socially administered punishment for the offender, the next best thing after the personal revenge that is legally impermissible.[15]

Resentment almost always precedes punishment. There is almost always a temporal gap between offense and punishment, a gap that need hardly exist between offense and personal retaliation. It is within this gap that resentment builds up, and once built up, resentment gravitates toward punishment through a double impetus, in that what began as the psychological urge for revenge is now also a moral imperative of justice. The vengeful aspect of resentment, which answers to the insufficiency of resentment as compensation, desires punishment for the offender. The self-righteous aspect of resentment justifies such a desire, turning it into an explicitly *moral* desire, the desire to see justice done.[16]

Punishment can serve as compensation for my unjust loss in exchange because it, like resentment, expresses the original conditionality of justice by restoring as much of it as possible in the face of breaches of reciprocity. Both punishment and resentment serve as compensation for those who practice justice unconditionally and yet whose motivation remains at bottom conditional. There is a sense, however, in which punishment approximates more closely to what but for the law would have been my personal response in kind to a breach of reciprocity. For punishment is characterized by a change in the *locus* of retaliation, from individual to social, whereas resentment is characterized by a change in the *kind* of retaliation, from material to psychological.[17] Punishment, though administered by so-

15. See Adam Smith, *The Theory of Moral Sentiments,* ed. D. D. Raphael and A. L. Macfie (Indianapolis: Liberty Classics, 1982), pp. 79–80. "The next best thing" because, as Judith Shklar remarks, even retributive justice "remains a frustrating substitute for revenge, neither eliminating nor satisfying its urging." Judith N. Shklar, *The Faces of Injustice* (New Haven: Yale University Press, 1990), p. 94; see also pp. 100, 101.

16. See Annette Baier, "Hume on Resentment," *Hume Studies* 6 (1980): 133–149, esp. pp. 138, 144.

17. There is a sense, however, in which resentment itself is a kind of punishment for the offender. As P. S. Greenspan points out, "unless the object of my anger has complete contempt for me (and even in some cases where he does), my viewing him with anger is normally itself a kind of punishment for him, whether or not I can punish him overtly." P. S. Greenspan, *Emotions and Reasons* (New York: Routledge, 1988), p. 68.

ciety rather than the offended individual, is carried out in deeds, and is a more direct expression of the relationship between justice and interest, and hence of the conditionality of justice. Resentment, by contrast, however personal, is still, as Nietzsche puts it, "the *ressentiment* of natures that are denied the true reaction, that of deeds, and compensate themselves with an imaginary revenge."[18]

Of course, punishment involves more than a mere shift in the locus of retaliation. By virtue of its social nature, punishment is considered *justifiable* revenge, so that the change in locus is simultaneously a change in kind. And the change in kind is in turn made possible by individual resentment, in which punishment finds both its impetus and its justification. Through his drop in moral standing, the offender has already (unwittingly) made payment for my loss. But that very drop in moral standing justifies yet further payment from the offender, in the form of punishment, for in the eyes of society a breaker of the law and of the morality implicit in it deserves to be punished. By virtue of its physical nature, its character as deed, punishment provides me with the compensation in kind that I need on top of the moral and psychological compensation I have contrived through resentment. By virtue of its social nature, the fact that it is administered by the state, punishment serves to validate the latter compensation by lending it society's seal of approval. Only when I consider punishment to have properly fulfilled this twofold function do I have a sense of closure to the exchange that constitutes justice. Punishment is the only definitive cure for resentment, the only way of purging resentment of its negative affects. As sickness and cure, resentment and punishment go hand in hand, and they do so because they derive from the same source, namely, the motivational conditionality of justice.

We may therefore expect to find a certain proportionality between resentment and (the likelihood of) punishment. Where resentment is strong and specific, punishment is usually available. If strong resentment is left unrelieved for a long time, the victims of injustice may well lose the moral incentive and the psychological equilibrium to practice justice unconditionally. A society that takes away the right to preserve the conditionality of justice from individuals but does not in return enforce that conditionality by social means risks the breakdown of justice, even revolt. Resent-

18. Nietzsche, *Genealogy,* I, 10. What Nietzsche means by *ressentiment* is different from, and vastly more complex than, the notion of resentment. When I draw on Nietzsche's remarks on *ressentiment,* I do so with reference only to what *ressentiment* has in common with resentment. This also applies to my earlier reference to Max Scheler.

ment, even as it accompanies the unconditional practice of justice, attests to the ineradicable conditionality of justice. It is the function of resentment, on the part of individuals who are not empowered to enforce the reciprocity of justice, to see to it that the state does so, that the state makes good its part of the social contract. In carrying out punishment, society at once recognizes the legitimacy of resentment and relieves it. The relief afforded in this way is a significant part of what John Stuart Mill calls the "pleasure" of punishment. "It would always give us pleasure," says Mill, "and chime in with our feelings of fitness, that acts which we deem unjust should be punished."[19] The pleasure of punishment—or the affective aspect of such pleasure—results in large part from the release of resentment and the consequent return of psychological equilibrium. Such release is made possible by what Mill calls "our feelings of fitness," which is none other than the knowledge—the cognitive aspect of the pleasure of punishment—that the conditionality of justice is preserved by society.

All the same, punishment does not always put a definitive closure to an exchange gone awry. By relieving the offended party of resentment, punishment sometimes creates resentment in the offender. This is because the offender may have committed the offense in the belief, however vague, that he had been unjustly treated in the first place, if only as a victim of unfortunate circumstances which society had not done enough to alleviate.[20] For such an offender, despite the guilt he may have felt in the wake of his conduct, the offense was a moment of justice (of sorts), the moment when he did not upset justice as he saw it but merely restored it and in so doing dissipated his own resentment. When punishment comes, therefore, he will experience it not as justice but as yet further injustice, to which he will respond with the recharging of resentment until he is able to vent it in yet further acts of a kind that society in turn will seek to punish—all of this as part of a never-ending cycle. This is especially true of a society in which factors such as class divisions make it impossible for people to reach genuine agreement on what constitutes justice. In such a society (how many societies are *not* like this?), punishment can produce resentment in the offender as easily as the perceived insufficiency of a punishment can cause resentment to linger in the offended.

More pervasively, there is a quieter war of daily clashes of interest in

19. John Stuart Mill, *Utilitarianism,* in John Stuart Mill and Jeremy Bentham, *Utilitarianism and Other Essays,* ed. Alan Ryan (Harmondsworth: Penguin, 1987), p. 321.

20. See, for example, Shklar, *Faces of Injustice,* pp. 84–85, 87, 94.

which punishment is not institutionally available and, by common consent, should not be. Punishment is even less available as a remedy for resentment where the blame for injustice cannot be easily assigned to particular individuals but the sense of injustice is nevertheless equally real. To be sure, the amount of injustice for which punishment is institutionally unavailable varies from society to society. But it is never wholly nonexistent, and where it exists, resentment itself is institutionalized in various forms,[21] reflecting the conditionality of justice and the psychological toll it takes.

21. See P. S. Greenspan, *Practical Guilt* (New York: Oxford University Press, 1995), pp. 72–73.

10

Individual Forgiveness, Social Resentment

Where breaches of reciprocity occur, resentment almost inevitably arises in response to them. Those who feel strong and persistent resentment but are powerless to do anything about its causes are often driven to violence, either inwardly directed against themselves or visited upon society. As long as agreement exists as to what injustice is and what instances of it call for punishment, the strain of resentment can typically be relieved, or at least lightened, through the institution of punishment. Society, which takes away from individuals the right to restore the reciprocity of justice through retaliation, must itself enforce the reciprocity of justice through the socialization of retaliation in the form of punishment. Punishment, we might say, is society's homage to the reciprocity of justice. Through punishment society restores the reciprocity of justice and thereby relieves individuals of such resentment as is caused by unilateral breaches of reciprocity.

As I noted toward the end of the last chapter, however, punishment does not always put a definitive closure to a cycle of injustice and resentment. Socially administered punishment, as Judith Shklar reminds us, is seldom sufficient to "wipe the slate clean."[1] Moreover, and this seems true of every society, punishment is unavailable for a wide range of injustices, which, though not treated as warranting legal redress, are serious enough to cause strong resentment.[2] In both cases, resentment must be relieved in

1. Judith N. Shklar, *The Faces of Injustice* (New Haven: Yale University Press, 1990), p. 94; see also p. 101.

2. Things are worse still when agreement is lacking as to what counts as injustice, with the likely result that some will routinely "get away with" what those at the receiving end perceive as gross injustice, leaving a trail of resentment that is not open to alleviation by legal or other institutional means. But this kind of resentment is different from the kind with which I am chiefly concerned in this book, that is, resentment caused by breaches of reciprocity against the background of agreement regarding norms of justice.

other ways if the unconditional practice of justice is to be maintained without an unbearable psychological cost. Since punishment is the only means *within justice* for relieving resentment,[3] this creates an extraordinary situation: Resentment, which reflects the conditionality of justice, must now be overcome, or prevented from arising in the first place, by means that rise above the conditionality of justice; or else there is the prospect of endless frustration and the potential for much of that frustration to turn into violence.

In desperation, individuals and societies sometimes turn to that rare virtue called forgiveness to break the moral and emotional impasse caused by unpunished or nonpunishable breaches of reciprocity. But what exactly is forgiveness? How is it related to justice and resentment? Can it work? And what are its powers and limits? These and other related questions form the subject of this chapter. Central to my argument is a distinction I draw between two types of forgiveness that are the expressions of very different psychological structures. One of these, conditional forgiveness, is an extension of the same kind of thinking in terms of exchange and reciprocity that is characteristic of justice; the other, unconditional forgiveness, is a form of psychic disposition altogether beyond justice. I try to show that as long as the circumstances of justice obtain, even conditional forgiveness cannot be expected to become the order of the day. More important, I argue, even when forgiveness, conditional or unconditional, is from time to time achieved under the circumstances of justice, it may promote the well-being of individuals by relieving them of the negative affects of resentment and yet may not necessarily promote the social cause of justice, of which resentment remains a necessary moral and psychological engine.

The Logic of Forgiveness

Hannah Arendt speaks of promising and forgiving as the two basic faculties that make human action possible. Although Arendt does not directly deal with justice, she would obviously take promising (including implicit

3. Reparation may be regarded as a milder form of punishment, inasmuch as it involves recognition of the injury of one party and the guilt and responsibility for compensation on the part of another but does not go so far as to require the latter's loss of freedom (in the form of imprisonment). Even public censure, with its strong disapproval of a breach of reciprocity, could serve as a form of punishment-like sanction, although it stops short of offering any material compensation to the injured party and exacting any financial loss on the part of the offender.

promising) to be the faculty that helps make justice—that is, the commitment to justice—possible. What about the role of forgiving in relation to justice? According to Arendt, forgiveness is necessary for human action because "trespassing is an everyday occurrence which is in the very nature of action's constant establishment of new relationships within a web of relations, and it needs forgiving, dismissing, in order to make it possible for life to go on by constantly releasing men from what they have done unknowingly. Only through this constant mutual release from what they do can men remain free agents."[4] We may add that forgiveness is also necessary for releasing people from what they have done *knowingly*. One of the things people do knowingly from time to time is to go back on their promises, including the usually implicit promise not to violate the reciprocity of justice. The self-centeredness (or egoistical forgetfulness) that makes promising necessary also makes the occasional breaking of promises inevitable.

The logical remedy for this comes from within justice, in the form of punishment. For punishment caters to the intrinsic conditionality of promising: one makes promises to those who themselves can make promises, indeed in return for their promises. This is true of implicit promising as well. Promising, based as it is on mutuality, calls for retaliation or punishment (or at least censure) when that mutuality is broken. Not surprisingly, Arendt places punishment and forgiveness side by side, in the belief that "both have in common that they attempt to put an end to something that without interference could go on endlessly."[5] What she neglects to point out, however, is that punishment follows from the nature of promising, whereas forgiveness does not—that punishment belongs within the realm of justice, as does promising, whereas forgiveness does not. It is these differences between punishment and forgiveness that explain both why punishment when available is generally the preferred response to breaches of promise and why punishment must sometimes give way to forgiveness.

The need for forgiveness invariably shows the insufficiency of justice. As I said earlier, punishment is not always available, and even when available may not succeed in putting an end to a cycle of injustice and resentment. It is here, even more than in the case of unintentional "trespassing," that

4. Hannah Arendt, *The Human Condition* (Chicago: University of Chicago Press, 1958), p. 240.

5. Ibid., p. 241.

forgiveness has an essential role to play. It serves as a safety valve when promises are broken but punishment is unavailable or would be counterproductive—in a word, when justice, made up of (implicit) promising and punishment, is insufficient.[6] Because forgiveness comes from outside of justice, it does not constitute a reaction, at least not a reaction in a sense that is true of retaliation, punishment, and resentment. When I forgive something, I act as if it had not happened. This means that my action will not be conditioned by it (hence no retaliation), nor even my state of mind (hence no resentment). As Arendt puts it, forgiving is "the only reaction that acts in an unexpected way and thus retains, though being a reaction, something of the original character of action. Forgiving, in other words, is the only reaction which does not merely re-act but acts anew and unexpectedly, unconditioned by the act which provoked it and therefore freeing from its consequences both the one who forgives and the one who is forgiven."[7] This line of reasoning could be carried further still. For what forgiving does to its antecedent act, the act forgiven, is to render it causally irrelevant, that is, to ignore it, and in so doing to enable action to go on as if it lacked that antecedent. In this sense, forgiving is not a reaction but rather an action that forestalls a reaction.

Unlike punishment, which responds to an act of injustice in accordance with the logic of justice (that is, the reciprocity and conditionality of justice), forgiveness responds by treating that logic as irrelevant and thereby prevents resentment from occurring. Forgiving a breach of the reciprocity of justice means not reacting to it, either in kind, even if I am permitted to do so by law, or in the form of resentment, no matter how much I may be morally entitled to it. In forgiving a breach of reciprocity in this way, I am acting contrary to the very reason for being just, namely, the mutual satisfaction of interests. In the act of forgiving, I am not doing justice to myself, for I am doing myself *less than* justice requires, and I am not doing justice to the breaker of reciprocity, for I am doing him *more than* justice requires. Thus, forgiving takes place beyond justice.

It follows from the nature of forgiving, as something beyond justice, that it is not at the discretion of the state, whose responsibility it is to en-

6. It is for reasons like this that "generosity—in the sense of a disposition to lay aside residues of resentment—is . . . an important adjunct to reciprocity." Lawrence C. Becker, *Reciprocity* (New York: Routledge & Kegan Paul, 1986), p. 155.

7. Arendt, *Human Condition*, p. 241.

sure justice, not to suspend or transcend it.[8] The state, having monopolized the power to enforce the conditionality of justice and imposed upon individuals the obligation to abide by the norms of justice unconditionally, has no right to forgive, to treat justice as nonreciprocal.[9] For individuals undertake to follow the norms of justice unconditionally only on condition that the reciprocity of justice—the mutual advantage accruing from justice—is protected by the state. When individuals give up the right to retaliate, to take the law into their own hands, they are not making a self-sacrifice but entering into an exchange with the state. Such an exchange would be put in jeopardy if the state were to forgive breakers of reciprocity without the consent of its reciprocity-abiding citizens. For the state unilaterally to forgive acts of injustice would be retroactively, as it were, to turn an exchange into a pure self-sacrifice for reciprocity-abiding individuals.[10]

Such self-sacrifice, for this is the price of forgiveness, is for individuals to make—or not to make. But they are in a position to make such self-sacrifices only in the domain not covered by law. This is because when the state takes it upon itself to enforce the reciprocity of justice, it thereby turns itself into the principal party—at least a party on a par with the offended individuals—whom lawbreakers offend when they offend individuals. In meting out punishment, therefore, the state is not only seeking justice—restoring the reciprocity of justice—for the offended individuals but also penalizing the offenders for shortchanging the state for the protection it has offered. In this latter regard, the offended individuals have no more right to forgive than the state does in the former.

The state, however, has no legitimate say in the matter *outside the domain of law.* Since justice is by nature conditional, I have an inherent right to treat it as such so long as the state does not, as part of an exchange, curtail that right by subjecting certain categories of action to punishment. In other words, where the state does not see fit to enforce the reciprocity of

8. This is why state pardons occur so rarely, and when they do, they are often timed to occur as part of a larger public occasion in which all citizens participate. In this way, the "forgiveness" issues—or at least has the appearance of issuing—not from the state alone but from the people as a whole.

9. Indeed, it is precisely because the state has the power to punish that it has no right to forgive. For a not dissimilar account of why the sovereign (or state) has no such right (with respect to "crimes of *subjects* against one another"), see Immanuel Kant, *The Metaphysics of Morals,* trans. Mary Gregor (Cambridge: Cambridge University Press, 1991), p. 145.

10. Although the state has no business doing the forgiving itself, it may legitimately encourage individuals to be forgiving.

justice by punishment, it is entirely up to individuals themselves to safeguard it, by retaliation or withdrawal of good will, or to forgo it, by forgiveness. In the absence of punishment, forgiveness is something entirely individual and voluntary. I am completely free to respond in kind to a breach of reciprocity, provided that I do not exceed the original provocation. By the same token, I am also completely free to forgive.

Beyond Good and Evil

It is tempting to think of forgiveness, because of the element of self-sacrifice involved, as something preeminently moral and, by contrast, to think of retaliation, even when legally permissible, as something less than fully moral. This is mistaken. To respond in kind to nonpunishable breaches of reciprocity is to act within justice, indeed, to act in the spirit of justice, and therefore such an act is no less morally respectable than society's punishment of lawbreakers, both having their source, and justifiability, in the conditionality of justice itself. To forgive, however, is to go outside of justice, and, when forgiveness is unconditioned by admission of guilt by the offender, to go beyond morality altogether. There are no *morally* comprehensible reasons for forgiveness, notwithstanding its status as a moral virtue in some systems of morality or religion. True forgiveness is beyond good and evil.

The best reason for forgiveness is, as Nietzsche sees it, physiological. Precisely because forgiveness takes one beyond good and evil, it can relieve one of the affects of resentment, of which consciousness of good and evil is a necessary condition. Through moral consciousness, a negative reaction to one's situation, typically involving some loss or disadvantage, is heightened into resentment of what is deemed the cause of that situation, which is thereby perceived as evil. Resentment, we might say, is the moralization of one's disadvantage. Such resentment tends to multiply in the absence of immediate release, and whenever it is denied adequate release in actions proportional to its source, it turns inward and saps one's energy in the manner of futile obsessions. That is why, according to Nietzsche, "nothing burns one up faster than the affects of *ressentiment.*"[11]

Against such affects forgiveness performs a function quite fittingly described by Nietzsche as "a kind of hygiene." By taking one beyond moral-

11. Friedrich Nietzsche, *Ecce Homo* (together with *On the Genealogy of Morals*), trans. Walter Kaufmann and R. J. Hollingdale (New York: Random House, 1967), "Why I Am

ity, forgiveness relieves one of the moral hatred that is resentment. By relieving one of resentment, forgiveness helps prevent the inwardly directed and self-destructive dissipation of one's energy. Thus, in forgiveness, moral consciousness gives way to physiological wisdom. In this context, it makes perfect sense for Nietzsche to depart from his usual position, most vehemently stated in the *Genealogy*,[12] and speak approvingly of the Buddha as "that profound physiologist" and of Buddhism for its "victory over *ressentiment*." Such a victory is achieved through following the doctrine "Not by enmity is enmity ended; by friendliness enmity is ended." These words, says Nietzsche, "stand at the beginning of the doctrine of the Buddha," and in them Nietzsche sees not moral insight but physiological wisdom: "It is *not* morality that speaks thus; thus speaks physiology."[13]

Physiology, if not physiology alone, seems to be speaking even in Kierkegaard's doctrine of forgiveness, of love "hiding a multitude of sins." When Kierkegaard says that "ridicule and insults really do no harm, if the one insulted does not harm himself by *discovering* them, that is, by becoming resentful,"[14] he is recommending not meekness but a certain, all too rare kind of wisdom. The wisdom is that of innocence, as epitomized by "a child in malice" who by not understanding evil does not notice it and by not noticing evil is not hurt by it. That is to say, wisdom is marked by a complete lack of moral consciousness. In this light, when Kierkegaard says that "wisdom is essentially the understanding of the good," that cannot mean good in any moral sense, for knowledge of such good implies knowledge of evil. Moral consciousness belongs rather to shrewdness, as distinct from wisdom. Shrewdness, says Kierkegaard, is "an understanding of evil," and since evil is necessarily a moral concept, such understanding implies an understanding also of the good in a moral sense. It is shrewdness, consciousness of moral good and evil, that makes possible "vainglorious comparison of one's self with the world and with other men."[15]

So Wise," 6. See also Max Scheler, *Ressentiment,* trans. Lewis B. Coser and William W. Holdheim, new ed. (Milwaukee: Marquette University Press, 1994), chap. 1. What Nietzsche and Scheler mean by *ressentiment* is different from, and vastly more complex than, the notion of resentment. When I draw on their remarks on *ressentiment,* I do so with reference only to what *ressentiment* has in common with resentment.

12. See Nietzsche, *On the Genealogy of Morals* (together with *Ecce Homo*), trans. Walter Kaufmann and R. J. Hollingdale (New York: Random House, 1967), III, 17.

13. Nietzsche, *Ecce Homo,* "Why I Am So Wise," 6.

14. Søren Kierkegaard, *Works of Love,* trans. David F. Swenson and Lillian Marvin Swenson (Princeton: Princeton University Press, 1946), p. 233.

15. Ibid., pp. 231, 230.

Through such comparisons one discovers a "multitude of sins" in others and goodness in oneself, and when one is personally harmed by such "sins," vainglory turns into resentment.

Through moral consciousness, one becomes capable of resentment; by jettisoning moral consciousness, one shakes free of resentment. One can become free of resentment only by becoming free of the categories of good and evil that make it possible. For Kierkegaard, freedom from resentment is not a symptom of weakness, which one would need to make up for by shrewdness, but a sign of strength, for which one needs no shrewdness. It is the strength to digest, to forget, to begin anew, to act, and the strength not to let moral consciousness produce negative feelings in oneself, not to let negative feelings sap one's energy. Kierkegaard calls this strength love, declaring, "Love hides a multitude of sins," where Nietzsche would say: thus speaks physiology.

It is tempting to take Kierkegaard, not to mention Nietzsche and Buddhism, to task for confusing forgiveness with condonation. But beyond good and evil there is no distinction between forgiveness and condonation.[16] Forgiveness, as distinct from condonation, requires the admission of guilt by the offender, but the idea of guilt makes sense only within the categories of good and evil. To the extent, therefore, that I have, if only temporarily, freed myself of such categories, I am incapable of distinguishing between forgiveness and condonation. Indeed, I am even incapable of being conscious of forgiving. Love, hiding a multitude of sins, discovers nothing to forgive. Such unconscious forgiving, if it is possible, represents a complete victory over resentment, in that it takes place outside of morality itself, transcending the very categories of good and evil that make resentment possible.

Conditional Forgiveness

Not surprisingly, this is not how forgiveness is usually understood. In everyday life, forgiving takes place within the categories of good and evil, and as a result, it is both conditional and conscious. Such forgiving lays down a condition that is thoroughly moral in character, namely, that the offender must in some way acknowledge his guilt.[17] There is an open

16. On the distinction between forgiveness and condonation, see, for example, Gabriele Taylor, *Pride, Shame, and Guilt: Emotions of Self-Assessment* (Oxford: Clarendon Press, 1985), pp. 105–106.

17. A more generous yet paradoxical kind of forgiveness occurs when the one who forgives recognizes a wrong and yet does not hold the perpetrator of the wrong responsible for

exchange here of acknowledgment of wrongdoing for forgiveness. The exchange is conducted in moral currency: mutual agreement about the wrongdoer's guilt, followed by the offended party's decision to stop placing blame on the wrongdoer, with the understanding that the wrongdoer will not repeat the wrong in the future.[18]

Underlying the moral exchange is an exchange in power. For the act of acknowledging one's guilt is an act of submission—to the offended party. In acknowledging one's guilt, one places oneself in the power of the offended party, the power to forgive. It is only when the offender admits his guilt that he will concede to me the power to forgive, and it is only when he concedes to me the power to forgive that he too will see my act as one of forgiveness. Therefore, when I make my forgiveness conditional on the offender's acknowledgment of guilt, I am in effect inviting him to concede that I am in a position to forgive—that I am in a position of power.[19] It is such a sense of power that I am after when I insist on the distinction between forgiveness and condonation.

The offender does not simply concede to me the power to forgive; he

---

it because of, say, the latter's ignorance. In a case like this, there is both something to forgive, since a wrong has been perpetrated, and nothing to forgive, since the perpetrator is not held responsible and therefore is not required to acknowledge her guilt as a condition for being forgiven. Thus, Jesus said of his executioners, "Forgive them; for they know not what they do" (Luke 23:34).

18. See P. S. Greenspan, *Practical Guilt* (New York: Oxford University Press, 1995), p. 153.

19. The converse of my (moral) power is my offender's (moral) weakness. The latter my offender also acknowledges when she admits her guilt and puts herself in my power to forgive. It may sometimes happen that the sense of release that comes from being forgiven is not enough to outweigh the sense of weakness. Therefore at no time does the offender need a greater sense of respect or power than when she is being forgiven. Forgiving that gives all the respect or power to the forgiver but leaves little for the forgiven is merely revenge in the guise of forgiveness. It is perhaps worse than not forgiving at all. It is, I believe, essentially this point that Nietzsche is trying to make, in his typically provocative fashion, when he says that even the best kind of forgiving—or even lack of punishment—is liable to damage the self-respect of the forgiven: "If you have an enemy, do not requite him evil with good, for that would put him to shame." Wrong that is not punished or returned in kind gives the wrongdoer a bad conscience, and "a gruesome sight is a person single-mindedly obsessed by a wrong." By inflicting "five little [wrongs]," we share the wrong, and "a wrong shared is half right." In this way punishment is a cure for the bad conscience. Therefore, "a little revenge is more human than no revenge," so much so that punishment should be "a right and honor for the transgressor." This kind of revenge—revenge motivated not by the need for power but by consideration of the wrongdoer—is what Nietzsche calls "justice which is love with open eyes." Friedrich Nietzsche, *Thus Spoke Zarathustra,* in *The Portable Nietzsche,* ed. and trans. Walter Kaufmann (New York: Viking Press, 1954), p. 180.

can do so only through moral categories. The power to forgive is a moral power, a power rooted in the categories of good and evil, right and wrong. It is only because he has done something wrong or evil that the offender is asking for forgiveness, and it is only because I, in not responding to wrong with wrong, have placed myself in the right that I am in a position to forgive. My power to forgive derives not from my status as the offended party as such but from my moral superiority, which entitles me to forgive or not to forgive. It is therefore integral to conditional forgiving that it is carried out through the categories of good and evil. These categories alone can confer power on the offended and render the offender powerless.

While these moral categories make conditional forgiveness possible, they turn it into something not very different from resentment. Like resentment, such forgiveness is part of an exchange, and as such it too bespeaks the conditionality of justice. Strictly speaking, when I forgive conditionally, I am not forgiving but trading, my generosity (to the offender) only an illusion caused by the fact that the currency I am trading in—power—is not so clearly visible. It is not merely true in a chronological sense that forgiving takes place after the acknowledgment of wrongdoing by the offender. After such acknowledgment, I am able to forgive because I have regained in a moral form the power that, as the victim of an offense, I have lost in the form of interests. Such forgiving is at best a partial victory over resentment, in that the forgiver overcomes resentment not by a generosity of spirit beyond good and evil but by a sense of power based on good and evil. Since it is based on moral categories, conditional forgiving may be said to consist in the self-righteous aspect of resentment uncoupled from its vengeful aspect. But the vengeful aspect of resentment disappears only because my offender, by acknowledging his guilt, has put himself in a position of (moral) weakness. I do not seek revenge on the weak—because I am powerful.[20]

Such a sense of power is necessarily rooted in moral categories, as we have seen, but it is only contingently dependent on the offender's acknowledgment of guilt. Although it is made easier by my offender's acknowledgment of guilt, my sense of power does not have to depend on it. I can grant myself the power to forgive as long as I see myself as good and my offender as evil. What gives me the power to forgive is *my* sense of good and evil as applied to a particular situation. My offender's acknowl-

---

20. It follows that to the extent that I draw a line between forgiveness and condonation, I am not really above resentment.

edgment of guilt serves merely to confirm it. Therefore, if my offender chooses not to admit his guilt, that does not by itself take away my power to forgive; it can do so only if it undermines my own moral judgment of the situation. This need not happen, especially if I can somehow see such a disparity in moral standing (power) between myself and my offender that his opinion can make no difference. This is indeed a psychological trick people sometimes perform when they are not generous enough really to forgive but still want to make a display of their broad-mindedness—saying, for example, in the very act of forgiving, that they will not be dragged down to the same (moral) level as the offender.[21] In a more positive vein, one need not put one's offender down in order to forgive him but instead can raise oneself to a higher than ordinary level of morality. There is no better way to do this than by partaking of some suprahuman power of forgiveness; small wonder that Alexander Pope called forgiving divine.

The motive behind conditional forgiveness is the exact opposite of the motive of sympathy. When I feel sympathy for others, I am concerned with their *lack* of power. Indeed, to be in a position to feel sympathy is to be in a position of power. It is not sympathy I feel when I forgive conditionally. In offering such forgiveness, I am concerned with my own lack of power, and I try to make up for it by somehow putting myself in a (moral) position that entitles me to exercise the power of forgiveness. The offender's acknowledgment of guilt, more than anything else, can help put me in such a position, which is why it is so important to those who are able to forgive only conditionally. Such acknowledgment of guilt is very different from a mere expression of sympathy, which would recognize my hurt but would not identify the offender as the one who should ask for forgiveness and me as the one who has the power to forgive. For this reason, the last thing I would be looking for from my offender is mere sympathy, which would only confirm *his* power and my lack of it.

This is not to say that sympathy cannot be a motive for my offender's acknowledgment of guilt. Sympathy is indeed a very appropriate motive, since the offender is the more powerful party until he brings himself to acknowledge his guilt. Sympathizing with my suffering caused by him, he finds himself in the wrong and makes an open acknowledgment of it. Hav-

21. There is, however, a corrective for this "arrogance" or "self-righteousness." As Arendt remarks, "The reflection that you yourself might have done wrong under the same circumstances may kindle a spirit of forgiveness." Hannah Arendt, *Eichmann in Jerusalem,* rev. and enl. ed. (New York: Viking Press, 1965), p. 296. This thought, however, if carried too far, would simply deprive one of the right or power to forgive.

ing made such an acknowledgment, he loses his power, and it is precisely this loss that I acknowledge as both deserved and adequate when I decide to forgive. Such a decision bears witness to my sense that the power I have lost has been adequately restored to me. It is only at this point that I may be in a position, if at all, to feel sympathy *for my offender*—not, of course, on account of what he has done to me but on account of what he has subsequently done to himself, allowing himself to be stricken with guilt and to lose his self-respect and peace of mind. Otherwise, sympathy, an emotion felt by the strong for the weak, is supposed to go to the offended, not to the offender. As John Stuart Mill observes, sympathy with the offended, along with the impulse of self-defense, gives rise to the desire to punish the offender.[22] In this case, I myself am the offended, and in sympathizing with myself, so to speak, I feel in relation to the offender the corresponding urge to punish. Such an urge is an expression of powerlessness, which, short of actual punishment, can normally be alleviated only by the offender's acknowledgment of guilt, which is also an expression of his willingness to be divested of the power wrongfully exercised. Only at this point, but not earlier, do I have the power to feel sympathy for my offender. For the offended, the power to sympathize and the power to forgive are the same power.

Forgiveness and the Circumstances of Justice

To forgive conditionally is to reach the limit of generosity *within* justice, while to forgive unconditionally—and by implication also unconsciously—is to go outside of justice altogether. Conditional forgiving is difficult enough, in that it involves shifting the exchange that is constitutive of justice a considerable distance away from the original site of justice, where interests are directly exchanged for interests. Needless to say, unconditional forgiving is much rarer—more an ideal (for some) than a reality. For by transcending the conditionality that makes justice what it is, unconditional forgiveness transcends justice itself, and it does so under the very circumstances of justice, circumstances that make justice necessary and breaches of it unavoidable. It is only under such circumstances that forgiveness, whether conditional or unconditional, has something to forgive. That is to say, forgiveness presupposes injustice; it does not eliminate injustice.

22. See John Stuart Mill, *Utilitarianism,* in John Stuart Mill and Jeremy Bentham, *Utilitarianism and Other Essays,* ed. Alan Ryan (Harmondsworth: Penguin, 1987), p. 324.

Kierkegaard is clearly putting the cart before the horse when he takes the prohibition of unjust acts to be the occasion for them: "The commandment, the prohibition, tempts, just because it wishes to constrain the evil, and now if sin takes occasion it *takes* that, because the prohibition *is* the occasion . . . But there is one environment which absolutely does not give and is not an occasion for sin: that is love. When a man's sin is encompassed by love, then it is outside its own element." He says further: "Oh, how many crimes have been prevented, how many evil purposes defeated, how many desperate resolutions consigned to oblivion, how many sinful thoughts halted on the way to becoming deeds, how many rash words repressed in time, because love gave no occasion! Woe to the man by whom the offense cometh; blessed the lover who by refusing to furnish the occasion covers a multitude of sins."[23] These passages contain much wisdom, but surely Kierkegaard goes too far in claiming, or at least implying, that forgiveness—the lifting of prohibition and censure—will eliminate injustice. For prohibitions are called for by the existence of injustice in the first place, although the latter is not *called* injustice until prohibitions, as part of a system of justice, are put in place. It is not that prohibitions call forth injustice but that the existence of injustice, though not named as such until being prohibited, requires prohibitions. Justice, the sum total of such prohibitions, is a solution to human conflict arising under the circumstances of justice. These circumstances are such that they inevitably give rise to acts of harm or violence which, given the concept of justice, would be deemed unjust, but such acts of harm or violence per se existed prior to, and independently of, justice. It follows that neither the circumstances of justice nor the acts of harm or violence occurring inevitably in them will disappear if the sum total of prohibitions ceases to exist. The problem of injustice will be not eliminated but only stripped of a certain conceptualization if the language of justice is removed.

This being the case, forgiving cannot possibly become the order of the day. The very circumstances in which there is injustice to be forgiven (or not forgiven) will necessarily make forgiving an exception rather than the rule. For it would be absurd to expect people constantly to rise above justice while they live under the circumstances of justice. Rather, as long as the circumstances of justice obtain, people can generally at best be expected to act in the spirit of justice, that is, in accordance with the conditionality of justice. Suppose, however, that such circumstances no longer

23. Kierkegaard, *Works,* pp. 241, 242.

obtained. If this were to happen, then forgiveness would simply no longer be necessary, because there would no longer be any injustice to be forgiven. It is a function of the very conditionality of justice that the need for forgiveness is in inverse proportion to the ability to forgive.

It is instructive in this connection to return to Arendt and consider her view that forgiving is immanent in human action, on a par with promising. Arendt is clearly right to see promising and forgiving as equally presupposed by action, that is, action as distinct from mere reaction. But her further move of seeing them as almost equally natural and indispensable seems questionable. She puts promising and forgiving on the same level both logically and, it seems, empirically when she writes:

> In so far as morality is more than the sum total of *mores,* of customs and standards of behavior solidified through tradition and valid on the ground of agreements, both of which change with time, it has, at least politically, no more to support itself than the good will to counter the enormous risks of action by readiness to forgive and to be forgiven, to make promises and to keep them. These moral precepts are the only ones that are not applied to action from the outside, from some supposedly higher faculty or from experiences outside action's own reach. They arise, on the contrary, directly out of the will to live together with others in the mode of acting and speaking, and thus they are like control mechanisms built into the very faculty to start new and unending processes.[24]

There is no doubt that the faculty of making and keeping promises (including implicit ones) is a condition of the possibility of human society.[25] The same cannot be said of the faculty of forgiving, however. If forgiving is, as Arendt sees it, "like a control mechanism built into the very faculty to start new and unending processes," this is so only in the sense that the ability to start new processes, if and to the extent that it exists, presupposes the ability to forgive. Empirically, this ability seems by no means common, especially in situations where forgiveness is most called for because resentment is at its strongest. Forgiving, unlike revenge, is not an instinctive act—except for those few (in our imagination, perhaps) who think beyond good and evil and who therefore find nothing to forgive. Most of us are accustomed to thinking in moral categories and thus are liable to be

24. Arendt, *Human Condition,* pp. 245–246.

25. Nietzsche sheds some light on how this faculty came about in *Genealogy,* II, 1, 2.

trapped in an ongoing chain of reactions that is powered by the conditionality of justice. If we are able from time to time to break this chain, it is usually not because we are able to forgive but because we are in the lucky position of not having a great deal to forgive.

When there *is* something serious for us to forgive, something that has the potential for setting off a chain of reactions, we usually, if we can, leave that chain to be broken by punishment. Arendt considers punishment an "alternative to forgiveness" in that both punishment and forgiveness "attempt to put an end to something that without interference could go on endlessly."[26] Forgiving is not indispensable, then, since there is an alternative to it. Or we should rather call forgiveness an alternative to punishment, in that it is generally the less preferred option. We should note, too, that often punishment "put[s] an end to something that without interference could go on endlessly" only for us, and not for the punished. It would serve this purpose for the punished only if they believed themselves to be in the wrong. But there is no guarantee that they will do that; on the contrary, the very fact that the offenders probably committed the prohibited acts in the first place with full knowledge of their illegality makes it likely that they will not. Even if they do see the justice of the punishment they receive, the chain is broken *for us* not because we have the ability to forgive but because society, in carrying out the punishment, and the offenders, in acknowledging their guilt, have made up for our inability truly, that is, unconditionally, to forgive.

When Arendt calls forgiveness an alternative to punishment, she is in effect saying that forgiveness is *an alternative to justice,* inasmuch as punishment is an instrument for restoring the reciprocity of justice. But in a society subject to the circumstances of justice, there can be no alternative to justice, except as an aberration. Forgiveness is an aberration because it constitutes a response to injustice not from the point of view of justice but from a point of view outside of justice, and this while the circumstances of justice still obtain. Therefore, forgiveness cannot generally serve as a solution to injustice but only as a way of relieving individuals of the negative affects of resentment. That is to say, forgiveness may be conducive to the well-being of individuals—both the forgiving and the forgiven—but not necessarily to the social cause of justice, insofar as the two can be separated.

26. Arendt, *Human Condition,* p. 241.

The Justness of Resentment

What is conducive to the social cause of justice, naturally enough, is the strict administration of justice. Since justice is by nature reciprocal, this means that the social response to injustice should reflect, and be such as to protect, the reciprocity of justice. In concrete terms, this means that injustice should not be forgiven but should whenever possible be punished in proportion to its seriousness. Punishment is not to be thought of as regrettable violence perpetrated for the sake of justice, nor even as morally justifiable violence administered in the interest of justice, if this is taken to mean that punishment, necessary as it is, is imposed from outside of justice. Rather, punishment is part and parcel of justice itself: it follows from the very reciprocity of justice and is none other than justice in response to injustice. Therefore, if one wants to condemn punishment, one must condemn justice itself. This is not to rule out the possibility that one may have good reason to find justice itself too narrow or too parsimonious, but one is not entitled to embrace the idea of justice and *at the same time* disapprove of practices, such as punishment, that derive from the nature of justice itself.

This way of looking at punishment may not be too offensive to our moral sensibility so long as the unpleasant responsibility for punishment rests with society—society in the abstract. But punishment of injustice is also what individuals, *qua members of society,* are supposed to desire. This desire takes the form of resentment. As Reinhold Niebuhr points out, the complete absence of resentment "simply means lack of social intelligence or moral vigor."[27] More precisely, the inability to feel resentment shows a total lack of any sense of justice. Just as punishment, as carried out by society, is justified by the very conditionality of justice, so the same must be said of resentment on the part of individuals. Despite the unpleasant ring to it, resentment is a perfectly appropriate moral response to injustice, a response dictated by the very logic of justice. Indeed, resentment, on the part of individuals qua members of society, is the only response to injustice that is in keeping with the conditional or reciprocal nature of justice itself. As such, resentment possesses more than the kind of instrumental value that Niebuhr sees in it. When Niebuhr writes, "Society must strive for jus-

27. Reinhold Niebuhr, *Moral Man and Immoral Society* (New York: Charles Scribner's Sons, 1960), p. 249. See also Annette Baier, "Hume on Resentment," *Hume Studies* 6 (1980): 133–149, for discussion of the role of "resentment as the watchdog of pride" (p. 139) and, via this role, resentment's indirect contribution to (the possibility of) justice.

tice *even if* it is forced to use means, such as self-assertion, resistance, coercion and perhaps resentment, which cannot gain the moral sanction of the most sensitive moral spirit,"[28] it sounds as if such means merely happen to be useful or necessary for promoting justice. Useful or necessary these means indeed often turn out to be, since they promote conditions of roughly equal power that are conducive to justice. But they are not incompatible, as Niebuhr seems to imply, with the spirit of justice itself. If such means "cannot gain the moral sanction of the most sensitive moral spirit," still less the approval of those who want to go beyond good and evil altogether, it is not because the means involved fall short of the spirit of justice but because justice itself falls short in the eyes of these people.

One important reason why Niebuhr finds resentment instrumentally valuable but morally suspect is that it contains what he calls an egoistic element. Niebuhr writes, by way of an example, that "a Negro who resents the injustice done his race makes a larger contribution to its ultimate emancipation than one who suffers injustice without any emotional reactions," but he immediately goes on to suggest that "the more the egoistic element can be purged from resentment, the purer a vehicle of justice it becomes."[29] To be sure, there is an egoistic element in resentment, but that element exists equally in justice itself. In resentment as in justice, the egoistic element is subsumed under the notion of reciprocity, which in its entirety is not purely egoistic because it is simultaneously self-regarding and other-regarding. When I resent injustice, I am not merely narcissistically complaining about the fact, say, that someone has failed to help me or to refrain from harming me. Rather I am angry at the fact that in so failing she has failed to live up to the reciprocity intrinsic to justice. Thus my resentment springs not directly from egoism but from a sense of justice, although the sense of justice contains a self-regarding element by virtue of its reciprocity. Resentment is an emotional response to breaches of justice—that is, to the *wrongful* hampering of my *legitimate* self-interest rather than my self-interest as such. It is therefore misleading to say, as

28. Niebuhr, *Moral Man,* p. 257, emphasis added. Niebuhr expands on this point as follows: "Society . . . makes justice rather than unselfishness its highest moral ideal. Its aim must be to seek equality of opportunity for all life. If this equality and justice cannot be achieved without the assertion of interest against interest, and without restraint upon the self-assertion of those who infringe upon the rights of their neighbors, then society is compelled to sanction self-assertion and restraint. It may even, as we have seen, be forced to sanction social conflict and violence" (pp. 258–259).

29. Ibid., pp. 249–250.

Niebuhr does, that "the more the egoistic element can be purged from resentment, the purer a vehicle of justice it becomes."[30] On the one hand, as noted earlier, the so-called egoistic element in resentment takes the form of reciprocity, which is distinct from egoism. On the other hand, as long as I act from motives in keeping with justice, neither my motive of justice nor my resentment of injustice can be entirely free of the self-regarding element that goes into the very making of reciprocity and hence of justice itself.

I can of course try to make my resentment a "purer vehicle of justice" by bringing it as close as humanly possible to the third-person emotion of indignation. To the extent that I succeed in this highly difficult endeavor, it may appear that I have removed all traces of egoism from my moral reactions to injustice. Since the emotion of indignation, however, does not preclude the ability to identify with victims of injustice, it is continuous with the first-person emotion of resentment and therefore cannot be free of the self-regarding element of justice any more than resentment is. Even when I am moved by indignation to selfless efforts to restore justice on others' behalf, I am still presupposing (legitimate) self-interest, as an element of reciprocity, on the part of those for whom I am fighting for justice, and I would be the last to blame them for being resentful of the injustice of which they are victims or for being less than self-denying in demanding reciprocity. Indeed, I must have an unreserved identification with their resentment, and by implication with their (legitimate) self-interests at least to the extent of strongly disapproving of the way in which these interests have been undermined.[31] In the final analysis, my very ability to feel resentment or to identify with the resentment felt by others expresses the knowledge, conscious or otherwise, of the reciprocal and hence partly self-regarding nature of justice.

Given that this is the case, attitudes such as self-assertiveness and resentment, though they may with good reason be deemed unattractive human traits from certain points of view external to and higher than justice, must be regarded as morally irreproachable in any context of human interaction regulated by the ideal of justice. In other words, they are an integral and legitimate part of the human economy of justice which could be eliminated completely only in a society in which the circumstances that make

30. Ibid., p. 250.

31. It is just as important to relieve the hurt of resentment as it is to remove the injustice responsible for it. The two things are causally related but to some degree conceptually distinct.

justice necessary in the first place no longer obtained. If in many situations such attitudes should perhaps not be encouraged too enthusiastically or even at all, it is not because they cease to be morally supportable and instrumentally valuable but only because they already exist in abundance, as they generally do in any society marked by the circumstances of justice.[32]

32. In such situations, it is perhaps the higher virtues of benevolence and forgiveness that should be cultivated, not only for the sake of individual "hygiene" but also in the interest of social justice. On the necessity to strike a balance between forgiveness and vigilance, and to avoid "dysfunctional weaknesses" at both extremes, see Annette C. Baier, *Moral Prejudices* (Cambridge, Mass.: Harvard University Press, 1994), p. 150.

11

Justice and the Moralization of Sympathy

I have examined, in separate contexts, two different kinds of attempts to overcome those problems or limitations of justice that arise from its reciprocal and conditional character. I discussed, in Chapter 8, the appeal to theistic conceptions for the creation of (apparently) unconditional motives, and then in Chapter 9 the possibility of purging resentment through forgiveness. Neither kind of attempt, as it turned out, can do the trick. Appeal to theistic beliefs will not work, because theistic beliefs are themselves fragile and, more important, because such appeals, even when successful, merely defer the expected reciprocity rather than changing the structure of conditionality. Forgiveness will not work either, because unconditional forgiveness not only is socially unavailable in sufficient abundance but also by its very nature stands outside the domain of justice, while conditional forgiveness, like the appeal to theistic conceptions, shares with justice the same psychological structure that is characterized by exchange, reciprocity, and the potential for resentment. Thus, either something (unconditional forgiveness) is brought in from outside the context of justice to lessen the psychological cost of justice, in which case it cannot possibly be regularly incorporated into the context of justice itself; or something (appeal to theistic conceptions, and conditional forgiveness) is invoked which is but a different, if less transparent, expression of the reciprocal and conditional nature of justice, in which case it cannot make any qualitative difference. The important thing is that in either case, though for opposite reasons, the disposition toward justice itself is left essentially unchanged.

It remains to consider a third possibility, namely, that the disposition to be just itself might be transformed by higher motives and thereby become a more intrinsic virtue. Reinhold Niebuhr held up just such a possibility when he remarked that "any justice which is only justice soon degenerates into something less than justice. It must be saved by something which is more than justice."[1] One of the most promising candidates for this role is sympathy, broadly construed. I devote this chapter to exploring the familiar yet still challenging question of whether sympathy can play this role and, if so, how.

Transcending Justice

It is worth recapitulating some relevant conclusions from previous chapters so as to be clear about what precisely is meant by the transformation of the disposition toward justice by higher motives into a more intrinsic virtue. We have seen that the characteristic of justice as a motive is its reciprocity or conditionality. Such conditionality of motive can nevertheless be made compatible with the unconditional practice of justice. This happens when the state makes itself solely responsible for enforcing the reciprocity of justice and in so doing relieves individuals of the need and the power to do so. That is to say, in exchange for the state's enforcement of the reciprocity of justice, individuals undertake to practice justice as if it were an unconditional imperative. It is important to note that the achievement in this way of the unconditional practice of justice, even of the apparently unconditional motive of justice, occurs within the logic of justice itself, since individuals are prepared to practice justice unconditionally (in relation to other individuals) only on condition that the reciprocity of justice is preserved by the state (in relation to each individual). That this is the case despite appearances to the contrary is shown by the fact that resentment is a characteristic emotional response to injustice, especially injustice unpunished, and as such it reflects the mentality of those who have learned to practice justice unconditionally but whose motive nevertheless remains conditional.

It is essential to keep these conclusions in view as I consider, later in this chapter, whether it is possible to overcome the conditionality of justice by transforming the motive of justice with higher virtues. These conclusions make clear what it is that can properly count as overcoming the conditionality of justice. To begin with, what is overcome has to be the conditionality of motive, as opposed to the mere conditionality of practice. Then, an individual's overcoming of the conditionality of motive must not in any way depend on the state's enforcement of the reciprocity of justice, as the

1. Reinhold Niebuhr, *Moral Man and Immoral Society* (New York: Charles Scribner's Sons, 1960), p. 258.

latter serves precisely to make such individual overcoming unnecessary. Finally, as the case of resentment reminds us, overcoming the conditionality of motive cannot be restricted to conscious motives alone but must include motives of which one need not be conscious but which can nevertheless be inferred from one's moral emotions, such as resentment. These are the criteria that have to be met if we are to speak in any strict sense of the overcoming of the conditionality of justice.

What these criteria rule out immediately is the possibility that the conditionality of justice can be overcome by means of duty. For what is overcome through duty is not the conditional *motivation* of justice but only what would otherwise be the conditional practice of justice. Instead of removing the conditionality of justice, the idea of duty merely reflects a transfer of the power to preserve it from individuals to the state. To the extent that such a transfer takes place, individuals have no choice but to practice justice unconditionally, although they must be made to understand this lack of choice also as a *moral* necessity. And they apprehend such a lack of choice in terms of duty, even in the most robustly moral sense, only to the extent that they would otherwise not sufficiently desire to practice justice unconditionally, that is, only to the extent that an unconditional motive of justice is originally lacking.

Such an unconditional motive will be lacking as long as an individual's duty to practice justice unconditionally does not rest on values external to justice itself. When individuals undertake to practice justice unconditionally in relation to one another provided that the state, through reward and punishment, maintains a conditional relationship to each, they are not motivated by values that are external to justice. Rather, they are motivated by the assurance that precisely the values of justice will inform the actions of the state, and indeed that the more they appear to rise above the reciprocity of justice, the more the state will be bound to stand by it. It is thus obvious that if the conditionality of justice is to be overcome (to whatever degree deemed desirable), it can be overcome only by values that come from outside of justice. This is presumably what Niebuhr means when he says that justice "must be saved by something which is more than justice."[2]

Justice and Friendship

This "something which is more than justice" takes the form of both premoral feelings and moral virtues, and it goes under a confusing array of

2. Ibid.

near-synonyms, most notably benevolence, love, altruism, sympathy, compassion, care, and kindness. It is not necessary at this point to make fine distinctions between these feelings or virtues. What is important for our purposes is not how they differ but what they have in common. Roughly, what they have in common may be characterized as a certain intrinsic concern for others, a concern that is independent of self-interest and is therefore free from the motive of exchange that is characteristic of justice.

I want to argue that the virtue of justice takes precedence, in both a logical and a developmental sense, over those higher feelings or virtues that may serve to elevate or transform it. I can perhaps best present this argument by considering the relationship between justice and friendship, as this relationship is conceived by Aristotle and as Aristotle in turn is interpreted by Alasdair MacIntyre. I have chosen the case of friendship because what is true of the relationship between justice and friendship is true, in those respects that concern us, also of the relationship between justice and the higher and warmer virtues in general. Let me hasten to add that I am not questioning MacIntyre's general historical-philosophical thesis as set out in *After Virtue,* nor his account of Aristotle as part of that larger thesis. I focus rather on the logical or conceptual relationship between justice and friendship, and thus for the most part analyze the relationship between justice and friendship in abstraction from its context in the ancient Greek polis.

Commenting on Aristotle's idea that "lawgivers seem to attach more importance to [friendship] than to justice,"[3] MacIntyre explains that "the reason is clear. Justice is the virtue of rewarding desert and repairing failures in rewarding desert within an already constituted community; friendship is required for that initial constitution."[4] Clearly, there is a sense in which true friendship is morally superior to a relationship based strictly on justice (that is, what Aristotle means by "particular" as opposed to "general" justice). In this sense, we might say that friendship has a certain *moral priority* over justice. It follows that, in relation to friendship, justice is a remedial virtue, in the sense that justice is required only to the extent that friendship is lacking. As Aristotle says, "Between friends there is no need for justice."[5] Since justice is a remedial virtue, it makes practical sense for lawgivers to try as much as possible to create conditions in which jus-

3. Aristotle, *The Nicomachean Ethics,* trans. J. A. K. Thomson, rev. ed., ed. Hugh Tredennick (Harmondsworth: Penguin, 1976), 1155a.

4. Alasdair MacIntyre, *After Virtue,* 2nd ed. (Notre Dame, Ind.: University of Notre Dame Press, 1984), p. 156.

5. Aristotle, *Nicomachean Ethics,* 1155a.

tice would not be necessary. Insofar as such conditions are akin to or characterized by friendship, it stands to reason that lawgivers should attach more importance to friendship than to justice or assign what may be called *legislative priority* to friendship.

This much seems roughly correct. The question is whether one can go further, as MacIntyre does, and think of friendship as having *logical priority,* in the sense that friendship is a condition of the possibility of justice. Something like this is obviously what MacIntyre means when he says that "friendship is required for that initial constitution"—namely, the constitution of a community in which justice may then have a role to play. Whether this is in fact the case, or whether the relation is the other way around, depends on the nature of the friendship Aristotle has in mind when he observes that lawgivers assign what we have called legislative priority to friendship.

There is little doubt that the friendship in question is civic friendship. If we are to determine the logical relationship between friendship and justice, however, it is not enough to identify a civic kind of friendship, even if it is then made clear, as by MacIntyre, that "the type of friendship which Aristotle has in mind is that which embodies a shared recognition of and pursuit of a good. It is this sharing which is essential and primary to the constitution of any form of community."[6] The problem is that a *merely* civic friendship is clearly dependent on the prior establishment of justice. Thus it is necessary to determine which of the three types of *personal* friendship distinguished by Aristotle might serve as the prototype of civic friendship and render it logically prior to justice. It appears that for civic friendship to preempt justice in the way Aristotle seems to suggest, and to have the moral quality (the sharing of substantive values) MacIntyre seems to claim for it, it has to be modeled on the type of personal friendship Aristotle calls friendship based on goodness. There are, however, at least two serious problems, one logical and one empirical, with treating such friendship as a precondition of justice. The *logical* problem is that friendship based on goodness is incompatible with there being a need for justice, for, as Aristotle says, "between friends there is no need for justice." This can be understood in the sense that people whose relationship is one of friendship based on goodness treat each other in ways that to an observer fully meet, indeed more than meet, what justice would require, but in so treating each other they need neither the conditional motive of justice nor the coercive

6. MacIntyre, *After Virtue,* p. 155.

enforcement of justice. If this is the case, what friendship does with regard to justice is not to make it possible but rather to make it unnecessary. This is what is meant by saying that justice is a remedial virtue in relation to friendship. The moral priority of friendship, which makes justice a remedial virtue in relation to it, is simply incompatible with friendship's having logical priority over justice.

The *empirical* problem with treating such friendship as a precondition of justice is that it is rare. Aristotle says in one place, "That such friendships are rare is natural, because men of this kind are few," and in another place, "To have many friends in the way of perfect friendship is no more possible than to be in love with many persons at the same time."[7] The rarity of this kind of friendship alone makes it incapable of serving as a precondition of justice on a society-wide scale, even if a society has only the scale of a polis. This difficulty can be resolved, it seems, only by treating civic friendship as being closer in spirit to the other two kinds of personal friendship identified by Aristotle, namely, friendship based on utility and friendship based on pleasure. Civic friendship, even as ambitiously conceived by MacIntyre as "the sharing of all in the common project of creating and sustaining the life of the city, a sharing incorporated in the immediacy of an individual's particular friendships,"[8] need not be at all incompatible with these kinds of friendship rooted in mutual advantage. Rawls, among others, has shown how a sense of common destiny or solidarity, as distinct from a common conception of the good, can develop on the motivational foundation of mutual advantage.[9]

Once civic friendship is understood in this way, the empirical problem noted earlier disappears—but only to be replaced by another problem. For the idea (whether attributable to Aristotle or to MacIntyre or to both) of civic friendship as *foundational* begs an important question: How does this kind of friendship come about?[10] Treating such friendship as foundational—as the starting point of everything else—precludes invoking any

7. Aristotle, *Nicomachean Ethics,* 1156b, 1158a.

8. MacIntyre, *After Virtue,* p. 156.

9. See John Rawls, *A Theory of Justice,* rev. ed. (Cambridge, Mass.: Harvard University Press, 1999), e.g., pp. 433–434.

10. Obviously, this does not apply to David Hume's idea of a narrower kind of friendship that (along with sexual love and familial bond) could serve as the psychological training ground, as it were, for the establishment of justice. For an analysis of this idea, see Annette C. Baier, *A Progress of Sentiments: Reflections on Hume's Treatise* (Cambridge, Mass.: Harvard University Press, 1991), p. 228.

prior notion of the circumstances of justice. But it is precisely this notion that is crucial to any account of the emergence of both justice and (civic) friendship. Aristotle hints at the circumstances of justice when he remarks on the rarity of perfect friendship or friendship based on goodness. And he can be interpreted as pointing to the logic of the circumstances of justice when he says that perfect friendship obviates the need for justice. In view of this, when he observes that lawgivers assign legislative priority to civic friendship, Aristotle must be treating the two kinds of personal friendship based on mutual advantage as the prototype of civic friendship.[11] Indeed, these kinds of friendship, including a civic friendship modeled on them, are the only ones that lawgivers are in a position directly to create or make possible on a large scale; it is not in the power of lawgivers to overcome the rarity of perfect friendship and thereby eliminate the circumstances of justice. Although they fall far short of perfect friendship, these kinds of friendship based on mutual advantage are sufficient for the goal of the lawgivers, for, as Aristotle says, "concord is their primary object."[12]

Since these kinds of friendship are based on mutual advantage, however, neither they nor a civic friendship modeled on them can be foundational in the sense in which MacIntyre takes friendship to be foundational. It cannot be said of such friendships that "between friends there is no need for justice"—a proposition that applies only to friendship based on goodness, which, as we have seen, cannot serve as a model for civic friendship. In the absence of universal friendship based on goodness, we must start with an account of the circumstances of justice, and this means assigning logical priority to justice and explaining everything else, including friendship, as being made possible by justice. In other words, given the circumstances of justice, mutual advantage presupposes the prior establishment of justice. By the same token, friendship based on mutual advantage, or a community based on such friendship, also presupposes the instituting of justice. Justice is a condition of the very possibility of friendship based on mutual advantage, and by implication also of civic friendship. In this regard, the polis is no different from a modern society.

Indeed, we can go further and see friendship based on mutual advantage as a natural, even inevitable outgrowth of justice. To the extent that *mutual advantage* is rendered stable by just institutions, ideally to the point where it can be taken for granted, it may be expected to give rise in

11. This interpretation is in keeping with Aristotle's general remarks about the necessity of friendship in the immediately preceding context and what he later has to say about the purposes of founding a political community. See *Nicomachean Ethics,* 1160a.

12. Ibid., 1155a.

due course to *mutual good will*.[13] Such mutual good will, a product of the institutionalization of mutual advantage by means of justice, constitutes what may be called utilitarian (that is, ultimately advantage-based) friendship. Once utilitarian friendship in turn is rendered secure through the uninterrupted accumulation of acts of good will, its utilitarian dimension may fade so much into the background—or, as Nietzsche would put it, be forgotten to such a degree—that those involved may act out of good will without thought of personal advantage, sometimes even in the absence of personal advantage. This does not mean, however, that the motive of mutual advantage is removed or transcended but only that it is rendered less conscious.

It is rendered less conscious by the fact, itself made possible by the instituting of justice, that mutual advantage no longer requires constant mutual suspicion and alertness. One can afford to drop one's guard, exercising good will in the (not fully conscious) knowledge that advantage will not be far behind. This kind of friendship or mutual good will is continuous with the original motive of justice as mutual advantage. It is the instinct of reciprocity lulled to sleep by favorable circumstances. We may thus see justice and utilitarian friendship as reflecting two phases of the same instinct of reciprocity. They share the same motive of mutual advantage and differ only in whether such a motive is overt or covert, which in turn depends on whether society succeeds in making mutual advantage a regular fact of life.

In the best scenario, as noted earlier, utilitarian friendship may become highly stable and, as a result, its utilitarian dimension may recede so much from consciousness that it may appear as if good will is an independent motive. This appearance, even if it is no more than mere appearance, represents a qualitative leap. For as soon as good will appears as a possible motive in its own right, it becomes something that can be socially promoted as such. That is to say, it can be socially promoted in the absence of personal advantage or even with the deliberate eschewal of personal advantage. To the extent that such social promotion is successful, good will as an independent motive ceases to be mere appearance and becomes instead a moral-psychological reality.

It is not inappropriate to regard such good will as a kind of "natural" sympathy, as long as we remember that it is natural, or can be made so, only in a context of stable mutual advantage that has been made possible by justice in the first place. Provided that we keep this in mind, we need

13. On the relationship between mutual advantage and mutual good will, see Chapter 7.

not regard good will as an outgrowth of mutual advantage, as I have been doing so far, but can treat it instead as something that is allowed to come to the fore under conditions of stable mutual advantage. In the end, it is perhaps immaterial which view we adopt. The important point is that once good will or sympathy (these terms are interchangeable for our purposes) is taken to be a motive in its own right, it can be socially promoted as such. In short, sympathy can be *moralized*. This means in turn that when we ask how sympathy impinges on the motive of justice, we must address the question *separately* for premoral sympathy and moralized sympathy. Thus, as we shall see, how sympathy affects the motive of justice depends on whether it is premoral or moralized, and on the modes of its moralization. Accordingly, the crucial distinction is not between sympathy as a natural motive and as a socially conditioned one, if such a distinction stands at all, but between premoral and moralized sympathy.

The Insufficiency of Premoral Sympathy

Hume is perhaps more responsible than any other philosopher for the idea that sympathy is insufficient as a motive of moral conduct. In Hume's view, sympathy is more an aid to moral judgment than a motive of moral conduct.[14] To assess the validity and coverage of this claim, we must distinguish between premoral and moralized sympathy. Once we do so, it is immediately apparent that Hume operates with a notion of sympathy that is thoroughly premoral. This is true not only of the *Treatise,* where a more or less mechanistic concept of sympathy is used to account for fellow feeling, but also of the second *Enquiry,* where Hume gives up any distinction between sympathy and fellow feeling in favor of a single, irreducible concept of fellow feeling that he terms the "sentiment of humanity."[15] In both cases, but especially in the *Enquiry,* Hume conceives fellow feeling as an original and natural instinct, that is, as something prior to and independent of any socially cultivated morality that comes into play only with the introduction of the "common point of view."[16] It should therefore come as no surprise that in Hume's view (though this is true more of the *Treatise* than of the *Enquiry*), sympathy or fellow feeling possesses relatively lit-

14. For an excellent discussion of this distinction, see Philip Mercer, *Sympathy and Ethics* (Oxford: Clarendon Press, 1972), pp. 45, 52–53.

15. On this change, see ibid., p. 42; and Brian Barry, *Theories of Justice* (Berkeley: University of California Press, 1989), pp. 159, 166.

16. David Hume, *A Treatise of Human Nature,* ed. L. A. Selby-Bigge, 2nd ed., ed. P. H. Nidditch (Oxford: Clarendon Press, 1978), p. 591.

tle conative force and is significant chiefly as a precondition, or an enabling condition, of moral judgment.

In fact, not only does premoral sympathy have little conative force in general, but also what conative force it can muster stands in an inverse relation to the need for sympathy as a motive of justice. In other words, sympathy is least present where it is most needed. We have seen how stable mutual advantage, brought about by the smooth working of just institutions under favorable conditions, has a tendency to generate good will, or, according to an alternative, equally plausible way of looking at the matter, to allow good will to come to the fore. Clearly, unless or until such good will is moralized, it is completely dependent on mutual advantage. This is the case regardless of whether such dependence is known to those who have developed good will. The fact that mutual good will is roughly proportional to and coexistent with mutual advantage shows that one's inability to perceive the dependence of good will on mutual advantage merely reflects one's ability to take mutual advantage for granted. Where mutual advantage can be taken for granted, or can at least be normally expected, it helps stabilize mutual good will, which in turn enables people to remain committed to just institutions that have brought about the mutual advantage in the first place.

This we can think of as the ideal situation of justice, a kind of situation that resembles what happens in Rawls's well-ordered society. In such a society, people can be expected to practice justice out of sympathy or spontaneous good will. But then, as Rawls shows, sympathy is the product of a system of justice that is established on the basis of the motive of reciprocal advantage in the first place. What sympathy does, therefore, is merely to reinforce the justice already achieved on the basis of other, lesser motives and to help keep the chain of justice going. In such an ideal situation of justice, sympathy is needed, if at all, only in a weak sense: it is in the first instance a *product* of justice and only subsequently a *motive* of justice.

Sympathy will be needed in a stronger sense—as a cause rather than an effect of justice—in less than ideal situations of justice, situations in which mutual advantage is not a stable fact of life. In such situations, a person committed to justice will often find himself having to follow the requirements of justice at a potential cost to himself, either because he is not certain whether other people will do the same or, worse, because he knows that others have failed to follow those requirements to his disadvantage in the past and may continue to do so in the future. What is needed in such situations is a motive that can cause the just person to remain committed to justice in the absence of guaranteed mutual advantage—that is, a motive that can raise her above the original purpose of justice. Premoral sympathy cannot supply that motive, for the simple reason that sympathy has a tendency to be suspended by breaches of reciprocity on the part of others.[17] This is true both for psychological reasons and by definition.

Psychologically, we do not sympathize with people who have acted unjustly and harmed our interests. Their very act of violating the reciprocity of justice makes them unfit objects of our sympathy. Therefore, if I refrain from retaliation, I cannot be doing so out of sympathy but at best out of a sense of duty to practice justice unconditionally. That sense of duty rests in turn, as we have seen, on the understanding that society will restore the reciprocity of justice, as well as my legitimate interests dependent on such reciprocity, through punishment or restitution. It is in the nature of premoral sympathy—as something that has to be made possible by justice before it can in turn help reinforce justice—that it can help prevent me from unilaterally breaking the reciprocity of justice but cannot cause me to give up the demand for reciprocity from others. After all, premoral sympathy is as reciprocal as justice itself.

The incompatibility between being harmed by injustice and continuing to practice justice out of sympathy can even be a matter of definition. It is not unreasonable to stipulate, as Philip Mercer does, that "the circumstances about which we sympathize with others are always unpleasant and involve some kind of suffering."[18] This rules out by definition, quite appropriately, even the relevance of sympathy to the motive of justice on the part of victims of injustice. Mercer makes an unnecessary concession, though, when he says that "although what a man does and what he is like may be made into psychological obstacles to sympathy, they can never be made into logical obstacles."[19] The stipulation that sympathy is directed at suffering presents something close to a logical obstacle to sympathy's serv-

17. For the opposite view, that is, the idea that empathy "can motivate the refusal to return evil for evil," see Lawrence C. Becker, *Reciprocity* (New York: Routledge & Kegan Paul, 1986), p. 159.

18. Mercer, *Sympathy*, p. 5. It is not necessary, though possible, to see this feature of sympathy in a negative light. Nietzsche, for example, has this to say: "*Sympathizers.*—Natures full of sympathy and always ready to assist in misfortune are rarely at the same time willing to join in rejoicing: when others are fortunate they have nothing to do, are superfluous, feel they have lost their position of superiority and thus can easily exhibit displeasure." Friedrich Nietzsche, *Human, All Too Human*, trans. R. J. Hollingdale, 2 vols. in 1 (Cambridge: Cambridge University Press, 1986), 1:321. This is unfortunately often the case, but not always or necessarily so.

19. Mercer, *Sympathy*, p. 5.

ing as a motive for practicing justice unconditionally in relation to those who are perpetrators rather than victims of suffering. So once again, and here by definition, the desire to continue practicing justice in spite of injustice cannot spring from sympathy.

If, as we have seen, premoral sympathy is not strictly required in an ideal situation of justice and is irrelevant in a situation of injustice, it also has a tendency to be weakened in an intermediate kind of situation. What characterizes the intermediate situation, perhaps the most common situation of justice, is a moderate degree of uncertainty concerning the prospect of mutual advantage. To the extent that such uncertainty exists, every act in conformity with the requirements of justice is potentially an unwilling act of self-sacrifice. This ever-present possibility of unilateral self-sacrifice presents the choice of what to do under the rubric of justice to one's consciousness in terms of a conflict between justice and self-interest. Instead of being guaranteed by the smooth working of just institutions and thus receding into the background, self-interest understandably becomes part of the conscious motive of justice. And to the extent that self-interest enters into the conscious motive of justice, justice turns into a reluctant virtue. Once this happens, sympathy has to contend with self-interest. But the very consciousness of self-interest as part of the motive of justice already represents the defeat of *premoral* sympathy. For whenever our self-interest is enlarged in our consciousness, our premoral sympathy for others is shrunk in proportion and is usually powerless to affect our behavior, except with the aid of moralization, in which case it ceases to be premoral sympathy. The conspicuous presence of self-interest in our motive of justice under relatively unfavorable circumstances is a reminder that, after all, our current motive of justice is not very far removed from the original purpose of justice, which was informed by the passive point of view and which made everyone more keen to benefit from justice than to sacrifice for it. And just as the original purpose of justice had little to do with sympathy, so our current motive of justice is hardly moved by it. The introduction of sympathy into that motive is a contingent event, one that occurs only when a stable situation of mutual advantage has generated a large amount of mutual good will and thereby caused, as it were, a partial forgetting of the original motive of justice. Until then, the context of deciding what to do under the rubric of justice is one in which we have to make a conscious effort to be willing potentially to give up our legitimate self-interest to some significant degree if we are to be able to keep our commitment to just institutions and practice justice unconditionally in the face of the uncertain prospect of reciprocity. That *conscious* effort in itself reflects the insufficiency of the premoral *instinct* of sympathy, and, as we shall see, if sympathy contributes at all to that effort, it can do so only after undergoing moralization.

All this goes to support MacIntyre's contention that "'sympathy' as used by Hume and Smith is the name of a philosophical fiction."[20] One must immediately emphasize, however, that it is the premoral character of Hume's notion of sympathy that makes it the philosophical fiction MacIntyre says it is. Having already clearly stated, as part of his conception of the circumstances of justice, that premoral altruism or benevolence is in short supply, Hume simply is not in a position to go on to invoke premoral sympathy (which belongs to the same family of other-regarding instincts) to make up for the insufficiency of enlightened egoism as a motive of justice. To invoke sympathy in this way, as MacIntyre charges Hume with doing in the second *Enquiry*, is either to contradict his own conception of the circumstances of justice or to resort to a philosophical fiction. Since Hume nowhere revokes his conception of the circumstances of justice, it seems reasonable to conclude, as MacIntyre does, that Hume invents the notion of sympathy or sentiment of humanity in order to fill a gap between enlightened egoism and justice that is unbridgeable, given the circumstances of justice.[21]

Such a gap, however, is not *entirely* unbridgeable if we distinguish between the cognitive and the conative uses of premoral sympathy and treat sympathy as fulfilling a primarily or exclusively cognitive function. In fact, this is essentially what Hume does in the *Treatise* when, after conceding

20. MacIntyre, *After Virtue,* p. 49. This view occurs in the following passage: "In the *Treatise* Hume posed the question why, if such rules as those of justice and of promise-keeping were to be kept because and only because they served our long-term interests, we should not be justified in breaking them whenever they did not serve our interests *and* the breach would have no further ill consequences. In the course of formulating this question he denies explicitly that any innate spring of altruism or sympathy for others could supply the defects of an argument from interest and utility. But in the *Enquiry* he feels compelled to invoke just such a spring. Whence this change? It is clear that Hume's invocation of sympathy is an invention intended to bridge the gap between any set of reasons which could support unconditional adherence to general and unconditional rules and any set of reasons for action or judgment which could derive from our particular, fluctuating, circumstance-governed desires, emotions and interests. Later on Adam Smith was to invoke sympathy for precisely the same purpose. But the gap is logically unbridgable [sic], and 'sympathy' as used by Hume and Smith is the name of a philosophical fiction." See also pp. 229–230.

21. Much fuller discussion, along similar lines, can be found in Chapter 5.

that "*Self-interest* is the original Motive to the *Establishment* of Justice," he immediately goes on to say that "a Sympathy with *public* Interest is the Source of the *moral* Approbation, which attends that Virtue."[22] The distinction here is between the original establishment of justice and the subsequent evaluation of justice. Hume suggests that sympathy (with the public interest) plays a role only in the latter. That is to say, sympathy serves a cognitive function in the forming of moral judgment, and this function is distinct from a conative function that sympathy is not strong enough to perform. As Hume puts it, "This latter Principle of Sympathy is too weak to controul our Passions; but has sufficient Force to influence our Taste, and give us the Sentiments of Approbation or Blame."[23]

It is not difficult to see why it is easier for sympathy to serve as an aid to moral judgment (cognitive function) than as a motive of moral conduct (conative function). For a moral judgment formed in a moment of abstract reflection does not directly and immediately impinge on our self-interest. Indeed, for this very reason, the ability to form moral judgments on the basis of sympathy is quite compatible with egoism. Such ability is attributable not to the overcoming of self-interest but to the (temporary) irrelevance or remoteness of self-interest, and the latter is possible as long as moral reflection is sealed off from any immediate adverse bearing on one's own self-interest. Once sympathy is understood strictly in this cognitive sense, then, it need not contradict Hume's conception of the circumstances of justice. In this sense—the sense in which Hume invokes sympathy in the *Treatise*—sympathy is not entirely a philosophical fiction, although it still cannot bridge the gap between acting from self-interest and acting consistently as justice requires. Significantly, however, this gap now takes the form of a gap between the cognitive and the conative functions of sympathy, and such a gap is one that can be bridged by the moralization of sympathy. Hume himself comes close to suggesting something like this when he describes sympathy as having "sufficient Force to influence our Taste, and give us the Sentiments of Approbation or Blame." For it is a short step from having a certain "taste" and certain "sentiments of approbation and blame" to turning them into principles of justice that form the substance of moral duty and even of law.

This kind of rationale is well captured by Brian Barry's example in which

22. Hume, *Treatise,* p. 670. This is an alternative version to the one on pp. 499–500.

23. Ibid., p. 670. Thus it is natural that "controlling our passions" is a function that Hume does not assign to sympathy in the *Treatise*.

"people who are prepared, say, to vote for a fair system for assessing contributions to some collective project may not be sufficiently motivated to pay their contributions voluntarily." The solution, Barry suggests, is "obviously, to vote also for a system of sanctions to ensure compliance."[24] It is assumed that those who are prepared to vote for the scheme in the first place will also be prepared to vote for the sanctions to back up the scheme. What makes both actions possible without contradiction is the temporal and psychological distance between moral judgment and the price one may later have to pay for it. In the real world, things are not always quite so straightforward, for egoism, whether in a crude form or in the more subtle form of settled political beliefs, may intervene to make people far-sighted enough, so to speak, not even to allow the acceptance of certain principles, let alone their enforcement. It is the function of cognitive sympathy to prevent such farsightedness. This is as far as premoral sympathy can take us, if indeed it can take us that far. Beyond that, if sympathy is to enable us to act on those principles it helps form in the first place, or to generate better principles, it must first be moralized.

Conscience, Self-Love, and the Moralization of Sympathy

Even Schopenhauer, for whom compassion (identical with sympathy for our purposes) is "the only genuine moral incentive,"[25] concedes the need for what amounts to its moralization. In the second chapter of *On the Basis of Morality,* Schopenhauer takes Kant to task for treating duty as the foundation of morality. Then, in the third chapter of the same book, he puts forward his rival theory of the basis of morality as consisting entirely and exclusively in compassion. Having thus rejected duty as the basis of morality and put compassion in its place, however, Schopenhauer finds himself having to bring principles back into the picture, if not in their Kantian form. "Without principles firmly held," concedes Schopenhauer, "we should inevitably be at the mercy of antimoral tendencies." The reason for this concession is his recognition, similar to Hume's, that compassion is in short supply or has a tendency to "come too late." This shortage calls for the introduction of principles, which amounts to the moralization of compassion. Thus: "*Rational reflection* raises *noble dispositions* to the *firm reso-*

24. Barry, *Theories,* p. 366.

25. Arthur Schopenhauer, *On the Basis of Morality,* trans. E. F. J. Payne (Indianapolis: Bobbs-Merrill, 1965), p. 141.

lution, grasped *once for all,* of respecting the rights of everyone, of never allowing themselves to encroach on them, of keeping themselves free from the self-reproach of being the cause of another's suffering."[26] Notice the crucial role assigned to "rational reflection," something reminiscent of Kant. But notice also—and this unmistakably separates Schopenhauer from Kant—that rational reflection can play this role only for those who possess "noble dispositions," that is, those who are capable of a significant degree of compassion (though, needless to say, not enough compassion to dispense with the need for rational reflection). The product, no less noteworthy, is "the firm resolution, grasped once for all"—in other words, duty, or to be more precise, duty based on the moralization of compassion.

On Schopenhauer's view, both compassion and duty, though the latter is not explicitly invoked, are indispensable for moral conduct, and this is how each is assigned its proper place: "Although *principles* and abstract knowledge generally are by no means the original source or first foundation of morality, they are nevertheless indispensable to a moral course of life: they are the receptacle or reservoir which stores the habit of mind that has sprung from the fount of all morality [that is, compassion], a habit of mind that does not flow at every moment, but when the occasion for its application arises, flows along the proper channel."[27] Put in simpler terms, compassion is the foundation of all morality, and yet it is not always available to a sufficient degree. So a sense of duty ("firm resolution") and the principles that make up its substance, both originally formed on the basis of compassion, enable us to act morally.[28] What makes Schopenhauer (somewhat) different from Hume is his stronger emphasis on the need for

26. Ibid., p. 150, emphasis added. "Once for all" does not exactly mean, however, that compassion will henceforth be irrelevant. As Schopenhauer says a little later: "Compassion, however, always remains ready to come forward *actu.* Therefore, when, in individual cases, the established maxim of justice shows signs of breaking down, no motive (egoistic motives excluded of course) is more effective for supporting it and putting new life into just resolutions than that drawn from the fountainhead itself, namely, compassion" (pp. 151–152).

27. Ibid., p. 150. This marks an obvious departure from Schopenhauer's earlier view that "no genuine virtue can be brought about through morality and abstract knowledge in general, but that such virtue must spring from the intuitive knowledge that recognizes in another's individuality the same inner nature as in one's own." Arthur Schopenhauer, *The World as Will and Representation,* trans. E. F. J. Payne, vol. 1 (New York: Dover, 1969), pp. 367–368.

28. Thus one way of understanding what Schopenhauer means when he describes compassion as the only moral motive is that we cannot *be* better than our spontaneous compas-

rational reflection and his greater attention to the concept of duty.[29] This pushes him in the direction of Kant. But what distinguishes him (very much) from Kant is his idea that duty must be based on compassion, that a sense of duty is nothing more than the desire to follow principles that have been established through the moralization of compassion in the first place.

Depending on the substance of the principles—"injure no one" or "help everyone as much as you can"—the moralization of compassion yields the virtue of justice or the higher virtue of benevolence. This way of viewing the relationship between compassion on the one hand and the virtues of justice and benevolence on the other is quite in keeping with Schopenhauer's overall theory, and it provides the key to a puzzle in his earlier work *The World as Will and Representation*. In that work, Schopenhauer argues for the existence of two degrees of compassion which happen to correspond to justice and benevolence, respectively. I have shown this to be an implausible view.[30] Now that we see that Schopenhauer (in *On the Basis of Morality*) is prepared to take justice and benevolence to result from the moralization of compassion, we can help him put the horse back before the cart. Instead of postulating two *preexisting* degrees of compassion that underlie justice and benevolence, respectively, we are now in a position to say that justice and benevolence are virtues that result from the moralization of compassion to different degrees. There are not two but innumerable degrees of premoral compassion, none of which corresponds precisely to any virtue. It is only because of the process of moralization that we can speak of two degrees of compassion, but then it would be more precise to speak of two degrees of the moralization of compassion—or two degrees of *moralized* compassion.

So interpreted, Schopenhauer's theory of moral motivation is a very plausible one, especially if we add the proviso that the prior establishment of justice on the basis of other motives, as described, for example, by Hume or Nietzsche, is a condition of the possibility of compassion. It is

---

sion can make us, but that we can *act* better than is possible with our short supply of compassion by deriving principles from compassion, which we then can be motivated to live up to by a sense of duty or "firm resolution." For an account of the need for principles that emphasizes the role of reasons, an account that might be complementary to Schopenhauer's, see Thomas Scanlon, *What We Owe to Each Other* (Cambridge, Mass.: Harvard University Press, 1998), chap. 5, sec. 3.

29. Or call it "the firm resolution, grasped once for all," since Schopenhauer abhors the Kantian and theological connotations of the very concept of duty.

30. See Chapter 4.

doubtful, however, whether moralized compassion retains the pure concern for others—"the absence of all egoistic motivation"—that Schopenhauer regards as the sole "criterion of an action of moral worth."[31] For with the shift of the burden of conative efficacy from compassion to the following of principles, there occurs also a shift from love of others to self-love. Once I form the "firm resolution" to follow principles that are established and comprehended on the basis of compassion, following such principles becomes part of my identity and my basis of self-esteem, such that I cannot respect myself, or live with myself, if I break these principles. In this way, my relationship with others is mediated by a relationship with myself.[32] Now it is my conscience rather than my compassion that enables me to tell right from wrong and to act accordingly, depriving me of peace of mind if I act otherwise. An important shift in ethical attention—from the effects of my actions on others' well-being to their effects on my own peace of mind—takes place here, a shift whose significance Schopenhauer does not fully appreciate. Having defined the criterion of moral worth as compassion or lack of *all* self-regarding motivation, Schopenhauer immediately goes on to say that "actions of moral worth have a characteristic that is quite *internal* and therefore not so evident, that is to say, they leave behind a certain *self*-satisfaction, called the approbation of conscience. In the same way, their very opposite, namely, actions of injustice and uncharitableness, and still more those of malice and cruelty, are affected by an inner self-censure."[33] Here, as elsewhere, Schopenhauer commits the mistake of placing compassion side by side with conscience as if they sprang from a single motive.

In order to give a more accurate account of the shift in ethical attention, it is necessary to distinguish *compassion-based conscience* from pure compassion on the one hand and from pure conscience on the other. I mean by pure conscience a kind of conscience whereby compassion is either absent or irrelevant, and this is close to what Gabriele Taylor means by guilt as distinct from remorse. According to Taylor,

> the crucial thought here is just that what I am doing is forbidden. It is

31. Schopenhauer, *On the Basis of Morality,* p. 140.

32. See Immanuel Kant, *Critique of Practical Reason,* in *Critique of Practical Reason and Other Writings in Moral Philosophy,* trans. and ed. Lewis White Beck (Chicago: University of Chicago Press, 1949), p. 258; and P. S. Greenspan, *Practical Guilt* (New York: Oxford University Press, 1995), pp. 200–203.

33. Schopenhauer, *On the Basis of Morality,* p. 140, emphasis added.

> quite natural, of course, that what is so ingrained in us as being forbidden should concern our behaviour towards others, for it is in this area that early childhood restrictions are most likely to be found, that "moral training" has its central place. But it is not the only area and hence not what delimits the appropriateness of the guilt-response. What is important for guilt is just that some form of action or abstention should present itself as obligatory to the agent, but the content of the demand is not restricted.[34]

It follows that, where one's actions do impinge on others, "causal responsibility is the type that is sufficient for guilt, and that much is also necessary." What the awareness of causal responsibility makes conspicuous to the agent is "not so much: 'I have done this terrible thing *to him'*; but is rather: '*I* have done this terrible thing to him.'" This focus on one's own guilt as the doer of the deed rather than on the effects of one's deed on the victim implies that one's main purpose for making amends is to relieve oneself of the guilt rather than to relieve the victim of the bad effects. These two purposes are only contingently related. Even if the action required for the first purpose happens, as it often does, to coincide with the action required for the second, it remains the case that the first purpose is what causes one to take action and hence what constitutes the meaning of one's action. In the final analysis, guilt or *pure conscience* is not "moral in the sense of being other-regarding, for the agent's chief concern is for himself."[35]

Compassion-based conscience, the kind of conscience valued by Schopenhauer, is clearly different from such purely self-centered conscience. In it there is an element of regard for others that is present not only in one's emotional response to having hurt others but also in the intention with which one tries to rectify the situation. This kind of conscience Taylor calls remorse: "Remorse . . . seems to be moral in just this [other-regarding] sense; though perhaps not necessarily, at least standardly the agent is here concerned with the effect of what he does on others. As it concentrates on the action rather than the actor it also seems the healthier emotion, for in turning the agent away from himself he is less threatened by the possibility of self-preoccupation and self-indulgence."[36] Even this kind of conscience, however, contains compassion chiefly in a moralized form, that is, in

34. Gabriele Taylor, *Pride, Shame, and Guilt: Emotions of Self-Assessment* (Oxford: Clarendon Press, 1985), pp. 88–89.

35. Ibid., pp. 91, 92, 97–98, 103, 101.

36. Ibid., p. 101; see also p. 107.

the form of principles. When Schopenhauer describes the moralization of compassion as accomplished "once for all," this means that pure compassion need be active only in forming the principles of moral conduct, and not in acting on them.

It is even more noteworthy that the very need for the moralization of compassion, at least in Schopenhauer's theory, implies the shortage of natural, premoral compassion. In acting on principles that are based on compassion, I am simultaneously showing my (moralized) compassion for others and betraying my lack of (premoral) compassion for them, which is why the moralization of compassion is necessary in the first place. What compassion-based conscience does is to make up for my lack of spontaneous concern for others by creating a kind of self-love that depends on my being able to treat others well in accordance with a set of general but ultimately compassion-based principles. Yet in this kind of case, as Schopenhauer realizes, "compassion operates in the individual actions of the just man *only indirectly*."[37] The indirectness here is a function, first, of the fact that compassion does its work by being translated into a set of general principles, and second, of the equally important fact that the concern for others that is the essence of compassion is mediated by a special kind of self-love whose direct object is one's moral standing in one's own eyes.[38] Both facts are essential for the constitution of compassion-based conscience. If the first shows the nature of the principles conforming to which makes the kind of conscience in question compassion-based, the second reveals the psychological mechanism that is at work in this type of conscience, an essentially self-oriented mechanism that compassion-based conscience has in common with what I have called pure conscience. It is the combination of these two features that gives compassion-based conscience its distinctness from pure compassion on the one hand and from pure conscience on the other and explains its unique character and power. That self-love is allowed to play an indispensable role in this otherwise other-regarding disposition stands perfectly to reason, since the insufficiency of premoral concern for others, which makes conscience necessary in the first place, can be no better compensated for than by a kind of self-love that follows other-regarding principles and satisfies itself by benefiting others. It is no mean achievement to be able to make one's self-love, and

37. Schopenhauer, *On the Basis of Morality*, p. 151, emphasis added.

38. See Becker, *Reciprocity*, pp. 83–84, for the idea that "once the disposition to reciprocate is acquired, it gets linked with the need for self-esteem."

with it one's self-respect, conditional on one's ability to treat others well, even with the aid of principles.[39]

Where Schopenhauer goes amiss is in taking little note of the element of self-love in conscience (even in compassion-based conscience) and in missing its implications. These are very important implications, too. On the one hand, moralized compassion, in the form of conscience, no longer meets his stringent standard of moral worth, namely, "the absence of all egoistic motivation." On the other hand, moralized compassion is potentially free of the insurmountable problem that besets premoral compassion, namely, its necessary shortage. If it is true, as Schopenhauer is at pains to make clear, particularly in *The World as Will and Representation,* that few people are endowed with a high degree of premoral compassion, it is equally true that most people are potentially capable both of some degree of such compassion and of a sense of duty. The latter being the case, it is possible for a morality worthy of the name to be built on the basis of the moralization of compassion. Indeed, this is just the kind of hope inspired by Schopenhauer's idea of compassion-based conscience in *On the Basis of Morality,* although it is the kind of hope one can entertain only after climbing down from the heights of pure, premoral compassion envisioned in *The World as Will and Representation.*

Two Degrees of Moralization and the Range of Conscience

It is no accident that when Schopenhauer discusses the moralization of compassion by principles, he does so, where he is specific, with reference to justice but not benevolence. This is because the establishment of general principles depends on a symmetry or balance between the active and the passive points of view, that is, between what I am able and willing to do for others and what I expect them to be able and willing to do for me. Such a symmetry is possible for justice but not for benevolence. Indeed, justice requires such a symmetry, in that an asymmetry between the active

39. Tillich calls conscience "the channel through which the unconditional character of the moral imperative is experienced." Paul Tillich, *Morality and Beyond* (New York: Harper and Row, 1963), p. 30. It would perhaps be more to the point to say that conscience is the vehicle whereby one's concern for others operates through self-love. Or from another, equally plausible point of view, we might describe conscience as the means by which self-love is transformed to incorporate concern for others. This means that through conscience *both* self-love *and* concern for others are transformed. One way of capturing the twofold nature of this transformation is through a conception that sees love and justice as mutually definable.

and the passive points of view would be either irrational or unreasonable. On the one hand, it would be irrational on my part if I were willing to do more for others than I expected them to do for me *with regard to justice,* since a rationally just person wants to be treated with justice no less than he or she should want to treat others with justice. On the other hand, it would be unreasonable on my part if I were to expect others to do more for me than I was willing to do for them *with regard to justice,* for the simple reason, among others, that reciprocity is the least requirement that one should be willing to satisfy in a reasonable scheme of cooperation.

Benevolence is subject to a totally different logic and would be undercut by the very idea of symmetry.[40] It consists precisely in the absence of expectation of reciprocity, that is, in the willingness to give more to others than one receives from them. A benevolent person, if she is also rational, will of course expect to receive just treatment from others, but what makes her benevolent is her willingness to do more for others than justice requires *and* to do so without expecting others to do the same for her. The moment a benevolent person finds her active point of view evenly balanced by her passive one—the moment she starts demanding benevolence from others—she ceases to be benevolent, for she has turned benevolence into precisely the kind of exchange, and the kind of conditional virtue, that is characteristic of justice. Thus symmetrical benevolence makes no *moral* sense, as the essence of benevolence is contradicted by the very symmetry between the active and the passive points of view.

Nor, indeed, does symmetrical benevolence make *prudential* sense, since what I gain from another's benevolent actions, whose beneficial effects on me are by no means always certain, is more than canceled out by the strain and inconvenience, which is certain, that I would feel as a result of having constantly to perform benevolent actions out of a less than

40. The important thing in benevolence so understood is its willing unconditionality or lack of insistence on reciprocity. Even if a benevolent person thus understood considers, say, in the Kantian spirit, the duty of benevolence as having the universality of a moral law, which thereby necessarily includes herself as an object as well, what makes her motive one of benevolence is her seeing herself as the subject of benevolence, and unconditionally so, rather than seeing herself equally as the object of benevolence and hence seeing benevolence as necessarily reciprocal. Thus the benevolent person will not, at least not as a necessary condition of her benevolence, entertain the thought that "by carrying out the duty of love to someone I put another under obligation; I make myself deserving from him." Immanuel Kant, *The Metaphysics of Morals,* trans. Mary Gregor (Cambridge: Cambridge University Press, 1991), p. 244. For Kant's emphasis on the universality of the duty of benevolence, see *Metaphysics,* p. 245, "The Doctrine of Virtue," sec. 27.

benevolent (because reciprocal) motive. In view of this, my best bet is to settle for justice, which alone allows a symmetry between the active and passive points of view that is both morally coherent and prudentially advisable. In terms of prudence, the balance I seek is between the least I need to require other people to do on a regular basis if my interests are to be protected and the most I can do for them on a regular basis if I am not to overstretch myself. In moral terms, this translates into a symmetry between what I feel *entitled* to expect others to do for me (my rights) and what I feel *obligated* to do for them (my obligations).

Such a symmetry helps to yield general principles of justice, principles that I am prepared to regard as equally binding on others and myself. This symmetry also makes me both ready and eager to support the legal enforcement of general principles. What makes me ready to offer such support is my prudential sense that I have the ability to follow these principles, backed up by my moral sense that I ought to exercise this ability. What makes me eager to do so is my prudential sense of the least that my basic needs require others to do or refrain from doing, and my moral sense of entitlement that goes with it. Since we tend to attach greater weight to our own needs than to the needs of others and, at the same time, tend to place less trust in others' moral ability than our own, the institution of law reflects everyone's sense of his or her own need for protection and of the unreliability of others. But since law represents the generalization of this sense on the part of everyone in relation to everyone else, the least that I expect others to do but cannot rely on them to do except through potential legal sanctions must come to mean the least that each has to do for all. Thus, in principle, I support the enforcement of justice even against myself, although, in practice, I may have enough (complacent) trust in my moral ability to consider such enforcement superfluous in my own case.

I trust my moral ability, however, only as far as justice goes, and where justice ends, so does my support for the legal enforcement of morality. We have seen how the very idea of symmetry rules out the requirement of benevolent *actions* on grounds of prudence, just as it makes nonsense of benevolent *motives* for reasons of self-contradiction. It is worth adding that ultimately it is the idea of symmetry (or reciprocity), rather than the specific content of the principles generated on the basis of it, that constitutes the essence of justice. In other words, *what makes a principle one of justice instead of benevolence is not how much it requires of each but the fact that what it requires is equally required of all.* Now we can see more clearly why prudence dictates that benevolent actions not be required by such principles.

From the foregoing arise important implications for *the range of conscience*. By this I mean the range of actions and abstentions with regard to which failure of performance can give one a bad conscience, and this range obviously depends on the range of the principles to which one subscribes. Given that both moral and prudential considerations dictate that the range of general principles coincide with that of justice, as we saw earlier, we can say that insofar as conscience is based on general principles—or on the moralization of compassion through subscription to general principles—the range of conscience coincides with that of justice rather than benevolence.[41] Something like this, I suspect, is the reason why Schopenhauer is reticent about benevolence when he discusses the moralization of compassion by principles. However that may be, the important point is that as long as we think of conscience in terms of conformity to general principles, we must conclude that conscience is conducive to justice but not to benevolence. This means that I will have a bad conscience only if I fail to be just, but not if I fail to be benevolent (beyond being just).

Insofar as the range of conscience coincides with that of justice, the same must be true of the range of compassion, mediated as it is by conscience and by the principles that make up its substance. What compassion does, at the stage of the establishment (or comprehension) of principles if not to the same degree subsequently, is to help represent to each the needs of all others and thus to provide a basis and rationale for the principles that need to be established (or understood). In this way, justice is indirectly influenced by compassion via the principles compassion helps establish, principles that are then internalized as the substance of conscience and externalized in the form of law. But inasmuch as compassion affects me through the general principles it helps establish, and inasmuch as those principles do not go beyond justice, compassion itself does not go beyond justice.

My compassion can go beyond justice only if there is an asymmetry between my active and passive points of view with regard to benevolent actions.[42] If, on the one hand, my passive point of view with regard to benevolent actions exceeds my active point of view, I sink below the reciprocity

41. It is possible that the range of conscience coincides, strictly speaking, not with justice but with what Scanlon identifies as the morality of "what we owe to each other," which is distinct from benevolence on the one hand and from (and broader than) justice on the other; see Scanlon, *What We Owe to Each Other,* chap. 6, sec. 4. If this is the case, what I say about the range of conscience here will need to be modified accordingly, but what I say about benevolence will be unaffected.

42. As we shall see, I need not, indeed had better not, be conscious of such an asymmetry.

that is characteristic of justice, to the level of unreasonableness or egoism. If, on the other hand, my active point of view with regard to benevolent actions exceeds my passive point of view—I still want others to be just to me but I am willing to be more than just to them—I rise above the reciprocity of justice, to the level of benevolence. To rise to the level of benevolence, however, it is not sufficient that I perform benevolent actions unconditionally or unilaterally. For it is also part of the very meaning of benevolence that I perform the actions involved without regard to my relationship to those at the receiving end of my actions; in this sense, benevolence is impersonal. Moreover, and this goes without saying, only the ability to perform benevolent actions on a regular basis can count as benevolence, that is, benevolence of character. It is very doubtful, barring highly improbable exceptions, that, being the tall order it is, benevolence can spring from a superabundance of premoral compassion. Where such superabundance seems to exist, its manifestation in the form of benevolence tends to be neither impersonal nor sustained. What happens here is that a relatively high level of premoral compassion falls short of benevolence, in the same way that a more pedestrian level of premoral compassion can fall short of justice. Thus, even a seeming superabundance of premoral compassion needs moralization before it can serve as the basis of benevolence.

Once compassion is moralized into benevolence, it undergoes a change not only from personal to impersonal concern, and from occasional to regular performance, but also from conditionality to unconditionality. This last change is what distinguishes the moralization of compassion into benevolence from its moralization into justice. In benevolence, compassion is raised to a level beyond justice, a level where it is immune to considerations of reciprocity. Something like this freedom from reciprocity (as well as from change) seems to be what Kierkegaard has in mind when he writes of the transfiguration of love by duty into something "immutable," "independent," and "everlastingly secure against every change."[43] It is not accidental, however, that Kierkegaard sees the relation of love to duty in terms

43. See Søren Kierkegaard, *Works of Love,* trans. David F. Swenson and Lillian Marvin Swenson (Princeton: Princeton University Press, 1946), pp. 15–36. As a matter of fact, Kierkegaard provides an example of freedom from reciprocity: "If one man, when another man says to him, 'I can no longer love you,' proudly answers, 'Then I can also stop loving you,' is this independence? Alas, it is only dependence, for the fact as to whether he will continue to love or not depends on whether the other will love. But the one who answers, 'Then I will still continue to love,' his love is eternally free in blessed independence" (p. 33).

of "the relation of love itself to the eternal."[44] For this relation to the eternal, with its inevitable theistic implications, is the only thing that makes possible the moralization of compassion into benevolence. Yet this relation undercuts the very idea of benevolence at the same time. Benevolence, as we have seen, is marked by an asymmetry between the active and passive points of view, and it is this asymmetry that keeps benevolence clear of the motive of exchange that characterizes the lesser virtue of justice. But the relationship with the eternal that is supposed to make this asymmetry possible is itself, at bottom, a relationship of exchange. We have seen how this is the case with regard to justice.[45] The same must apply to the moralization of compassion into benevolence. In the final analysis, moralization, even as it appears to raise compassion to the level of benevolence, betrays a deficiency of unconditional fellow feeling that can be made up for only by appealing to a theistically mediated kind of exchange.

There is yet another sense in which benevolence is vitiated by its dependence on the moralization of compassion. Since my benevolence is the product of the moralization of compassion, I may be said to follow *principles* of benevolence, principles that I must see as binding on myself only, given the necessary asymmetry of benevolence. But the very consciousness of following such asymmetrical principles may imply an asymmetry of moral assessment, a sense of moral superiority to others that goes against the very spirit of true, that is, truly other-regarding, benevolence.[46] That spirit must show itself in the ability to practice the asymmetry of benevolence without the slightest consciousness of such asymmetry and hence also without the slightest reliance on moralization. It must therefore be premoral or, better still, beyond morality. As Nietzsche writes, "Whatever is done from *love* always occurs *beyond good and evil*."[47] Yet, because genuine benevolence is incompatible with moralization, it is also incompatible with social promotion. It must be left a mystery—beyond comprehension and contrivance.

44. Ibid., p. 32.

45. See Chapter 8.

46. It is possible to argue that my consciousness of the asymmetry of benevolence may result from trying to make myself believe not in my own moral superiority but in other people's greater worth. But the inevitable loss of self-esteem caused by the latter belief is likely to need some balancing by the former belief.

47. Friedrich Nietzsche, *Beyond Good and Evil,* trans. Walter Kaufmann (New York: Random House, 1966), p. 153, emphasis added.

12

Justice as a Conscious Virtue

Since my concern throughout this book has been with the disposition toward justice, it is only fitting that I should end with an examination of justice as a mode of moral consciousness. In a way I have been doing just that for the greater part of the book, and thus what I do in this chapter is to shift the focus of attention from the structure of the disposition toward justice, as a mode of moral consciousness, to its quality of self-consciousness and conscientiousness itself. In so doing, I try to bring out the fact that justice, in its deliberate balancing of self-interest and the interest of others, is a socially achieved virtue, whether or not it is also in part a natural individual disposition. Such a virtue, with its particular form of regard for the interest of others, is achieved at a considerable moral-psychological cost, a cost that is built into the disposition toward justice itself. Both the achievement and its cost are reflected in the fact that justice is a conscious virtue. It is therefore appropriate to conclude this account of justice by looking at the ways in which justice is a conscious virtue and thereby shedding some light in general on the possibility and limits of justice, of which the self-consciousness of the virtue of justice serves as perhaps the most revealing mirror.

Williams on Conscious Virtues

What, precisely, is it to be conscious, or unconscious, of one's virtue? Or what is it to be self-conscious in performing an action that is typically ascribed to a virtuous motive? Bernard Williams provides some especially precise and suggestive answers:

> If one has a certain virtue, then that affects how one deliberates. We need to be clear, however, about the ways in which it can affect delib-

> eration. An important point is that *the virtue-term itself usually does not occur in the content of the deliberation.* Someone who has a particular virtue does actions because they fall under certain descriptions and avoids others because they fall under other descriptions. That person is described in terms of the virtue, and so are his or her actions: thus he or she is a just or courageous person who does just or courageous things. But—and this is the point—*it is rarely the case that the description that applies to the agent and to the action is the same as that in terms of which the agent chooses the action.* The road from the ethical considerations that weigh with a virtuous person to the description of the virtue itself is a tortuous one, and it is both defined and *pitted by the impact of self-consciousness.*[1]

This is not the case with justice, however, and the passage from Williams can help us pin down exactly what is not the case with justice. Williams also has something explicit to say about what is the case with justice. Justice is exceptional among the virtues, though not the only exception, in that "a just or fair person is one who chooses actions *because* they are just and rejects others *because* they are unjust or unfair."[2] The accent is on "because," which helps define just actions in terms of the reasons for performing them: it is a necessary condition for an action to be just that it is performed for the principal reason that it is just. Put another way, the content of justice is *directly* linked to the motive of justice. Where such a link is posited, a theory of justice is seen as doing two things simultaneously. As Brian Barry puts it, "A theory of the motivation for being just must at the same time be a theory of what justice is. For the content of justice has to be such that people will have a reason for being just."[3] That this should be the case does not follow, however, simply from the practical nature of justice, as Barry seems to believe, but follows only under the assumption, which I examine later, that the motive of justice is, or ought to be, identical with the content of justice.

This assumption points to one sense in which justice is a conscious virtue. Applying Williams's metaphor to justice, we can say that the path leading from the ethical considerations that move a *just* person to the description of the virtue of justice itself is a *straightforward* one. Or as we

1. Bernard Williams, *Ethics and the Limits of Philosophy* (Cambridge, Mass.: Harvard University Press, 1985), p. 10, emphasis added.

2. Ibid., emphasis added.

3. Brian Barry, *Theories of Justice* (Berkeley: University of California Press, 1989), p. 359.

might say in terms of Barry's somewhat different way of looking at the matter, the motive of justice comes from subscribing to a particular substantive conception of justice. In both cases, a just person is conscious of the reasons for performing just actions, *and* he or she is conscious of those reasons under an explicit description in terms of justice. For both Williams and Barry, it seems, this twofold consciousness is a necessary, if not a sufficient, condition for being a just person. No explanation is given, however, of why justice *has to be* a conscious virtue.

Elsewhere in his account, Williams describes a particular approach to the virtues that *can* make justice the conscious virtue it sometimes is. It is an approach in which self-consciousness is a function not of an ethical effort's being self-directed but, paradoxically, of such an effort's being not self-directed enough. The resulting consciousness of one's being just has to do with putting up a public appearance of being just, with trying to be just *in the eyes of others*. Williams explains:

> Deliberation toward satisfying those second-order desires must be in a special degree directed toward the self. The trouble with cultivating the virtues, if it is seen as a first-personal and deliberative exercise, is rather that your thought is not self-directed enough. Thinking about your possible states in terms of the virtues is not so much to think about your actions, and it is not distinctively to think about the terms in which you could or should think about your actions: it is rather to think about the way in which others might describe or comment on the way in which you think about your actions, and if that represents the essential content of your deliberations, it really does seem a misdirection of the ethical attention.[4]

This is indeed a particular, and perhaps not uncommon, way for justice to be a conscious virtue, and one wonders whether a virtue marked by such a type of consciousness is a virtue at all. But it is of crucial importance to see that such a misdirection of the ethical attention, as Williams aptly calls it, is not *intrinsic* to justice as a conscious virtue (Williams does not suggest that it is). It is therefore possible that justice, as an instance of ethical attention, can be entirely or primarily self-directed, in Williams's sense, and still remain a conscious virtue. If so, the factor or factors that make justice *necessarily* a conscious virtue, or that are intrinsic to justice as a conscious virtue, have to be sought elsewhere.

4. Williams, *Ethics*, p. 11.

Justice as Self-Overcoming

Justice is necessarily a conscious virtue, I submit, not because it can be insufficiently self-directed (in Williams's sense), but because, even when entirely self-directed, justice involves the overcoming of contrary inclinations. It is the effort at overcoming such inclinations that leads to a description of one's own motives and actions in terms of justice and to a corresponding kind of consciousness. This is why, as Stuart Hampshire puts it, "we think of justice as *a restraint upon . . . the desire for a greater share of rewards, the desire for dominance.* It is *the denial of pleonexia,* as Plato wrote, of getting more than is due, of unmeasured ambition, of overreaching, and of self-assertion without limit. When justice needs to be enforced and is enforced, the scene is not one of harmony; some ambitions are frustrated. A barrier is erected, an impossibility declared."[5]

Now, the very idea of restraint or overcoming implies the existence of contrary inclinations, which it is the object of a sense of justice, and, in the absence of that, the institutional enforcement of justice, to overcome. What a sense of justice allows one to do is to turn the overcoming of such inclinations into at least in part *self*-overcoming. It is only in something like this sense that we can, as J. R. Lucas does,[6] speak of justice as an unwilling or reluctant virtue, a description that would otherwise amount to a contradiction in terms. Justice is an *unwilling* or *reluctant* virtue in that there is something in oneself to overcome or restrain; and it is an unwilling or reluctant *virtue* in that the overcoming or restraining is carried out by oneself, that is, for moral rather than purely prudential reasons. The self-overcoming that goes together with this reluctant virtue implies the *simultaneous* existence of inclinations contrary to justice and the willingness regularly to overcome them. Thus, even at its best, even in the form of self-overcoming, justice represents the conquest of a natural egoism, the refraining from injustice to which one would otherwise be naturally prone by virtue of egoism. It is because justice is not a natural instinct that it has to be a conscious virtue. Conversely, it is from the fact that justice is a conscious virtue that we know it is not a natural instinct. In this regard, Hume

5. Stuart Hampshire, *Innocence and Experience* (Cambridge, Mass.: Harvard University Press, 1989), pp. 71–72, emphasis added. See also Abraham J. Heschel, *The Prophets* (New York: Harper and Row, 1962), p. 209. According to Heschel, "justice bespeaks a situation that transcends the individual, demanding from everyone a certain abnegation of self, defiance of self-interest, disregard of self-respect."

6. J. R. Lucas, *On Justice* (Oxford: Clarendon Press, 1980), p. 3.

is right and Hampshire wrong, for precisely the reason Hampshire himself so clearly recognizes, namely, that justice bespeaks more a restraint upon than an expression of (natural) desires.[7]

It is arguable, of course, that certain natural instincts, such as envy, are among the rudiments that could go into the making of a sense of justice. But by themselves these natural instincts are sufficient only to generate a construal of justice from what Schopenhauer calls the passive point of view,[8] and such a point of view can lead only to rational egoism rather than a proper sense of justice. A proper sense of justice has to contain an equal measure of the active point of view, the willingness and ability to overcome oneself in the interest of others to an extent determined by some broadly reasonable conception of justice. Insofar as the active point of view emanates from any natural instinct, its source must be the premoral instinct of sympathy or compassion. In the extremely unlikely event, however, that the active point of view emanates *entirely* from sympathy (extremely unlikely given the rarity of a superabundance of premoral sympathy), justice will cease to be distinguishable from benevolence, since premoral sympathy by itself knows no boundary between justice and benevolence. By contrast, if the sense of justice is to be distinguishable from benevolence by regularly stopping short of it, it cannot flow entirely from the natural or premoral instinct of sympathy.[9] The upshot is that a distinct sense of justice can (at best) rest only *in part* on the natural instinct of sympathy, and this means in turn that the need remains for the cultivation of a conscious virtue to combat natural inclinations that militate against the desire to be just. This is, I think, a reasonable sense in which we can say that justice is not a natural disposition, at least not a fully natural disposition. The same can indeed be said of conscious virtues in general. All conscious virtues, including justice, result from, and exist for the sake of, overcoming contrary inclinations. This is the case even when one natural instinct (say, the sum total of those natural inclinations subsumable under the rubric of egoism) is overcome with the aid of another, equally natural instinct (say, the arguably equally natural instinct of sympathy), unless the latter instinct is sufficient *by itself* for the overcoming, which it seldom is.

Where it appears sufficient, this is usually in the context of family or close friendship. In such relationships, a stable situation of mutual advan-

7. See Hampshire, *Innocence,* p. 82.

8. See Chapter 4 for an explanation of the distinction between the active and passive points of view of justice.

9. See Chapter 4.

tage and good will seems to obtain without the need for a sense of justice. But even here a sense of justice is dispensable, to the extent that it *is* dispensable, not necessarily because of an abundance of sympathy, but perhaps more because of the relative ease of establishing instinctively regulated rather than consciously contrived cooperation. These relationships by their very nature and scale allow for an implicit, seemingly spontaneous reciprocity that generally makes self-assertion unnecessary and counterproductive as a way of securing interests and over time gives rise to the instinctive knowledge, itself constitutive of such relationships, that things work best in the absence of self-assertion.[10] It is arguable that some such instinctive knowledge is, for the kind of evolutionary reasons suggested by Allan Gibbard,[11] the cause rather than the effect of what to an outside observer seems an especially high degree of sympathy or fellow feeling characteristic of kinship and close friendship.

Such instinctive knowledge is contradicted at every turn outside of these special relationships. Hence the need for self-assertion. And where self-assertion is needed to promote self-interest, justice in turn is needed to prevent self-assertion from turning into aggression against others. Justice, once internalized in the form of a sense of justice, then becomes the basis for a lesser friendship in the shape of civic friendship. By acquiring a sense of justice, people become conscious of one another's legitimate claims—the kinds of claims whose near counterparts in the setting of family and friendship could be attended to instinctively and without the aid of a conscious virtue of justice. For this reason, the acquisition of a sense of justice tells an ambiguous story. Even as a sense of justice bespeaks the resolve to overcome one's egoism, to place limits on one's self-assertion, it implies a sufficient degree of assertive egoism to require self-overcoming, even external coercion, in the first place. Therefore, as Michael Sandel reminds us (albeit in a context of argument somewhat different from my own), an increase in the sense of justice need not indicate moral improvement, either for an individual or for a society as a whole.[12] It could equally be the case that there has somehow emerged a greater amount of assertive egoism that needs to be overcome, and the inculcation of a heightened sense of justice aimed at combating this new level of assertive egoism may well end

10. See Chapter7 for more detailed discussion of conditions of reciprocity.

11. Allan Gibbard, *Wise Choices, Apt Feelings* (Oxford: Clarendon Press, 1990), pp. 257–264.

12. Michael J. Sandel, *Liberalism and the Limits of Justice* (Cambridge: Cambridge University Press, 1982), p. 32.

up also naturalizing it by incorporating it into a new understanding of "human nature."

There is a further, related reason why justice has to be a conscious virtue, and this has to do with a just person's distinctness at once from a benevolent person and from a sheer egoist. A just person is characterized by a set of motives (I will discuss the nature of such motives shortly) that regularly cause him to do what justice requires but that nevertheless do not regularly cause him to perform actions that are beyond the call of justice, such as acts of benevolence.[13] If we think about the implications of this distinctness of the just person for the nature of the self-overcoming that justice is designed to accomplish, we will immediately see a further sense, over and above the sheer need for self-overcoming, in which justice has to be, or at any rate has to begin as, a conscious virtue. Unlike both benevolence and egoism, justice is marked by precise limits, though such limits can change over time and vary from society to society. The ability neither to transgress those limits nor to transcend them requires a precise degree of self-overcoming. Such a precise degree of self-overcoming in turn is made possible only by a precise form of consciousness. This precise form of consciousness is what we call a sense of justice.

What such a precise form of consciousness does for the just person is to enable him or her to overcome egoism to the degree required by justice (as justice is defined substantively by the society of which one is a member)—neither more nor less. It is this conscious quality of the virtue of justice that distinguishes it at once from egoism and from benevolence, neither of the latter necessarily involving self-consciousness on the part of an agent. A sense of justice, necessarily highly conscious until it becomes habitual through frequent exercise, enables one to be just but at the same time stops one from being more than just. It lifts one above egoism but at the same time holds one back from benevolence. Together, rising above egoism and stopping short of benevolence point to a precise form of consciousness that we customarily name a sense of justice. It is the consciousness that one *ought to* rise above egoism but that one *does not have to* go beyond the call of justice. Without such consciousness, one would not be able to overcome egoism to precisely the degree required by justice. Egoism can be unconscious, and so can natural benevolence, if it exists. Self-overcoming is absent in one case and unnecessary in the other. If justice is to be distinct from benevolence and egoism alike, it must be a conscious

13. See Chapter 1 for more detailed discussion of justice as distinct from benevolence.

virtue. A sense of justice that is both distinct and unconscious is simply impossible.

Self-Overcoming and Its Rewards

Being in conscious possession of the virtue of justice has yet another side, and inevitably so. It is one's consciousness of *others* as just or unjust, particularly in relation to oneself. Thus, the disposition to be just involves what Williams calls "a disposition to assess others." Williams thought-provokingly suggests the need to resist "the idea that having a virtue or admirable disposition of character should also involve a disposition to assess others," one of the reasons for such resistance being "a conception of innocence, the image of a virtue that is entirely unselfconscious and lacking the contrast with self that is implied by judgment of others."[14] For better or for worse, this quality of unself-consciousness and innocence is impossible for justice, because the disposition to judge others follows from the expectation of reciprocity that is part and parcel of the disposition to be just. If the need for self-overcoming makes justice a conscious virtue, our demand for similar self-overcoming on the part of others makes justice a doubly conscious virtue. As a doubly conscious virtue, justice consists in the vigilance, ideally of equal measure, against egoism in ourselves (as potential cause of injustice to others) and egoism in others (as potential cause of injustice by others to others, but particularly to ourselves). But since generally it is much easier to see egoism and injustice in others and altruism and justice in ourselves, a sense of justice often goes together with a measure of self-righteousness.[15] The hallmark of the self-righteous is just that one is as prone to find justice in one's own motives and deeds as one is to notice injustice in the motives and deeds of others. And when one finds oneself at the receiving end of an unjust deed, self-righteousness will be compounded by resentment.

Resentment is marked by consciousness at once of our own self-over-

14. Williams, *Ethics,* p. 36. This is precisely the kind of quality that is lacking in justice, which is one reason why Williams objects to the centrality of duty that is characteristic of justice and of what he calls "morality" as a whole (see chap. 10 of his book).

15. Thus Hume observes, "Tho' a present interest may thus blind us with regard to our own actions, it takes not place with regard to those of others; nor hinders them from appearing in their true colours, as highly prejudicial to public interest, and to our own in particular." David Hume, *A Treatise of Human Nature,* ed. L. A. Selby-Bigge, 2nd ed., ed. P. H. Nidditch (Oxford: Clarendon Press, 1978), p. 545.

coming in accordance with the requirements of justice and of others' failure to do so or, more precisely, their failure of reciprocation to our disadvantage. It is the anger of those who, we might say, consciously practice the self-overcoming required by justice as if it were a categorical imperative, but unconsciously, or at any rate less consciously, do so in the spirit of a hypothetical imperative. Such anger or resentment would disappear if we could stop treating justice as a categorical imperative, that is, if we could suspend the effort of self-overcoming in relation to those who have not bothered to practice self-overcoming themselves. But we cannot, since we are less conscious, if at all, of the original motive of self-overcoming as rooted in mutual advantage than of the socially prescribed status of self-overcoming as an unconditional duty, which we violate on pain of self-disapproval. When our commitment to the self-overcoming required by justice has been raised through socialization to the level of an unconditional duty and yet our (unconscious or less conscious) motive of self-overcoming remains tied to the reciprocity and conditionality of justice, our inevitable reaction to a breach of reciprocity by others to our disadvantage is resentment.

Such a reaction, itself conscious, serves in an unconscious manner to compensate for our sense of loss in an exchange (either of actions or of abstentions) in which others have not done their part as justice requires. This compensation, which will work only if it is not consciously perceived as such, takes the form of attributing a loss of moral standing to the violator of reciprocity. Whoever is guilty of a breach of reciprocity has lost morally what he has gained materially (and if the breach is of a kind that is subject to legal sanctions, the material advantage will be taken away too in due course). By thus attributing moral inferiority to the reciprocity-breaker, we are implicitly attributing moral superiority to ourselves for our unilateral self-overcoming. As long as we are imbued with a sense of justice, that is, as long as we are more conscious of the unconditional duty of self-overcoming than of its underlying conditional motivation, we will attach more importance to how well we have lived up to *justice as morality* than to what we have lost in terms of *justice as exchange*. Accordingly, strong as our resentment is, it will nevertheless be submerged under our self-righteousness, in which another's material advantage gained through unjust self-assertion will be eclipsed by our own moral triumph achieved through self-overcoming.

In self-righteousness, then, one finds a reward for self-overcoming, a reward all the more needed in the absence of similar self-overcoming on the part of others. That reward is one's consciousness of oneself as a just and righteous person, and this self-consciousness is confirmed by society in the form of a good name. Although a good name, or socially recognized trustworthiness, stands one in good stead in all kinds of practical ways, it is not tangible advantage that self-righteousness seeks first and foremost. Far more important, owing to its self-conscious quality, self-righteousness has the appearance, even to the righteous person himself, of being its own reward.

In the Name of Justice

It is a necessary condition of self-righteousness, indeed of a sense of justice even when it is not accompanied by self-righteousness, that one sees oneself not only as the object of overcoming but also as its subject. That is to say, one has to perceive one's overcoming of inclinations contrary to justice in terms of *self*-overcoming. But such a perception is necessarily a misperception with regard to the *origin,* as opposed to the current motive, of self-overcoming. I noted earlier that a sense of justice implies the simultaneous existence of inclinations contrary to justice and the ability regularly to overcome them. What I must now add is that such coexistence is the product of socialization, which takes the impulses contrary to justice as given (and hence as natural, for practical purposes) and sets about correcting them by inculcating a sense of justice. There is thus a sense in which the impulses contrary to justice are prior to the sense of justice needed to counteract them—"natural and active in us even prior to the moral law," as Kant puts it.[16] This means in turn that the impulses contrary to justice are properties of the individual while a sense of justice is, in the first instance, a social creation. The self-overcoming that is constitutive of justice does not *originate* with the individual.

Justice is, in the first instance, that *in the name of* which society compels individuals to overcome themselves. Individuals have no choice but to overcome themselves when it comes to justice. To borrow a formulation from Hume,[17] justice is a "certain form of words" used by society in constituting a convention whereby a certain degree of self-overcoming is made to take place. When self-overcoming is thus performed in the name

16. Immanuel Kant, *Critique of Practical Reason,* in *Critique of Practical Reason and Other Writings in Moral Philosophy,* trans. and ed. Lewis White Beck (Chicago: University of Chicago Press, 1949), p. 181.

17. Hume, *Treatise,* p. 522.

of justice, the resultant *action* falls under the description of justice, but the *motive* need not. In this sense, one may be said to be conscious of the reasons for performing just actions, and conscious of those reasons under the heading of justice. Such reasons, however, make up the public description of socially required actions rather than necessarily one's private motives for performing those actions. They are the terms, the "form of words," in which we can *represent* our actions and our motives intelligibly and acceptably to others, and they to us, and both to society. Such representation is possible (intelligible and acceptable) only because, or to the extent that, one's putative reasons for self-overcoming can be found among those public reasons for which society has compelled individuals to overcome themselves in the first place. Justice is, in the first instance, that in the name of which society imposes its requirements on individuals, and only then that in the name of which individuals represent and justify themselves to one another and to society.

I earlier described a sense of justice as the conscious realization that one ought to rise above egoism but that one does not have to go beyond the call of justice. It should now be added that the origin of the belief that one *ought to* (rise above egoism) is the knowledge that one *has to* (rise above egoism). And that knowledge can only be the product of socialization. "A barrier is erected, an impossibility declared," as Hampshire succinctly says of the nature of justice.[18] It is society that erects the barrier and declares the impossibility. In other words, it is society that sets the (minimal) requirements of individual self-overcoming. Individuals, qua individuals, are not in a position to set those requirements, but can only choose how to relate to them: to treat the requirements as essentially external to themselves and hence as something to be followed out of fear or prudence, or to internalize them in the form of a conscience so that they become part of their identity and basis of self-respect.

When the requirements are set somewhere between unbridled egoism and self-denying altruism, as they often are, individuals have yet another choice. On the one hand, because unbridled egoism is treated by society as impermissible, individuals have to overcome their egoism to some degree. On the other hand, because self-denying altruism or benevolence is treated by society as supererogatory, individuals can choose to overcome their egoism only to the degree that society designates in terms of justice. A sense of justice, itself based on the socially acquired knowledge of the

18. Hampshire, *Innocence*, p. 72.

coercive nature of justice, goes hand in hand with the knowledge, also acquired in the course of socialization, of the absence of coercion regarding acts of benevolence. Without this twofold knowledge, namely, that justice is obligatory but anything beyond justice is supererogatory, one would not be able to overcome oneself to such a precise degree. We might say that a sense of justice consists in the intersection of the most one is socially compelled to do and the least one should be personally willing to do.

The Diversity of Motives and Their Vicissitudes

The reasons in the name of which society compels individuals to overcome themselves should not be confused with the motives from which individuals bring themselves to accept such compulsion. The fact that justice is the rationale (the "form of words") in the name of which self-overcoming is *socially* imposed seems to impart a unity to *individual* motives of self-overcoming. But this is only a specious unity. From the fact that society justifies its imposition of self-overcoming *in the name of justice*, it does not follow that when individuals have accomplished such self-overcoming they must have done so *from the motive of justice*.[19]

Indeed, it is impossible for individuals to accomplish such self-overcoming from the motive of justice (alone). For they can be made to absorb the social rationale for self-overcoming only from *preexisting* motives. The desire to be just, as we have seen, is not among these preexisting motives; at least, it is not a preexisting motive of sufficient strength independent of external compulsion. Otherwise there would be no need for *socially compelled* self-overcoming in the first place. The very need for social compulsion shows that the self-overcoming that is constitutive of justice has to be accomplished from motives other than the desire to be just. Before self-overcoming can be motivated by the desire to be just, the desire itself has to be created, and it cannot be created on the basis of its own natural absence or at least natural shortage. Nietzsche expresses this idea concisely when he remarks that "to become moral is not in itself moral."[20] In this sense, representations of one's actions in terms of justice are invariably false as representations of one's *original* motive of justice. They can be

19. As Niebuhr reminds us, "only the agent of an action knows to what degree self-seeking corrupts his socially approved actions." Reinhold Niebuhr, *Moral Man and Immoral Society* (New York: Charles Scribner's Sons, 1960), p. 258.

20. Friedrich Nietzsche, *Daybreak,* trans. R. J. Hollingdale (Cambridge: Cambridge University Press, 1982), 97.

true only as representations of one's *subsequent* or *current* motive of justice, and this later motive, as we have seen, is a product of socialization which itself must rely on preexisting motives. Thus the isomorphism between social rationale and individual motive is achieved, if at all, only when individuals, who had no choice but to act on the social rationale for self-overcoming to begin with, have come to absorb that rationale as their own motive. Only then does the socially prescribed "form of words" called justice become also the description by which they represent their actions and their motives *to themselves.*

It follows from the nature of justice, in its aspect as promise-keeping, that there will always remain the possibility of simulacrum even after the internalization of the socially prescribed rationale for just behavior. As Nietzsche says, one can promise only actions, not motives or feelings,[21] and just actions are no exception. For this reason, just motives cannot be *required* as part of the duty of justice.[22] In other words, the overcoming of egoism that is constitutive of justice cannot require the overcoming of (overly) egoistic intentions but only of (overly) egoistic deeds. Lucas is quite right to insist that "unwilling justice is still justice." Given the obligation to perform just actions and the impossibility of promising just motives, it would be unrealistic and unreasonable to require justice to be a "whole-hearted and inward virtue." Rather, "although it might be better that I should do these things [required by justice] gladly, justice is satisfied if I do them at all."[23]

What is important is just that egoism be overcome, and overcome to an extent that is socially determined and described in terms of justice. The

21. See Friedrich Nietzsche, *Human, All Too Human,* trans. R. J. Hollingdale, 2 vols. in 1 (Cambridge: Cambridge University Press, 1986), 1:58: "*What one can promise.*—One can promise actions but not feelings; for the latter are involuntary. He who promises someone he will always love him or always hate him or always be faithful to him, promises something that does not reside in his power; but he can certainly promise to perform actions which, though they are usually the consequences of love, hatred, faithfulness, can also derive from other motives: for several paths and motives can lead to the same action. To promise always to love someone therefore means: for as long as I love you I shall render to you the actions of love; if I cease to love you, you will continue to receive the same actions from me, though from other motives: so that in the heads of our fellow men the appearance will remain that love is still the same and unchanged.—One therefore promises the continuation of the appearance of love when one swears to someone ever-enduring love without self-deception."

22. See Immanuel Kant, *The Metaphysics of Morals,* trans. Mary Gregor (Cambridge: Cambridge University Press, 1991), p. 56.

23. Lucas, *On Justice,* pp. 3, 4.

motive for such self-overcoming, as already noted, cannot have been the desire to be just, to begin with. It is arguable that the motive need not be such a desire afterwards, either. The best reason for insisting that the (subsequent) motive of just actions be the desire to be just itself would be to suggest that this is the most effective way of self-overcoming. But whether this is the case is an open question, at least one that does not lend itself to an a priori answer. Nietzsche for one suggests (in his early work) that the insistence on achieving an identity of good conduct and good motive is not only unrealistic but unwise and counterproductive as well. Of crucial importance is what Nietzsche sees as a fact of moral psychology, namely, that different people, at the point when their moral education begins, are already predisposed to develop what appears to be the same virtue from quite diverse motives. In an aphorism titled "The Ineptest Educator," Nietzsche remarks, by way of illustration, that "in the case of one man all his real virtues have been cultivated in the soil of his spirit of contradiction, in the case of another in his inability to say no, that is in his spirit of assent; a third has developed all his morality out of his lonely pride, a fourth his out of his strong drive to sociability."[24] Whether or not we find these specific cases convincing, the point they are meant to illustrate seems a valid one: the diversity of what Nietzsche calls the "seeds of virtue," the diversity of motives behind the apparent unity of virtue.[25] It follows, again abstracting from the validity or lack thereof of the specific cases, that if "the seeds of virtue had . . . not been sown in that region of [their] nature where the topsoil was richest and most plentiful, then they would be without morality." This can happen, according to Nietzsche, through the "ineptitude of teachers," and "the ineptest of all educators" is a "moral fanatic, who believes that the good can grow only out of the good and upon the basis of the good."[26]

The "moral fanatic" is further mistaken, according to Nietzsche, in that he does not realize that what begins as a simulacrum of virtue does not

24. Nietzsche, *Human,* vol. 2, pt. 2, 70.

25. As Nietzsche puts it in another aphorism, "Several paths and motives can lead to the same action" (ibid., 1:58).

26. Ibid., vol. 2, pt. 2, 70. The prototype of the "moral fanatic" is presumably Kant. But such a description, as Nietzsche meant it, could apply only to Kant's strictly *moral* philosophy, as expounded, for instance, in the *Groundwork.* In what may be considered his political philosophy, for example, *The Metaphysics of Morals,* Kant shows as much wisdom or shrewdness as Nietzsche in not insisting on such so-called moral fanaticism—the kind of wisdom that is also found in thinkers as diverse as Vico, Hume and Adam Smith, and Hegel and Marx. It is worth noting that Nietzsche was later, in a vein of thinking "beyond good and

have to remain as such. Nietzsche suggests that the simulacrum of virtue, if practiced long enough, can become virtue itself. This claim has two sides to it, and Nietzsche puts the accent now on one side and now on the other. He insists, as noted earlier, that *becoming moral is not in itself moral*—in other words, goodness originates from its simulacrum. This is one side of Nietzsche's claim, having to do with the question of origins and leaving open the question whether something that originated in a certain way should be regarded as goodness. The other side of his claim gives an affirmative answer to the latter question, the concern being not so much with origins as with what can develop from them. Here Nietzsche suggests that what originates from the simulacrum of goodness can indeed end up being more than mere simulacrum. For Nietzsche, it is both the case that goodness originates from its simulacrum and the case that what originates from the simulacrum of goodness can develop into goodness worthy of the name. Both ideas, or both sides of the same claim, are captured in an aphorism titled "Dissimulation as a Duty," in which Nietzsche begins by saying that "goodness has mostly been developed by the protracted dissimulation which sought to appear as goodness" and ends by counterpoising this idea with the suggestion that "what is dissimulated for a long time at last becomes *nature:* dissimulation in the end sublimates itself, and organs and instincts are the surprising fruit of the garden of hypocrisy."[27] What is here vaguely called sublimation Nietzsche elsewhere explains in terms of forgetting. As he remarks in an aphorism on the very topic of the virtue of justice, sublimation and forgetfulness go hand in hand, as reciprocal cause and effect, indeed as two ways of describing what is in fact the same process:

> Since, in accordance with their intellectual habit men have *forgotten* the original purpose of so-called just and fair actions, and especially because children have for millennia been trained to admire and imi-

evil" and deeply critical of morality, to reverse his position and see in such wisdom not only unwisdom but also untruth. When, for example in *Twilight of the Idols*, in *The Portable Nietzsche*, ed. and trans. Walter Kaufmann (New York: Viking Press, 1954), "The Improvers of Mankind," 5, he says, in what is clearly a condemning tone, "neither Manu nor Plato nor Confucius nor the Jewish and Christian teachers have ever doubted their *right* to lie . . . [*A*]*ll* the means by which one has so far attempted to make mankind moral were through and through *immoral*," he himself has become what he used to call a "moral fanatic." We need not, however, go into the reasons for this complete change of heart.

27. Nietzsche, *Daybreak*, 248.

tate such actions, it has gradually come to appear that a just action is an unegoistic one: but it is on this appearance that the high value accorded it depends; and this high value is, moreover, continually increasing, as all valuations do: for something highly valued is striven for, imitated, multiplied through sacrifice, and grows as the worth of the toil and zeal expended by each individual is added to the worth of the valued thing. *How little moral would the world appear without forgetfulness!* A poet could say that God has placed forgetfulness as a doorkeeper on the threshold of the temple of human dignity.[28]

If Nietzsche is right,[29] then it is both the case that justice necessarily has its starting point in simulacrum and the case that it does not have to remain as simulacrum. Justice ceases to be simulacrum, or *mere* simulacrum, when one comes to represent self-overcoming *to oneself* (not only to others and to society) in terms of justice. Such self-representation begins to be possible when self-overcoming has become so habitual or so habitually successful that one no longer needs to rely (consciously) on the motives that made self-overcoming possible in the first place and as a result can, without any (conscious) hypocrisy, take the public description of one's actions in terms of justice to be also a description of one's own private mo-

28. Nietzsche, *Human,* 1:92. Such forgetfulness is in turn solidified, as it were, or enshrined, in what Nietzsche calls "suprahuman concepts"—in his sense all moral concepts are suprahuman concepts—through which people are both compelled to virtue (in the process of education—see ibid., vol. 2, pt. 1, 91) and made to forget the origins of virtue in social compulsion. What "suprahuman concepts," along with the institutions that embody and support them, do is to turn something transitory and human, including transitory forgetfulness, into something permanent and suprahuman by virtue of transcending the immediacy of the senses. In this connection, Nietzsche invites us to "think of institutions and customs which have created out of the fiery abandonment of the moment perpetual fidelity, out of the enjoyment of anger perpetual vengeance, out of despair perpetual mourning, out of a single and unpremeditated word perpetual obligation" (*Daybreak,* 27). And, as one might add, out of the momentary forgetfulness of the origins of morality the permanent lapse of memory that is (the condition of the possibility of) morality itself.

29. These insights of the early Nietzsche remain highly illuminating and suggestive regarding the nature of socialization and moral education. In his later work, however, Nietzsche came to doubt that this is how socialization and moral education ought to be carried out, and even whether moral education, at least of a kind conceived in terms of good and evil, ought to be carried out at all. What began as a celebration of the creation of morality through forgetfulness ended up, in Nietzsche's later work (for example, *On the Genealogy of Morals, Twilight of the Idols, Antichrist,* and *The Will to Power*), as a critique of *ressentiment* and decadence. This change, important as it is, is beyond the scope of my concerns here.

tives for performing such actions. At this point, one's self-representation, though still mistaken with regard to one's original motives of self-overcoming, can be treated as accurate with regard to one's subsequent—that is, current—motives. It is the aim of socialization and moral education to make such self-representation *retrospectively* true, as it were—true after the fact. As we have seen throughout this book, given the dual character of the virtue of justice as arising from the conditionality of interest and the unconditionality of morality, such a task is a perpetual challenge to any society that stands in need of justice.

Index